Object Oriented Technologies:

Opportunities and Challenges

Rick Gibson
American University, USA

IDEA GROUP PUBLISHING
Hershey USA • London UK

Senior Editor:	Mehdi Khosrowpour
Managing Editor:	Jan Travers
Copy Editor:	Brenda Zboray Klinger
Typesetter:	Tamara Gillis
Cover Design:	Connie Peltz
Printed at:	BookCrafters

Published in the United States of America by
Idea Group Publishing
1331 E. Chocolate Avenue
Hershey PA 17033-1117
Tel: 717-533-8845
Fax: 717-533-8661
E-mail: jtravers@idea-group.com
Website: http://www.idea-group.com

and in the United Kingdom by
Idea Group Publishing
3 Henrietta Street
Covent Garden
London WC2E 8LU
Tel: 171-240 0856
Fax: 171-379 0609
http://www.eurospan.co.uk

Library of Congress Cataloging-in-Publication Data

Gibson, Richard G.
Object oriented technologies : opportunities and challenges / Rick Gibson.
p. cm.
Includes bibliographical references and index.
ISBN 1-87828-967-5 (paper)
1. Object-oriented methods (Computer science) I. Title

QA76.9.O35 G53 1999
005.1'17--dc21 99-046092

British Cataloguing in Publication Data
A Cataloguing in Publication record for this book is available from the British Library.

Object Oriented Technologies: Opportunities and Challenges

Table of Contents

Preface

The continual evolution of object oriented technologies creates both opportunities and challenges. The chapters in this book were selected to represent a variety of perspectives concerning the present and future of this broad sub-field of software development. Practical considerations limited the size of this book to twelve chapters, which forced the omission of several important topics such as object oriented programming.

The first four chapters are presented in systems development life cycle order. The opening chapter, written by Edward Sim, examines object oriented analysis (OOA), reviews some of the fundamental concepts on which OOA is based and discusses the acceptance of this new technology. Recently, many new techniques and methodologies have been introduced to assist analysts and users in efforts to identify and specify system requirements. One of the newest approaches to be used in this effort to improve requirements analysis is the application of object oriented analysis. Proponents of object technologies argue that the use of objects facilitates communication and problem understanding because people naturally think about their environment in object oriented ways. The solution for improving analysis and the requirements produced by that analysis, they argue, is to adopt an object oriented approach to doing analysis. However, despite these claims, the use of OOA has not achieved the levels of adoption that other object oriented technologies (i.e., programming languages) have achieved.

In the next chapter James Nelson, Kay Nelson, Mehdi Ghods, and Holly Lee discuss the use of structured design techniques in an object oriented environment. Their research examines specific traditional structured methods for their contribution to traditional development team performance. The attitude of the team toward structured methods and the satisfaction of the team with training in structured methods are used as mediating variables in this examination. Correlation analysis and stepwise regression are used as analysis methodologies. The results of these analyses are then mapped to the object oriented environment.

Samuel Agyemang describes object oriented testing. Most researchers and practitioners seem to agree that object oriented testing is a challenge. The main reason for this view seems to revolve around the fact that the objects and the code are inseparable, and also because of inheritance. Nevertheless, object oriented systems, when successfully tested, leave a better maintained product than traditional non-object oriented software.

Jozsef Komlodi examines the technical and market viability of object database technology. Object databases represent a revolutionary new technology and provide a superior storage facility for complex data structures and types. They also enable close language binding and a unified development process. It is a mature technology with advanced database management and development features, and has several proven and robust deployment examples. Besides its current technical excellence, this technology is also demonstrating future potential through such emerging technologies as Java, Application servers, and XML-a markup meta-language for documents containing structured information. The past failure of object databases to proliferate the market was mainly due to unawareness, lack of skills, and the overwhelming existing investment in relational systems. These factors are changing and new technology adoption is accelerating, so object databases are looking forward to a slow but sure take off.

A second grouping of chapters illustrates one of the main benefits of object technology-reuse, along with one of the main challenges-what to do with legacy systems. Jane Fedorowicz and Denis Lee provide an overview of software reuse and object technology. They surveyed practitioners with extensive systems development experience to evaluate their experiences with object oriented tools and techniques. A related goal of the study was to focus on reuse-to determine what is being reused and by whom.

The chapter by Gretchen Irwin and Chamini Wasalathantry provides an empirical study of reuse of object models. The aim of their study was to explore the effect of a reusable example on the cognitive processes associated with object oriented modeling.

Cobo and Mauco discuss transforming legacy systems into object oriented. They discuss how the development of new architectures and the improvements in programming methods and languages have created a need to reverse engineer and reengineer existing program code in order to get as much value as possible from legacy systems, while exploiting the latest technology.

Gerald Cameron considers integration and migration issues associated with upgrading legacy applications. Conversion of a COBOL legacy application to an object oriented application requires a complete restructuring of the legacy application. Objects and their inheritance structure must be identified, data usage and data flow must be analyzed, and instructions must be allocated to objects. Dynamic Object Oriented Programming allows parts of an application design that are represented by objects to be modified dynamically. Integrating or migrating legacy applications with newer more advanced client/server architectures can be a very expensive and time-consuming undertaking.

The final four chapters address some of the more complex issues associated with object technologies. Alex Podaras introduces distributed object systems. The purpose of his chapter is to provide a clear understanding of what distributed object oriented systems are, no matter how complex they may appear to be. It will be shown that, fundamentally, distributed object oriented systems must have two object oriented properties or characteristics: encapsulation (the ability to hide code from the user) and messages (the way objects communicate). Additionally, it will be shown that software components (objects) of the distributed object oriented systems must have certain inherent features. Aside from the two object oriented properties and the certain inherent features, any critical system must have the ability to keep its data in a consistent state. This is particularly important when concurrent transactions are executed.

David Patton provides a discussion of distributed object business engineering. His chapter presents a framework for architecting enterprise-wide object based information systems. These next-generation systems maximize information value throughout the enterprise, while reducing development time and effort throughout the system lifetime.

Luis Proano examines industry trends in order to make recommendations for training approaches for object technology skills. He offers some ideas regarding the current needs in the information technology industry in terms of object oriented technology skills and knowledge. He also analyzes factors like the lack of mainstream products and object standards influencing the development of skilled professionals in working with object databases.

Robert Gittins brings together two important trends by questioning the use of object oriented technology for business process reengineering. He asserts that although the potential for object oriented technology has information technology and business professionals extremely excited, the burgeoning field is undeniably immature and currently lacks the stability necessary to be considered mainstream or a reliable option for companies that are about to reengineer their business processes. Despite the growing popularity of object oriented technology, there are numerous issues that have contributed to its inability to firmly entrench itself and take over from the older, proven technologies. Object oriented technology's image problem has created a highly difficult decision-making process for corporations about to embark on business process reengineering (BPR) projects. At this time, reengineering with object technologies is a significant risk for companies to make and those who have moved forward with object technologies have not, for the most part, seen the results that they were hoping for and their organizations are now suffering as a result of this decision.

Chapter I

Object Oriented Requirements Analysis: Its Challenges and Use

Edward R. Sim
Loyola College, USA

Introduction

The ability to correctly identify system requirements is seen by most Information Systems (IS) researchers and practitioners as essential to the design and development of effective information systems (Yadav, Bravoco et al. 1988; Vessey 1994). Requirements are used to drive all subsequent stages of systems development and are critical to system validation. Incorrect requirements or poorly specified requirements usually produce systems that require major revisions or are abandoned entirely (Pressman 1996). Recently, many new techniques and methodologies have been introduced to assist analysts and users in efforts to identify and specify system requirements (Coad, North et al. 1995) (Pancake 1995). One of the newest approaches to be used in this effort to improve requirements analysis is the application of object oriented analysis (OOA).

Proponents of OO argue that the use of OO concepts improves communication and the formation of accurate conceptual models because OO's fundamental concepts are more "natural" (Booch 1991). They argue that the use of OO facilitates communication and problem understanding because people naturally think about their environment in object oriented ways (Martin and Odell 1992). The solution for improving analysis and the requirements produced by that analysis, they argue, is to adopt an OO approach to doing analysis. However, despite these claims, the use of OOA has not achieved the levels of adoption that other object oriented technologies (i.e., programming languages) have achieved. This chapter examines OOA, reviews some of the fundamental concepts on which OOA is based and discusses the acceptance of this new technology.

OO Requirements Analysis

Requirements drive the function to structure transformation that occurs during IS development. The requirements for a particular IS development effort represent the goals or tasks that system must meet in order to be successful (Davis 1993). Most often these goals or requirements are specified as a set of functions and constraints that the system must meet (Yadav, Bravoco et al. 1988). Usually these requirements are expressed at a relatively high level of abstraction (i.e., the system must provide customer purchase information) and are later refined to detailed specifications.

Many researchers and developers of IS methodologies divide the requirements activities into discrete stages: problem analysis and description (Norman 1988). During the problem analysis the analyst seeks to understand the problem by identifying essential problem elements and structuring those elements into a coherent problem description. The problem description becomes the basis on which a solution is proposed and subsequent specifications are written. These two major activities of requirements are referred to as requirements elicitation and requirements specification (Whitten, Bentley et al. 1994). Various techniques for performing the activities of each of these stages have been proposed. In most cases the techniques suggested by the particular development methodology attempt to guide the user in constructing various graphical models (sometimes augmented by textual descriptions) that describe the current and future systems. The requirements output consists of a set of models and/or textual descriptions produced by following the techniques and heuristics suggested by the methodology.

The specific output products of the requirements activities vary according to the IS development methodology being followed. In most cases, structured analysis leads to the development of data flow diagrams, textual process specifications and a high level data dictionary [Demarco, 1978, p. 352]. In Object Oriented Analysis the output products vary according to the specific OOA methodology used, but at minimum most OOA methodologies attempt to model both the structure and behavior of the system.

The most important OO model produced during the requirements phase is the high level object model (Jacobson 1993). The object model shows the basic structural relationship between the elements in the system (i.e., business objects). To produce the object model, the analyst must identify the basic objects of interest in the system and their relationships or associations and important attributes. The behavior or dynamics of the system are often represented in a separate model (i.e., a dynamic model or event schema). These models are often merged into a single object model that represents objects that include both structure (i.e., attributes) and behavior (i.e., services or methods) (Rumbaugh, Blaha et al. 1991). In addition, inheritance relationships and message passing connections are sometimes shown. Typical outputs of OOA would include an object model, use cases, and an event schema model (Yourdon, Whitehead et al. 1995).

Object Oriented (OO) Software Development

Progenitors of the object oriented approach to software development argue that at its most basic level OO is a way of modeling reality (Martin and Odell 1998) (Booch, Rumbaugh et al. 1995). OO provides a robust conceptual framework for developing models that can be used to assist in the development of software and information systems. The proponents of OO suggest that as the complexity of software systems has increased, so too has the developer's need to have effective modeling concepts that can accurately capture the developer's understanding of reality. The promise of OO is its ability to provide a more powerful method to derive the models that are necessary to create complex software systems (Henderson-Sellers and Edwards 1990; Loy 1990).

Fundamentally, all software development methodologies provide heuristics for mapping our understanding of some real world entity or process into a model that the computer can manipulate. However, with conventional approaches the representations within the computer are usually very different from the real world entities and processes that are being modeled. This "conceptual" difference is a constraint on the software developer's ability to build complex software systems. OO attempts to overcome this limitation by providing a method for creating models that is more flexible and can more closely represent the reality that is being modeled (Weinberg, Guimaraes et al. 1990).

OO more closely models the way the we actually understand reality because we think in terms of concepts which are derived from our ability to abstract similarities from distinct objects in our environment (Martin and Odell 1992). These concepts, real and abstract, are represented as objects in object modeling. We organize our understanding of reality around the generalizations we derive from our concepts.

Since object oriented software development is a new approach to software development, it is important that the basic principles of "object" orientation be described.

OO Concepts

Objects

In the OO approach to modeling reality and developing software, all concepts whether real or abstract can be referred to as objects. The unifying theme of all object oriented methodologies is the object. An object represents a thing or concept. Some typical definitions of objects are:

> Something you can do things to. An object has state, behavior, and identity. The terms instance and object are interchangeable (Booch 1994).
>
> A concept, abstraction, or thing with crisp boundaries and meanings for the problem at hand; an instance of a class (Rumbaugh, Blaha et al. 1991).
>
> Anything real or abstract, about which we store data and those methods that manipulate the data (Booch 1986).

Objects are used to model the basic concepts and entities in the "problem space." By examining the problem space we are able to identify a set of objects that are the components of the "problem space" (Henderson-Sellers and Edwards 1990).

Encapsulation and Inheritance

Objects combine both data and processes. Objects respond to requests for services (called messages) by invoking internal procedures (called methods). The internal procedures and data are referred to as the private parts of the object and are not accessible to other objects. The data and procedures within the object are encapsulated by the object. The encapsulation of the object's private parts make objects highly modular and effectively hides the information of the object from other objects.

Objects share attributes and procedures by inheriting those attributes and procedures from one or more parent classes. For example, a sports car object may be a member of a more general set of objects (cars) and may have inherited from the car parent class those attributes that are associated with the car class (maker, has wheels, has an engine, etc). Multiple inheritance allows objects to inherit properties from several classes. The use of inheritance allows the designer to incrementally specialize a specific object (called an instantiation) without recoding those attributes and behaviors that are common to the class. Objects may inherit attributes and behavior from a single parent class or from multiple classes.

Classification

The grouping of similar objects into classes is referred to as classification and is a critical component of OO analysis. The grouping of objects into classes creates a hierarchical object structure. Booch distinguishes between class-structure hierarchies which he refers to as "kind-of" hierarchies and object structure hierarchies which he refers to as "is a part of" hierarchies. Booch believes that both kinds of hierarchies are necessary to model a complex system (Booch 1991).

Identifying hierarchical structure is a critical mechanism for reducing the complexity of modeling complicated systems. Since most hierarchical systems are "usually composed of only a few kinds of different elements" (Simon 1969), the inheritance mechanism supported by most OO methodologies can be used to reduce the difficulty associated with modeling the complex systems.

Proper classification of objects is essential to effective object oriented analysis and design. Booch argues that object classification is particularly hard because there is no "perfect" classification and intelligent classification requires creative insight. Booch points out that the classification of objects depends in large part on the perspective of the observer (Booch 1994). The three general approaches to classification are classical classification, conceptual classification, and prototype theory (Sowa 1984).

In the classical approach to classification, all objects or entities that share a similar set of features or characteristics are grouped into a class. Although a particular object may have many features or characteristics, only those that are considered relevant from the perspective of the system are considered. Most of the approaches used for classification in object oriented methodologies are classical (Booch 1994). An example of the classical approach to classification is the approach suggested by Coad and Yourdon.

Coad and Yourdon suggest the following approach for finding and classifying objects (Coad, North et al. 1995):

Structure (is-a and part-of relationships);
Other systems;
Devices;
Events remembered;
Locations; and
Organizational units.

In conceptual classification, classes are formed by associating objects into classes when they share a general conceptual description of a shared property (Michalski and Stepp 1983). In the classical approach, the features or characteristics that a set of objects share are distinguishable and measurable (i.e., employee name, account balance, etc.). If the particular features that associate a given set of objects are more conceptual (e.g., is tall), then conceptual classification is being used.

The behavior analysis used by Wirfs-Brock (Wirfs-Brock, Wilkerson et al. 1990) is a form of conceptual clustering. In the Wirfs-Brock object oriented methodology, the concept of an object's "responsibilities" is used to group objects into classes that have or share a common set of responsibilities. According to Wirfs-Brock, responsibilities are used to denote the knowledge that an object contains and the actions that it can perform. The analyst using the Wirfs-Brock methodology uses the concept of responsibilities to define classes of objects that provide a particular system behavior.

Classical and conceptual classification approaches are sufficient for most object oriented analysis; however, for situations where these approaches are inadequate, prototype theory can be used to assist in classification (Booch 1994). In this form of classification, objects are classified according to their resemblance to a "prototypical" object. In prototype classification, objects are grouped according to family resemblance to the prototypical object. The example used by Booch to illustrate this idea is the notion that we can perceive beanbag chairs, barber chairs, and contour chairs as being "chairs" not because they share a distinguishable common property, but because they share a common resemblance to our conceptual prototypical object of a chair (Booch 1994). Prototyping classification is not currently directly supported in any of the object oriented methodologies.

Polymorphism

Polymorphism allows certain objects in a system to respond in different ways to the same message. For example, a "show" message may be applied to a text document, graphical image, or audio object. In each case the object would interpret the show command in a way that is meaningful for that object. Polymorphism reduces the complexity associated with dealing with multiple objects by allowing a single message to have multiple meanings.

The origins of polymorphism can be seen in the use of generic or overloaded operators in traditional programming languages. The specific operation of a generic operator is determined by the context in which it is used (Pratt and Zelkowitz 1996). For example, in traditional programming languages a "+" can be interpreted as meaning integer addition or real number addition, depending on the data types of its argument. Polymorphism extends this concept to objects.

Behavior and States

The dynamic behavior of an object refers to the changes of the object over time and in response to events. Each object exists in a certain "state". The state of the object is defined to be the value of the object's attributes and associations or links with other objects. For example, a car object could be in a state of "running" or in a state of "off." The car object's response to the event "ignition key turned" would be different depending on the state of the car object. The response of an object depends on a given input (message) and the state of the object. Events can change an object's state. The complete history of all events that can happen to a given object is the object's lifecycle. Events can be categorized into event classes or event types. An event schema (or event trace) can be used to show the sequence in which the events occur and how the events affect the state of the object. Scenarios or Use cases can be used to describe the sequence of events that occur in one particular execution of the system (its lifecycle). State transition diagrams are used to show the state sequence of a given object caused by the events occurring to that object. A collection of state diagrams can be used to show the complete behavior of a system.

Origins of Object Orientation Concepts

One of the most interesting aspects of object orientation is that the concepts it represents are pervasive throughout computer science, information system and software development literature. In addition, object orientation is also used in cognitive psychology, hardware design and many other areas. Object oriented concepts are currently being used in the design and development of human computer interfaces (HCI) (Collins 1995), databases (object oriented databases) (Kim 1990; Edelstein 1991), analysis and design methodologies, artificial intelligence research and many other computer science, information system and software endeavors (Khoshafian and Abnous 1990). Since fundamentally object orientation represents the concepts behind good engineering and design, it makes sense that these concepts have broad applicability.

Many areas can be identified as making a significant contribution to the object-orientation paradigm: programming languages, databases, and research in artificial intelligence are the most frequently mentioned areas.

Programming Languages

Ideas in programming language design have contributed significantly to object orientation. In earlier programming languages the primitives provided by the language were very limited (Pratt and Zelkowitz 1996). This forced programmers to work at very low levels of abstraction. Real world concepts had to be represented and modeled at nearly machine level using constructs like linked lists, arrays, variables, etc. The cognitive distance between these two worlds (i.e., the real world and the world inside the computer) was very wide; consequently, general programming and the associated problem solving it represented were difficult (Henderson-Sellers and Edwards 1990).

One of the first ideas to assist the programmer was the use of data types. Data types are constructs that represent data structure and a set of prescribed operations that can be applied to the data structure (Pratt and Zelkowitz 1996). For example, real numbers would be considered a data type. Real numbers are implemented by the programming language and represented in the machine architecture to have a particular defined data structure and a set of operations that can be applied to them (i.e., addition, etc.).

The data type concept defined by the language implementation was later extended by allowing user defined or abstract data types. Abstract data types are "types" constructed and defined by the programmer. The abstract data type allows the user (i.e., programmer) to define structure and corresponding operations once, and then apply the type definition to new instances of the data type. The idea of the abstract type laid the foundation for the "object" in object oriented programming languages. However, abstract data types lack object oriented characteristics like encapsulation, support for inheritance, and message passing.

Many authors have cited Simula as the language that introduced many object oriented concepts into programming languages (Khoshafian and Abnous 1990; Bourne 1992; LaLonde 1994; Pratt and Zelkowitz 1996). Simula was developed by Dahl and Nygaadas as a simulation language. Simula took the concept of block structure from ALGOL and the abstract data type and extended it to the concept of an object to promote encapsulation.

Simula was also significant because it introduced the concept of classes, inheritance, and communication between objects by message passing. Simula took this approach because it was a simulation language and needed to model the real world of complex interactions between objects [Khoshafian, 1990 #27]. The world view Simula perceived was already packaged in objects and messages; consequently, these concepts became natural constructs in the Simula language.

The implementation of the class construct in Simula was significant because it supported the notion of inheritance. Classes, which describe the structure and behavior of objects, are similar in concept to abstract data types. However, class structures extended the capability of abstract data types by directly supporting the sharing of similar structure and behavior through inheritance. The effect of the class construct at the programming level was to greatly reduce the amount of work necessary to represent a problem in the computer.

The ideas in Simula were further extended by the researchers at the Xerox Research Park at Palo Alto, California into a language called Smalltalk (Bourne 1992; LaLonde 1994). Smalltalk is considered by many people to be the quintessential object oriented programming language because it supports the major concepts of object orientation. Smalltalk has grown in importance since its inception; however, it has not been considered a language useful for large system development. Some of the major criticisms of Smalltalk have been its lack of support for static-type checking, poor portability, and its general poor performance. In addition to these limitations, Smalltalk has been criticized for limited support of concurrency (Bourne 1992; LaLonde 1994).

A major goal of all object oriented programming languages is to enable the programmer to use constructs that model the real world as closely as possible. A significant aspect of this goal is the ability to model concurrent activities or processes. Real world interactions occur concurrently; consequently, the objects that represent those real world entities must interact concurrently. Smalltalk supports concurrency by providing a construct called a "process." However, the "process" feature in Smalltalk has been criticized as being limited (Yokote and Tokoro 1987). Other OOPLs have made attempts to support concurrency with various language features. The major examples of these concurrent OOPLs are Hewitts Actor Model and ABCL/1 (Khoshafian and Abnous 1990).

In addition to the OOPLs, many other languages that were not developed as OOPL have been extended to support object oriented concepts (e.g., C++) (Pratt and Zelkowitz 1996). The success of these object oriented extensions to the various programming languages has been varied (Khoshafian and Abnous 1990).

In addition to Smalltalk, the work done at PARC (Xerox's Palo Alto Research Park) which was led by Alan Kay, Adele Goldberg, Daniel Ingall and others, applied object oriented ideas and technology to many other areas. One of their most notable applications of object oriented design principles was the design of the objected oriented computer interface (Collins 1995). The object oriented interface developed at PARC influenced the design of the Apple Macintosh and led to the development of the graphical user interface (Shneiderman 1988).

Graphical user interfaces (GUI) use the concepts of objects to represent a desktop metaphor wherein icons appear for files, applications, and devices. Each icon on the desktop represents an object that can be selected and used according to its specified behavior (Collins 1995) (Foley 1987). Message passing and communication protocols between the objects are implemented with constructs similar to those described above for programming languages. Current operating systems like Windows, Mac OS, and Warp support dynamic information exchange between applications by using object message passing protocols. The object oriented paradigm has effected not only the design of the interface itself, but all aspects of the operating system and system resource management and communication.

Artificial Intelligence

Independently of the research in the software community, artificial intelligence (AI) researchers were struggling with essentially the same problem of modeling and structuring knowledge that beset software developers and program language designers. Scripts and frames were developed by AI researchers as constructs for organizing and representing real world knowledge. Marvin Minsky used the concept of a frame as a way of packaging both declarative and procedural knowledge into a single representation (Minsky 1975). Objects in object oriented programming languages are similar in concept to the frame used for knowledge representation in artificial intelligence (Parsaye, Chignell et al. 1989).

A frame is a data structure that includes all knowledge about an entity or concept. Frames represent a unit of knowledge that combines both declarations (structure) and procedures (behavior). Detail about the frame is included in the slots and facets of the frame (Turban 1993). The slot can contain procedural knowledge or declarative knowledge about the frame. Frame based programming languages (Finin 1986) are similar in concept to object oriented programming languages and many of the ideas for knowledge representation have been used in the implementation of object oriented programming languages. Although the two concepts, frames and objects, emerged from different groups, it is clear that there are many similarities.

Databases

Databases and their design have also contributed and benefited significantly from the object oriented paradigm. Data modeling concepts have had a significant influence on object oriented analysis and design methodologies. Many object oriented analysis and design methodologies have been built on data and information modeling concepts in entity-relation (ER) diagrams and other semantic data models. In the ER diagram, first proposed by Chen, the information domain is modeled in terms of entities, attributes, and the relationships between entities (Chen 1976).

Entities in the ER diagram share many similar characteristics to objects or classes in object orientation. For example, a customer entity can be seen as a template (i.e., class) for holding instances of customers (i.e., individual customer objects). Strategies for transforming ER entities and their relations into relational database tables are well defined in the database literature (McFadden and Hoffer 1994). The attributes of the entities in the ER diagram become the columns in the relational tables and linkages between tables are established through the use of common link fields (i.e., attributes). Entities, as described in database literature (Parsaye, Chignell et al. 1989; Khoshafian and Abnous 1990; Kim 1990; Ozsu and Valduriez 1991; McFadden and Hoffer 1994), have only data structure and do not encapsulate behavior or code; consequently, they are significantly different than objects (which encapsulate both code and data).

Object oriented Databases (OODB) based on the concepts of object orientation currently exist and many more are under development (Kim 1990). The advantage of OODB, according to Khoshafian and Abnous (Khoshafian and Abnous 1990), is that they overcome many of the limitations of current relational database architecture by providing more expressiveness in modeling complex and nested information (e.g., the information in CAD and engineering databases) (Edelstein 1991).

Since OO concepts have shown great potential for improving programming languages, database design, interfaces, and other aspects of information technology, many developers and experts are now attempting to apply OO concepts to the analysis and design issues in software development. Many new software development methodologies have adopted these OO concepts as a basis for their approach. The following sections discuss the general approach used by these OO methodologists.

OO Analysis Methodologies

According to Booch, "a method is a disciplined process for generating a set of models for describing a software system under development, using some well defined notation" (Booch 1991). Peters and Tripp assert that a "methodology is a collection of methods for developing coordinated by some general philosophy" for developing a system (Peters and Tripp 1977). The general philosophy used in OO software development is based on OO concepts. An overview of the general approach used by many object oriented methodologies follows.

Steps in OOA

The purpose of OO analysis is the same as traditional approaches to analysis; that is, to produce a complete description of the problem domain and the requirements for the proposed system (Fichman and Kemerer 1992). The difference between an object oriented approach to analysis and a traditional approach is the method for understanding and representing the problem domain. For example, with structured analysis, problem decomposition is based on processes or functions. Top level functions or processes are identified and decomposed into subprocesses. These subprocesses are in turn decomposed into other processes (Yourdon and Constantine, 1979).

The basic understanding of the problem domain comes from understanding what processes must occur and how the data is transformed by these processes. The basic approach of structured analysis is top-down (Page-Jones, 1988). OO analysis, on the other hand, organizes the problem statement around objects that exist in the user's view of the world. These objects can be implemented in a top-down, bottom-up, or middle-out approach (Henderson-Sellers and Edwards, 1990). A typical approach to object analysis is as follows:

1) An initial problem statement is identified. The focus of the problem statement should be on what is to be done, not how. Since the initial problem statement is usually incomplete, it becomes only the basis for developing a full analysis.
2) From the problem statements the potential objects are identified. Since not all objects are explicit in the problem statement, general and application domain knowledge should be used to identify additional candidate objects. Once all potential objects have been identified, similar objects can be grouped into classes. The initial object model is refined by eliminating all irrelevant, vague, or redundant classes.

3) A data dictionary is prepared to provide a complete description of all classes.
4) Associations between classes are identified. Associations, which are dependencies between classes, can usually be identified by looking for the verbs in the problem statement. For example, "works-for" might describe an association between a person object and a company object.
5) Identify the attributes. Attributes are properties of classes. Adjectives can be used to identify object attributes.
6) Refine the model by using inheritance to share common structure.
7) Define the behavior of the objects by defining the operations and the messages that pass between them (Tkach, 1994, pp. 323).

Steps in OOD

OO Design, like traditional design, focuses on the "how." The overall system architecture is developed during system design and implementation details are added to the basic object model. Unlike structured design, most authors of OO design advocate a single notation centered around the object concept (Bailin 1989; Wirfs-Brock, Wilkerson et al. 1990; Rumbaugh, Blaha et al., 1991; Martin and Odell, 1998). This single notational schema can be applied to all the activities of the software development. An example of this approach is Rumbaugh's OMT (Object Modeling Technique).

OMT uses the same notation for all the activities of software development. The shift from analysis to design is largely a matter of changing emphasis from problem domain concepts to solution domain concepts. Since some of the objects in the solution domain have no direct analog in the problem domain, new objects must be added to represent the solution constructs necessary to implement the solution (i.e., interface objects, control objects). The use of a single notation facilitates the addition of new objects in the design process.

The benefits of using the same conceptual unit to address issues of analysis and design are twofold. First, unlike the shift from structured analysis to structured design, the notation remains the same. This reduces the need to map analysis notation into design notation, i.e., data flow diagrams into structured charts. The benefit here is a reduction in system development complexity. A second major benefit is that the consistent notation supports an iterative approach to system development. This encourages a more pragmatic and realistic approach to design which Booch characterizes as "analyze a little, design a little" (Booch 1994). A typical approach to design is as follows:

Refine the work during OOA by looking for subclasses and message characteristics, and the details associated with implementation constructs; then, represent the procedural detail associated with each object attribute, and the procedural detail associated with each operation.

The above approach to design represents the basic approach used by Pressman and Booch (Booch 1991; Pressman, 1992). Other authors approach object oriented analysis and design differently (Bailin 1989; Weinberg, Guimaraes et al. 1990; Wirfs-Brock, Wilkerson et al., 1990). Rumbaugh, for example, divides design into two parts which he calls system design and object design. During system design overall system architecture is developed. The relationships between the subsystems which are organized around a given set of functions (called a service by Rumbaugh) are specified. During object design, internal data structures and implementation details (specifications of algorithms) for operations are detailed (Rumbaugh, Blaha et al., 1991).

The Unified Modeling Language (UML) has recently been developed to address some of the problems caused by conflicting notation and concepts in OOA. The UML approach brings together much of the work of Booch, Rumbaugh, and Jacobson and attempts to provide a common framework (meta-model) that can used to represent the semantics of different approaches to OOA (Martin and Odell, 1998).

Diffusion of OOA

Although OO analysis and requirements modeling has great potential for addressing many of the problems associated with modern IS and software development, its acceptance has not been widespread. The study of the adoption of OOA can be based on the diffusion literature.

Research based on diffusion of innovation (DOI) investigates the evaluation, adoption, and implementation of innovations (Rogers, 1983). Although there exists a large body of research that has used DOI theory to investigate the induction of new information technologies and information systems into organizations, very little literature exists that has used DOI to investigate the adoption of new "methodologies" aimed at improving the analysis phase of software development (Raghaven, 1989, p. 214). Currently, most of the literature that has addressed new practices or techniques in software engineering has focused on either design or code level activities.

The diffusion of innovations has been studied since the early 1940s and comprises a substantial body of literature(Prescott, 1995, p. 439). Diffusion is defined as " the process by which an innovation is communicated through certain channels over time among the members of a social system" (Rogers, 1983). Factors which affect the diffusion of innovations include the characteristics of the innovation, the social system which is the target of the innovation, and the various communication channels over which information about the innovation is communicated.

The diffusion process consists of two stages: adoption and implementation. The adoption stage is often broken down into stages of knowledge acquisition, persuasion and learning and decision leading to the actual adoption decision. The implementation stage includes change to work organization, work processes and the technology necessary for the innovation deployment within the organization (Prescott and Conger 1995). DOI has been used to study a variety of IS technologies including e-mail, multimedia, data administration, and object oriented methods. The DOI research within the IS community has been influenced by the formation of DIGIT (Diffusion Interest Group in Information Technology) which was formed in 1988.

Diffusion literature suggests that the successful introduction of innovations and technologies (e.g. OOA) depends in part on the characteristics of the innovation, organizational influences, and the personal characteristics of potential users.

DOI Factors

Characteristics of the innovation are conceptualized in diffusion literature as relative advantage, compatibility, complexity, trialability, and observability. The relative advantage of an innovation is the degree to which it is perceived as being an improvement over the current practice or technology it is replacing. Relative advantage can be measured in economic terms or an increase in social prestige or some other benefit. If an innovation is perceived to have a large relative advantage then its adoption rate would be positively affected. The compatibility of an innovation is the degree to which the innovation is perceived to be consistent with existing practices. Innovations that are very dissimilar to existing practices will be less likely to be accepted than innovations that are similar or built on current practices. Complexity is the degree to which an innovation is perceived to be difficult to understand and use. Innovations that are perceived to be complex or complicated will be adopted less readily than innovations that are perceived to be easily to understood and used. Trialability refers to the degree which an innovation may be used or experimented with on a limited basis. Innovations that are easier to use on a limited basis are usually adopted faster.

Observability refers to the degree to which the results of an innovation are visible to others. If the use of an innovation results in positive benefits that are easily observed, then the innovation will be adopted more quickly.

Organizational factors do influence the adoption of innovations. These factors can include organizational reward structures, training, management support, and the role of various change agents. Organization reward structures and job performance criteria can be used to encourage the adoption of an innovation. Often, however, organizations fail to align their reward and job performance criteria with the new practices and procedures required to support the innovation. Consequently, potential users of the innovation fail to see the benefits of adopting the innovation at a personal level even though they recognize that the innovation does produce a superior product. This discrepancy can result in a lack of motivation on the part of the potential adopters and even cause resistance to the innovation.

Training and management support are also factors that can influence the adoption of innovations within organizations. Training in a new technology can positively influence the acceptance and use of the new technology; however, in order for the training to be effective it must be of sufficient duration to ensure a minimal competence level. Strong management support can also encourage the adoption of a new technology; however, reward structures must be aligned to reinforce management efforts.

The importance of change agents in the successful induction of new technologies is well established in the DOI literature. However, the effectiveness of these change agents does vary between organizations and type of innovation.

Traditional DOI literature, some based on marketing research studies, has hypothesized a positive correlation between some demographic descriptors and adoption rate. However, recent studies relating to the diffusion of information technologies and software engineering innovations have shown a more mixed result (Leonard-Barton 1987).

Characteristics of OOA: Diffusion Perspective

Although all of the above mentioned factors have influenced the adoption of OOA, this discussion will focus only on the characteristics of the innovation itself. According to Rogers, 49% to 87% of the rate of adoption can be explained by the attributes or characteristics of the innovation.

The lack of widespread adoption of OOA can be explained, in part, by comparing it with the dominant approach currently being used in the IS field-structured analysis. Compared to structured analysis (SA), OOA ranks lower on most of the attributes necessary for a fast rate of adoption. However, with respect to SA, OOA can be said to have a higher relative advantage. Evidence for this assertion abounds in the literature (Fichman 1993). Most practitioner literature has been uniformly positive about the potential of OO technologies based on the perceived potential of this approach. The main argument presented here is that OOA represents a more natural way of model-

Table 1: DOI Factors

Factors	Variables
Characteristics of the Innovation	relative advantage compatibility complexity trialability observability
Organizational Influences	job performance criteria reward system training management support advocates for the innovation access to consulting help client preferences
Personal Characteristics of Potential Users	demographics technical skills years of experiences

ing reality, whereas SA forces the developer into a conceptionalization of reality based on processes and functions. This can be a significant disadvantage when designing applications for client-server environments or for highly dynamic systems. OOA also offers an advantage over SA because the concept of the object can be used consistently in both the analysis and design phases of development. Implementation constructs (e.g., interface and control objects) can be added during the design of the system using the same notation and models as analysis. In SA, design is usually implemented with different constructs (structure charts). This switching of concepts and notation can add a cognitive burden to the developer.

Overall, the compatibility of OOA with existing approaches is low. OOA, and OO concepts, in general, represent a paradigm shift in thinking about problems. SA which is based on the familiar concept of process is significantly more compatible with traditional imperative programming and system development. Currently, standards are being established that will address some compatibility issues with existing legacy systems (i.e., CORBA). However, fundamentally the incompatibility of OOA with existing approaches is based on the paradigmatic shift in thinking that is required to analyze and design a system using object concepts.

OOA rates unfavorably on the complexity attribute because it requires developers to learn a whole new set of concepts. Successful application of OOA requires that the developers learn basic object oriented concepts and a methodology for applying these concepts to analysis. A whole host of strategies is offered to assist developers in finding objects (i.e., use cases), classifying objects (domain analysis), and describing object behavior (object life cycles, object interaction diagrams). Understanding this new skill set requires a significant effort on the part of the developer.

OOA is difficult to use on a trial basis because of the high cost of training and implementation. In addition, many of the benefits of OOA can only be achieved after a significant investment of time and effort to create a database of reusable objects. Although reuse is a concept that has been applied mostly at the code level, reusable analysis and design objects are also a promise of object orientation. However, this benefit would not likely be achieved in a trial period.

It is difficult to observe the benefits and effects of OOA, given that metrics for OO techniques are poorly defined. This is especially true

Technology Characteristics	OOA	Structured Analysis
relative advantage	high	medium
compatibility	low	high
complexity	high	medium
trialability	low	medium
observability	low	medium

for OOA, which addresses the complexity of analyzing and defining requirements. The analysis and requirements stage is the most unstructured part of the development life cycle. Any benefits that would accrue from an improved analysis and requirements definition would not likely be observable until the final stages of the development.

In summary, although OOA rates high on relative advantage with respect to SA, it rates less favorably with respect to the other characteristics. However, this does not necessarily imply that OOA will not be as widely adopted as SA in the long run. But it does imply that the rate of adoption for OOA will be relatively slow and that the role of change agents and effective adoption management strategies will be critical to OOA's success in the marketplace.

Management must take an active role to ensure widespread adoption of OOA. Effective training as well as effective reward structures are essential. In addition, projects must have measurable milestones that will show the effectiveness of OOA. Reuse, a significant benefit of OOA, can only be achieved through management policies that encourage reuse and the development of organizational repositories of objects.

Conclusion

Determining requirements has always been a difficult phase of IS and software development. Mistakes made during requirements are difficult to correct and can lead to an ineffective or abandoned system development effort. The difficulty of determining requirements and doing analysis has increased because of complexity of new systems and technologies. Previous approaches based on structured analysis and process decomposition provide limited support for developing the dynamic and highly interactive systems required today. A new approach to requirements analysis based on object concepts has emerged as a potential solution to the problems associated with requirements analysis. However, object oriented concepts represent a distinctly different set of concepts that require a paradigmatic shift in thinking on the part of developers, managers, and users. An understanding of the concepts, their origins, and the basic approaches used in OO software and system development is essential to effective use and management of OOA projects.

Although OOA has potential to address many of the issues in developing requirements its adoption has not been widespread. The difficulty of adopting and using OOA is similar to most new technologies and innovations. Many factors influence the adoption of an innovation: characteristics of the innovation, organizational factors, and the attitudes and abilities of the potential adopters. Effective management of the adoption process requires an awareness of these factors and capable management policies to address the problems and difficulties of adopting OOA. While the "relative" advantage of OOA is high, it lacks characteristics that ease the resistance to an innovation or technology; consequently, effective management policies are critical to adopting and using OOA.

Training, effective reward structures, and realistic project selection and milestones can help encourage the adoption of this exciting new technology. However, understanding the basic concepts, their origins, and uses in OO software and system development is a necessary prerequisite to developing management strategies for its adoption and use.

References

Bailin, S. (1989). "An Object Oriented Requirements Specification Method." *Communication of the ACM*, 32 (May), 608-623.

Booch (1991). *Object oriented Design with Applications.* Redwood City, CA., Benjamin/Cumming Co.

Booch, G. (1986). "Object Oriented Development." *IEEE Transaction on Software Engineering*, 12 (February), 211-221.

Booch, G. (1994). *Object Oriented Analysis and Design with Applications.* (2nd ed.). Redwood City, CA: Benjamin/Cummings Co.

Booch, G., J. Rumbaugh, et al. (1995). The Evolution of Object Methods. Santa Clara, CA, Rational Software Corporation.

Bourne, J. (1992). *Object Oriented Engineering: Building Systems Using.* Smalltalk-80.Homewood, IL: Irwin

Chen, P. (1976). "The Entity-Relationship Model-Toward a Unified

View of Data." *ACM Transactions of Database Systems*, 1(1), 9-36.
Coad, P., D. North, et al. (1995). *Object Models: Strategies, Patterns, & Applications*. Englewoods Cliffs, NJ: Yourdon Press.
Collins, D. (1995). *Designing Object Oriented User Interfaces*. Redwood City, CA., Benjamin/Cummings Co.
Davis, A. (1993). *Software Requirements: Objects, Functions, & States*. Englewood Cliffs, NJ: Prentice-Hall.
Edelstein, H. (1991). "Relational vs. Object Oriented." *DBMS* (November): 68-79.
Fichman, R., &. Kemerer, C.. (1993). "Adoption of Software Engineering Process Innovations: The Case of Object Orientation." *Sloan Management Review* (Winter), 7-22.
Fichman, R. and C. Kemerer (1992). "Object Oriented and Conventional Analysis and Design Methodologies." *Computer* (Oct.), 22-39.
Finin, T. (1986). "Understanding Frame Languages." *A1 Expert* (November): 44-50.
Foley, J. (1987). Interfaces for Advanced Computing. *Scientific American*. October.
Henderson-Sellers, B. and J. Edwards (1990). "Object-Oriented Systems Life Cycle." *Communication of the ACM*, 33 (September), 143-159.
Jacobson, I. (1993). *Object oriented Software Engineering*, Reading, MA: Addison-Wesley.
Khoshafian, S. and R. Abnous (1990). *Object-Orientation: Concepts, Languages, Databases, User Interfaces*. New York, NY: Wiley.
Kim, W. (1990). "Object Oriented Databases: Defintion and Research." *IEEE Transactions on Knowledge and Data Engineering*, 2(3), 327-341.
LaLonde, W. (1994). *Discovering Smalltalk*. Redwood City, CA: Benjamin/Cummings Co..
Leonard-Barton, D. (1987). "Implementing Structured Software Methodologies: A Case of Innovation in Process Technologies." *Interfaces* 17(3), 6-17.
Loy, P. (1990). "A Comparison of Object Oriented and Structured Development Methods." *ACM SIGSOFT: Software Engineering Notes*, 15(1), 44-48.
Martin, J. and J. Odell (1992). *Object Oriented Analysis and Design*. Englewood, NJ: Prentice Hall.
Martin, J. and J. Odell (1998). *Object Oriented Methods A Foundation*.

Englewood, NJ: Prentice Hall.

McFadden and Hoffer (1994). *Database Management*, Redwood City, CA Benjamin/Cummings Co.

Michalski, R. and R. Stepp (1983). Learning from Observation: Conceptual Clustering. In R. Michalski, J. Carbonell and T. Mitchellm (Eds.), *Machine Learning: An Artificial Intelligence Approach*, Palo Alto, CA: Tioga.

Minsky, M. (1975). A Framework for Representing Knowledge. In P. Winston (Ed,), *The Psychology of Computer Vision*, New York:, NY: McGraw-Hill.

Norman, D. (1988). *The Design of Everyday Things*, New York, NY: Doubleday Currency.

Ozsu, M. and P. Valduriez (1991). "Distributed Databases: Where Are We Now?" *Computer IEEE* (August), 68-78.

Page-Jones, M. (1988). *The Practical Guide to Structured Systems Design*, Englewood Cliffs, NJ Yourdon Press.

Pancake, C. (1995). " The Promise and Cost of Object Technology: A Five Year Forecast." *Communications of the ACM*, 33 (10), 22-49.

Parsaye, K., M. Chignell, et al. (1989). *Intelligent Databases*. New York, NY: Wiley.

Peters, L. and L. Tripp (1977). "Comparing Software Design methodologies." *Datamation* (November), 89-93.

Pratt, T. and M. Zelkowitz (1996). *Programming Languages: Design and Implementation*. Englewood, NJ: Prentice Hall.

Prescott, M. and S. Conger (1995). Information Technology Innovations: A Classification by IT Locus of Impact and Research Approach. Working Paper.

Pressman, R. S. (1992). *Software Engineering: A Practitioner's Approach*. (2nd ed.). New York, NY: McGraw-Hill

Pressman, R. S. (1996). *Software Engineering: A Practitioner's Approach*. (3rd ed.). New York, NY: McGraw-Hill.

Rogers, E. (1983). *Diffusion of Innovations*. New York,: NY: Free Press.

Rumbaugh, J., M. Blaha, et al. (1991). *Object oriented Modeling and Design*. Englewoods, NJ: Prentice Hall.

Shneiderman, B. (1988). *Designing the User Interface*. Reading, MA: Addison-Wesley.

Simon, H. (1969). *The Science of the Artificial*. Cambridge, MA: MIT Press.

Sowa, J. (1984). *Conceptual Structures: Information Processing in Mind and Machine*. Reading, MA: Addison-Wesley.

Turban, E. (1993). *Decison Support and Expert Systems,* (3rd ed.) MacMillan.

Vessey, I., & Conger, S. (1994). "Requirements Specifications: Learning Object, Process, and Data Methodologies." *Communications of the ACM*, 37(5): 102-113.

Weinberg, R., T. Guimaraes, et al. (1990). "Object Oriented Systems Development." *Journal of Information Systems Management*, 7, 4, 18-26.

Whitten, J., L. Bentley, et al. (1994). *Systems Analysis and Design Methods*. Homewood, IL: Irwin.

Wirfs-Brock, R., B. Wilkerson, et al. (1990). *Designing Object-Oriented Software*. Englewoods Cliffs NJ: Prentice-Hall.

Yadav, S., R. Bravoco, et al. (1988). Comparison of Analysis Techniques for Information Requirement Determination. *Communications of the ACM*, 31, 9:1090-1097.

Yokote, Y. and M. Tokoro (1987). Concurrent Programming in Concurrent Smalltalk. In A. Yonezawa and M. Tokoro (Eds.), *Object Oriented Concurrent Programming*. Cambridge, MA: MIT Press.

Yourdon, E. and L. Constantine (1979). *Structured Design*. Englewoods, NJ: Prentice Hall.

Yourdon, E., K. Whitehead, et al. (1995). *Mainstream Objects: An Analysis and Design Approach for Business*. Upper Saddle River, NJ: Prentice Hall.

Chapter II

Building on Structured Design Techniques in the Object Oriented Environment

H. James Nelson
University of Utah, USA

Kay M. Nelson
University of Utah,USA

Mehdi Ghods
The Boeing Company, USA

Holly E. Lee
University of Kansas, USA

Introduction

The term structured methods refers to a philosophy of software development which emphasizes an adherence to a set of consistent rules or methods throughout a project (Yourdon, 1989). These methods include broad programs such as Systems Development Lifecycles and Methods and Information Engineering as well as individual techniques such as structured programming, data flow diagramming, data modeling, and Object Oriented methodologies. Perhaps the newest, most visible, but least understood of these methodologies are the Object Oriented methods. The specific set of rules or methods that organizations use can come from a variety of sources. Organizations often implement their own methodologies for software development, using tools and techniques borrowed from a variety of formalized methodologies. Commercially produced methodologies are also widely used, usually obtained from software vendors and consultants.

The primary objectives of traditional structured methodologies can be summarized as follows: (Martin and McClure, 1988)

- Achieve high-quality programs of predictable behavior
- Achieve programs that are easily modifiable (maintainable)
- Simplify the development process
- Control the development process
- Speed up system development
- Lower the cost of system development

Structured methodologies seek to attain these objectives through the decomposition of complex problems and constructs into simpler ones, the use of modeling and diagramming techniques, achievement of code clarity and readability, improved communication with end users, improved documentation, and earlier error detection (Chapin, 1979; Topper et.al., 1994). Some methodologies also provide for repositories and libraries of code and modules which encourage reuse (Banker and Kauffman, 1991).

Graham (1994) summarizes the benefits of Object Oriented (OO) methodologies as:

- reuse
- higher quality due to reuse of tested objects and modules
- flexibility
- more naturalistic applications
- ease of maintenance
- ability to reverse engineer and trace requirements

The focus of traditional structured methods is function and procedure with data shared by functions or processes (Bordoloi and Lee, 1994). In OO methodologies, data and procedure are encapsulated within the object. Therefore, the primary focus is on data modeling rather than process modeling. This difference in focus does not require that all of the knowledge gained through the use of traditional structured methods be put aside when adopting OO languages and methodologies. Rather, a need exists to map traditional methods that have shown performance results in the organization to the OO paradigm. This mapping should be a conceptual one in that the logic remains the same while the mechanics and focus of the methodology are adapted for OO. Janet Conway, of GE advanced Concepts Center, states that, "The largest single cost in converting to OO methodology is training." (Conway, 1993). Reusing knowledge gained from the traditional structured methods environment is one way of reducing these training costs by focusing on the concepts that produce the best results and adapting them to new development paradigms.

This research examines specific traditional structured methods for their contribution to traditional development team performance. The attitude of the team toward structured methods and the satisfaction of the team with training in structured methods are used as mediating variables in this examination. Correlation analysis and stepwise regression are used as analysis methodologies. The results of these analyses are then mapped to the OO environment.

Why Structured Methods Make a Difference

Structured methods, as a general concept, can make a difference to application development projects in many ways (Atkas, 1987; Graham, 1994; Topper et.al., 1994). Using structured methods can effect development team efficiency and effectiveness. The overall quality and business value of the delivered system can be improved. User satisfaction with product attributes such as the format of information, the content of information, ease of use of the system, timeliness of information, and accuracy of information, as well as overall user satisfaction are also impacted by structured methods.

Yourdon (1986) states that application programmers are not very productive and that structured methods can increase programmer productivity through standardization of work methods and outputs. This can be accomplished on two dimensions, efficiency and effectiveness. Efficiency is the rate at which programmers produce programs. Efficiency can be measured in terms of meeting user needs or meeting specified deadlines. It can also be measured as how much of the work is performed correctly the first time and does not need reworking. Effectiveness addresses the quality of the product produced by programmers. Does it capture the needs of the business process? Is it delivered bug free? Does it produce the right information at the right time? These concepts apply to both the traditional and OO development environment.

Structured methods can reduce the impact of differences in programmers' abilities (Yourdon, 1986). Structured methods seek to formalize the instinctive good practices of experienced programmers in a way that can be taught to programmers of all experience and ability levels. This is especially critical in a new paradigm such as OO, where most of a development team may be relatively inexperienced. Examples of programming practices are the breaking down of a large system into modules, well organized coding or classes, and complete and accurate documentation (Topper et.al., 1994).

Yet another reason why structured methods impact developer efficiency and effectiveness is the percentage of time developers actually spend programming. Brooks (1995) states that normally only one sixth of development time is spent writing code. OO programming requires even less code than structured programming with procedural languages because of its feature of inheritance and polymorphism (Bordoloi and Lee, 1994). Structured methods not only structure the programming process, but the management processes which are involved in application development, such as meetings, reporting, documenting, inspecting, testing, and communicating (Topper et. al., 1994). These processes exist in both the traditional and OO environments.

Structured methods can also impact the quality and business value of a system. The structured methods performed at the beginning of application development are especially critical for quality and business value. Estimation provides an early analysis of costs to benefits. Data/process models, enterprise models, and design inspections can insure that the system being developed is the one needed for the business (Topper et.al., 1994). The role of users in enterprise modeling and design inspections can result in increased quality and business value. Code or object inspections and other forms of testing can contribute to quality by insuring delivery of a minimum defect product (Chaar, Halliday, Bhandari, and Chillarege, 1993).

The user satisfaction measures of timeliness, accuracy, format, and content of information in the system, as well as ease of use of the system are impacted by structured methods. High levels of initial user satisfaction will result in lower system maintenance costs (Yourdon, 1986; Topper et.al., 1994). While maintenance to keep pace with changes in the business process will always be a reality, a system that meets user needs up front will require fewer changes to meet users' current needs.

The Role of Attitudes in Structured Methods

The attitude of developers toward structured methods can make a difference in performance. The Theory of Reasoned Action (TRA) (Fishbein and Ajzen, 1975; Ajzen and Fishbein, 1980) provides a way of understanding the relationship of attitudes toward technology and technology performance. In this theory, a person's performance of a behavior is a result of behavioral intention (BI) to perform the behavior. This BI has two components, the person's attitude (A) and subjective norms (SN) about the behavior.

$$BI = A + SN$$

BI is defined as the strength of a person's intention to perform a behavior. A is defined as positive or negative feelings about performing the behavior, and SN refers to a person's perception of how people important to him or her feel about performing the task.

Davis (1986) adapted the TRA into a Technology Acceptance Model (TAM) specifically designed to model user acceptance of information systems. TAM differs from TRA in that it does not include SN as a determinant of BI. Davis, Bagozzi, and Warshaw (1989) tested this model and confirmed that for user acceptance of information systems, SNA is not a significant indicator of BI. This same study demonstrated that BI is determined by A and perceived usefulness (U).

$$BI = A + U$$

This implies that all else being equal, people form intentions to perform behaviors which they hold positive attitudes towards and perceive they can have positive results with.

Sherif, Sherif and Nebergall (1965) found in several studies that groups exhibit group behaviors and attitudes. As the knowledge base, expectations, and realities of a group become more cohesive, cooperation and group behaviors begin to appear (Sherif, 1962). Groups begin to exhibit a single attitude which can exhibit itself in contrast to that of other groups, such as an "us against them" group attitude.

Ancona (1990) also found that the external interactions of groups have patterns similar to the internal patterns of the members of the group. In this research, when individual members of a development team exhibit attitudes toward structured methods, the group itself will display these attitudes. These attitudes, according to the TAM model, will lead to behavioral intentions and usage of structured methods.

The Role of Training

Formal training in structured methods also impacts both structured methods and CASE usage and team performance. It is not only the quantity and quality of training received that matters, it is the level of satisfaction with this training on the part of developers which impacts usage and performance. In other words, great training is only great training if the student perceives it as such. The ability to conceptualize the ideas behind structured methods and to see potential benefits from using them can be gained through good training programs.

Structured Methods in This Study

This study measures the structured methods of estimation, data/ process modeling, enterprise modeling, standards, design inspection, code inspection, user training, and metrics collection. These methods were chosen using a traditional systems development lifecycle model and an information engineering type of model (Topper et.al., 1994). Figure 1 shows these models and the structured methods constructs they represent in the center of the figure.

Data was not available for all of the constructs listed in Figure 1, so only the methods listed above were chosen for measurement and analysis. Each of the constructs chosen are defined below.

Estimation is defining application priorities and dependencies, product scope, and preliminary project feasibility. Estimation allows I/S organizations to forecast the time and cost required to produce a system. This information can be communicated to users and be used as a project management tool.

Data/process modeling is defined as producing data models, process/function models, and modeling the distribution of data and process. Data/process modeling allows system developers to capture the nature and flow of information in the system during early phases in development.

Enterprise modeling is defined as using observation and interview data to model the business model. Enterprise modeling depicts

Figure 1. Initial models and constructs

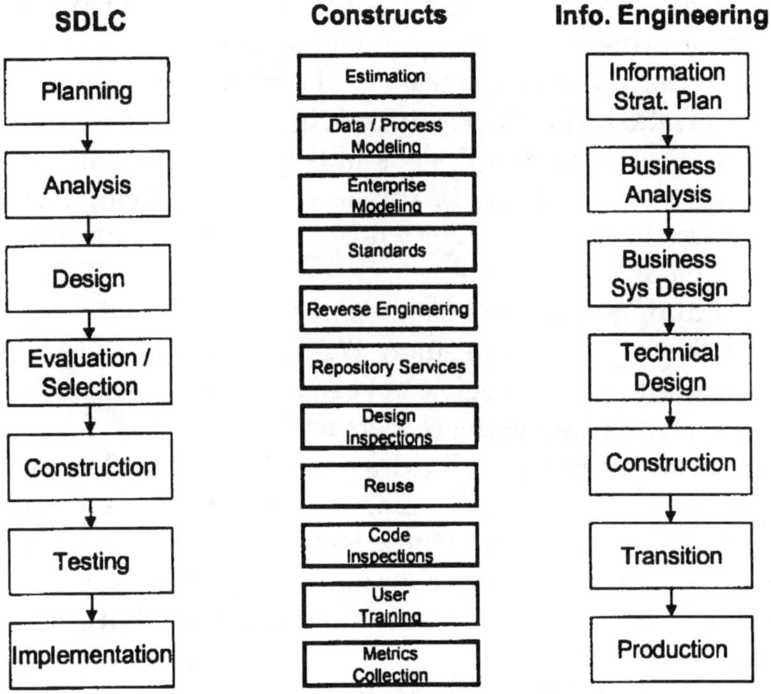

the tasks and activities as well as the flows of the business process. It can be used to generate process diagrams for the information system. Another purpose of enterprise modeling is to communicate the flow of information in a way comprehensible to the user.

Standards is defined as the enforcement of compliance with standards. Standards are put in place for software development for a variety of reasons. Standards can force developers to produce a product that is compatible with other systems in the organization. Standards in documentation allow easier maintenance by people other than the original developer. Standards can enforce both the way which systems are developed and the composition of the final system. An example of a structural standard would be that the span of control of a program module cannot exceed four layers of programming. An example of a process standard would be that every programmer conducts a code inspection once a week.

Design inspection is defined as performing walkthroughs and reviews of the system design with users. The purpose of design inspection is to look for flaws, weaknesses, errors, and omissions in the design before the code is written (Chaar, et al., 1993).

Code inspection is defined as performing walkthroughs and reviews of the code once it has been written. Code inspections are normally performed by the programmer(s) who wrote the code, other members of the development team, and perhaps other programmers in the organization. The purpose of code inspection is to look for flaws, weaknesses, errors, and omissions in the code before it is put into production (Chaar, et al., 1993). This is especially critical since defects are much less likely to be detected once a system is in production (Yourdon, 1986).

User training is defined as the percent of users who have been trained on the software application. Training is not included as a part of all structured methodologies, but can be a useful tool in the hand-off of the system from the developers to the users.

Metrics collection is defined as metrics data collected for the purpose of productivity measurement. Many measures are collected by organizations. Examples of these metrics and measures are source lines of code, function points, labor hours, cost, and complexity. This data is used by organizations to calculate the productivity of software development activities.

The structured methods described above were tested for direct effects on development team performance. In addition, two other constructs were used as mediating variables to test for effect on performance: attitude toward structured methods and satisfaction with training in structured methods. Attitude toward structured methods is defined as the attitude held by developers on the power, reliability, value, usefulness, and speed of structured methods. Structured methods use is defined as the extent to which structured methods are used in the development team. Satisfaction with structured methods training is defined as satisfaction with the amount and quality of formal education given in structured methods.

The next section details the analysis performed on these variables.

Methodology and Results

In order to compare results across organizations, this study focused on large companies that had extensive in-house Information Systems departments. To control for project size, development projects had to be 12-to-18 months in planned duration. The selected projects were business applications with some strategic relevance to the company. Data was collected on 105 projects at 22 sites of 15 organizations in the US and Canada. Contributing organizations represent financial services, manufacturing, and high-technology industries from the Fortune 500. For each project, we surveyed the development team at the end of the requirements phase of the project. All of the 105 teams provided information on structured methods usage, attitude, and training. The projects consisted of a variety of computing infrastructures including mainframe, local networks, uncoupled work stations, mixed vendor shops, and rudimentary client-server systems. Studied projects made use of more than 20 different CASE tools. Data on structured methods use, training, and attitude was given by the developers. Performance data was collected from information systems and user managers who are considered the stakeholders of the systems.

The specific structured methods defined in the previous section were tested for impact on performance using stepwise regression. In stepwise regression, all of the structured methods are added to a model of performance based on a specific dependent variable such as quality. The regression procedure adds variables one at a time, testing for contribution to performance, and keeping variables which contribute while dropping those that do not. Figures 2 and 3 show the results of the stepwise regression procedures. The number of teams in these regressions was 54.

Figure 2 shows the structured methods which contribute to team efficiency, overall user satisfaction, business value and quality. Design inspections are shown to be a significant contributor to team efficiency at the .02 significance level. Design inspections and enterprise modeling both contribute to overall user satisfaction with a system. Design inspections are significant at the .05 level, while enterprise modeling is significant at the .10 level. Design inspection also contributes to system quality as rated by the stakeholders of the system. Design inspection is significant at the .004 level. Estimation contributes to the business value as perceived by stakeholder of the system. Estimation is significant at the .04 level.

Figure 3 shows that structured methods also contribute to the timeliness, accuracy, content, and format of information, as well as ease of use of the system. Code inspection, enterprise modeling, and metrics collection contribute to timeliness of information rated by the end users of the system. Code inspection is significant at the .10 level, enterprise modeling at the .06 level, and metrics collection at the .10

Figure 2. Structured methods contribution to performance

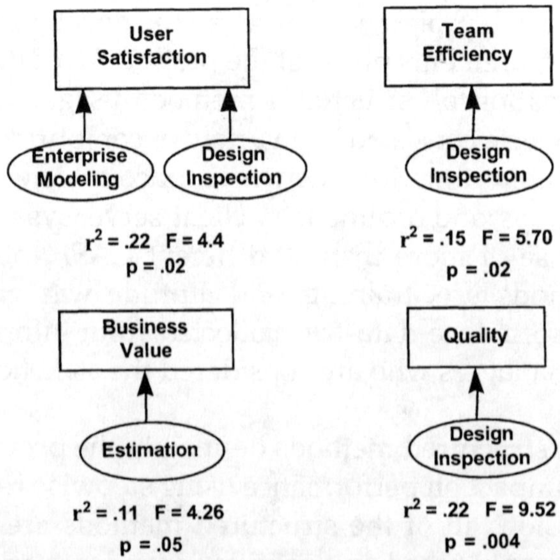

level. Enterprise modeling and design inspection contribute to accuracy of information and format of information. Enterprise modeling is significant at the .10 level for both accuracy and format, while design inspection is significant at the .02 level for accuracy and the .08 level for format. Content of information is impacted by enterprise modeling and code inspection. Enterprise modeling is significant at the .09 level, while code inspection is significant at the .07 level. Design inspections contribute to the ease of use of the system. Design inspection is significant at the .01 level.

Structured methods were also analyzed for direct effects on performance with attitudes toward structured methods and satisfaction with training in structured methods used as mediating variables. Correlation analysis was used to detect relationships. Table 1 shows the relationship of structured methods to performance for teams with positive attitudes toward structured methods.

Table 1 shows that design inspections, code inspections, and enterprise modeling have the strongest relationship to performance for teams with positive attitudes toward structured methods. Design and code inspections are related to user satisfaction, ease of use, accuracy and content of information. Enterprise modeling is related to the user satisfaction, ease of use, and content of the system. Table 2

Figure 3. Structured methods contribution to performance.

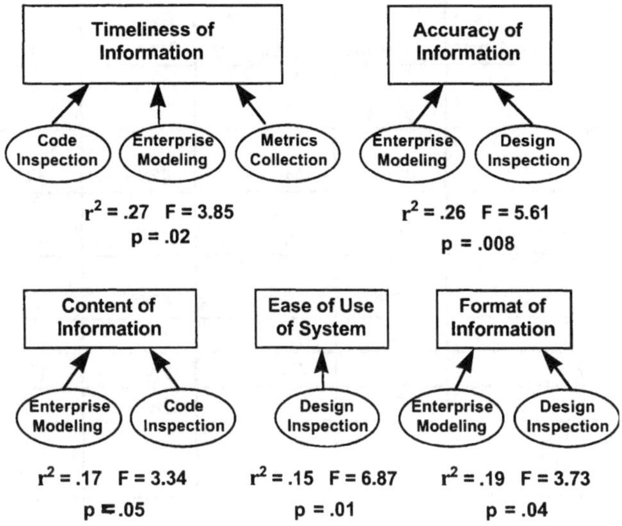

*Table 1: Relationship of Specific Structured Methods on Performance (T3 part V) for Teams with Positive Attitudes Toward Structured Methods. N= 30, *<.05, **<.01*

Method/ Measure	User Satisfaction	Format	Accuracy	Ease of Use	Content
Data/ process modeling	.35	.28	.22	.25	.31
Design Inspection	**.42***	.34	**.51****	**.40***	**.36***
Code inspection	**.41***	.32	**.49****	**.35***	**.37***
Enterprise Modeling	**.39***	.34	.32	**.36***	**.37***
User Training	.35	.36	.22	.36	.33
Estimation	.00	-.02	.05	-.14	.01
Standards	.00	-.22	.04	-.32	.06
Metrics Collection	.03	-.14	.17	-.06	.15

*Table 2: Relationship of Specific Structured Methods on Performance for Teams Satisfied With Training in Structured Methods. N= 30, *<.05,**<.01*

Method/ Measure	User Satisfaction	Format	Accuracy	Ease of Use	Content
Data/process modeling	.52	.57	.45	.54	.55
Design Inspection	.42	.42	.41	.47	.34
Code inspection	.43	.38	.45	.38	.40
Enterprise Modeling	.69**	.70**	.59	.67**	.67**
User Training	.08	.16	.12	.13	.04
Estimation	.20	.26	.13	.25	.16
Standards	.20	.15	.18	.18	.18
Metrics Collection	-.00	-.13	.03	.09	-.09

shows the relationship of structured methods to performance for teams satisfied with training in structured methods.

Enterprise modeling is the only structured method which shows a positive correlation to performance for teams satisfied with training in structured methods. Enterprise modeling is related to user satisfaction, ease of use, format and content of information.

Mapping the Results to OO Methods

This research indicates that structured methods have a direct impact on the development team's performance. Design inspections contribute to user satisfaction, team efficiency, the quality of the work performed on the final product, the accuracy and the format of the information, and the ease of use of the final system. These results support results (Chaar et. al., 1993) that indicate that design inspections detect defects in system documentation, system function, and system interfaces. These defects must be detected early in the lifecycle to insure that the system delivered is the system ordered. Design inspections can also lead to confidence on the part of the users that the development team is performing the work ordered (Yourdon, 1986). In addition to being a method for error detection, design inspection is a management tool for good developer - user interface.

Design inspections are critical to Object Oriented development. OO development is by its nature incremental, concurrent, and iterative (Bordoloi and Lee, 1994). One of the more popular software development life cycle models for OO development is the spiral model (Boehm, 1986). Paper designs and prototype subsystems are released to the users and/or experts for comment, verification, and validation (Graham, 1994). The users see the system much earlier than they would under the waterfall development model, and design mistakes can be corrected much more quickly. Additional benefits to this prototyping approach include the much earlier testing of technical feasibility, the finalizing of reusable components and library classes, and the elimination of the duplication of functionality among classes. By releasing parts of the system to the users, transitioning to the new system is much easier, and developers- enhanced credibility and communication with the user community is greatly facilitated.

This research also shows the importance of code inspections to the timeliness of information and to the content of information. Code inspections reveal many checking and documentation errors (Chaar et al., 1993). A second inspection can be critical in eliminating operational semantic errors. The first code inspection can detect content defects; whereas the second code inspection can detect operational defects that can impact performance measures (for example, timeliness). It should be noted that design and code inspections are primarily manual processes which are difficult to automate with tools such as CASE.

Object Oriented methods blur the lines between analysis, design, and implementation. In traditional structured methods, each phase of development creates a different model. In systems analysis, the high level flow of the software is developed and is modeled in a data flow diagram or a flowchart. Systems design breaks the software into detailed functional components and models these in a functional decomposition diagram. Coding creates the actual software. Each of these phases requires a sort of "translation" of the phase before it.

Object Oriented software development, on the other hand, is "seamless." The same model is used for analysis, design, and implementation. This places much more emphasis on rigorous inspection to ensure that the design elements required by each step is actually produced. It is very tempting in a seamless environment to step directly from analysis into coding without passing through the detailed design step. Graham (1994) recommends testing every object as it its produced, and testing it again as it becomes part of a classification structure.

This research indicates that enterprise modeling contributes to the timeliness, the accuracy, the format, and the content of information, as well as to user satisfaction with the final software product. Enterprise modeling is used extensively in the Object Oriented paradigm. However, frequently OO enterprise modeling follows traditional data modeling: entities and their attributes are identified, and then their behavior is modeled. This generally produces a system that may not meet the needs of the user and may require a great deal of rework. This problem suggests that Object Oriented enterprise modeling must be tied much closer to the user's business processes. Some sort of process model must be produced and objects identified from it rather than "in the blind."

Other problem areas in Object Oriented enterprise modeling include abstraction, problem decomposition, separating analysis (the problem space) from the design (the solution space), and distributing the behavior of the enterprise. These problems may be addressed by focusing a relatively larger proportion of development time on enterprise modeling issues by using examples, discussions, and analysis and design evaluations. This allows analysts to explore alternative representations of a problem from different perspectives (Puhr, Nelson, Monarchi, 1995). As in traditional structured methodologies, time spent up front in enterprise modeling pays off throughout the OO development process.

Estimation contributes to the business value of delivered systems and metrics collection contributes to the timeliness of information. Traditionally, metrics have been used for two purposes: for the estimation of development effort and for the prediction of maintenance effort (defects). Although Object Oriented metrics research has received considerable interest lately, few metrics have emerged from academic research into commercial practice, and there are even fewer commercially available tools for collecting and evaluating OO metrics.

This research also investigated the effect that structured methods have on the performance of the development team when the teams have a positive attitude towards methods in general, or when they are satisfied with the training they received in the methods. Once again design inspection, code inspection and enterprise modeling are significantly related to development team performance. This suggests several things. The early verification, validation, and error detection provided by design and code inspections lead to a better overall product. However, these methods are time consuming and must be included as part of the original time schedule estimates.

The same holds for the Object Oriented paradigm. From a managerial viewpoint, the OO paradigm promises reuse and easy extensibility due to OO's richer semantic constructs. However, this requires much more effort "up front" and consequently more time before a product is seen by the customer. Estimating practices must change to reflect this change (Graham, 1994). Teams that have positive attitudes towards the methods are more likely to be willing to take the time needed to perform these activities and are more likely to defend the methods to an anxious customer. Enterprise modeling, prototyping, design inspections, and code inspections bring the customer into the development process and help enhance communication. These methods allow early detection of disparities between user expectations and developer understanding.

Teams who are satisfied with training in structured methods achieve results through the use of enterprise modeling. Perhaps it is this training that "sells" a development team on the value of this method. Mangers have long recognized the need to link development activities to the enterprise (Yourdon, 1986), and training in structured methods appears to be a way of transferring this need to developers. Puhr, Nelson, and Monarchi (1995) have found that the concepts of OO methodology by themselves are not difficult to grasp, but that difficulty occurs in seeing how the concepts are manifested in designs and programs. Therefore, training may be even more critical to the successful use of OO methods than it is to traditional methods use.

This study has shown the importance of the structured methods of design inspection, code inspection, and enterprise modeling in traditional software development projects. Organizations should consider the importance of these activities when implementing a structured methodology, be it in the traditional or OO paradigm. This study shows a clear link between the use of methods and the performance of internally developed software. The lessons learned from these traditional versions of design inspection, code inspection, and enterprise modeling can be used by both practitioners and future researchers of the Object Oriented paradigm.

References

Ajzen, I., & Fishbein, M. (1980). *Understanding Attitudes and Predicting Social Behavior*, Prentice Hall, Englewood, NJ.

Aktas, A. Z. (1981). *Structured Analysis & Design of Information Systems*, Prentice Hall, Englewood, N.J

Ashok, S. (1981). An Approach to Structured MIS Development, *MIS Quarterly*, 5,4, 19-33.

Baker, F. T. (1977). Chief Programmer Team Management of Production Programming. *IBM Systems Journal*, 11, 1,.56-73.

Banker, R., & Kauffman, R. (1991). Reuse and Productivity in Integrated Computer-Aided Software Engineering: An Empirical Study. *MIS Quarterly*, 15,3, 375-402.

Boehm, B. W. (1986). A Spiral Model of Software Development and Enhancement. *Software Engineering Notes*, 11 (4).

Bordoloi, Bijoy & Min-Hwa Lee (1994, Winter). An Object-Oriented View. *Information Systems Management*.

Brooks, F. P., Jr. (1995). *The Mythical Man-Month.* Addison-Wesley Publishing Company, Reading, Massachusetts.

Chaar, J.K., Halliday, M.J., Bhandari, I.. S., & Chillarege , R. (1993). In-Process Evaluation for Software Inspection and Test. *IEEE Transactions on Software Engineering*, 19,11, 1055-1070.

Chapin, N. (1979). Some Structured Analysis Techniques. *Data Base*, 10,3,. 16-23.

Chen, P. P. Entity-Relationship Model: Toward a Unified View of Data. *ACM Transaction on Database*, 1,1.

Conway, J. (1993). OOP: An academic perspective., *Education and Training Supplement to SIGS Publications*, 4-7.

Crinnion, J. (1991). *Evolutionary Systems Development: A Practical Guide to the Use of Prototyping Within a Structured Systems Methodology.* Plenum Press, NY.

Davis, F. D.(1986). A Technology Acceptance Model for Empirically Testing New End-User Information Systems: Theory and Results. Doctoral Dissertation, *Sloan School of Management, Massachusetts Institute of Technology*.

Davis, F. D., Bagozzi, R. P., & Warshaw, P. R. (1989). User Acceptance of Computer Technology: A Comparison of Two Theoretical Models. *Management Science*, 35,8.

DeMarco, T. (1978). *Structured Analysis and System Specification*. Yourdan Press, New York.

Dolk, D. R. (1988). Model Management and Structured Modeling: The Role of Information Resource Dictionary Systems. *Communications of the ACM*, 31,6. 704-718.

Downs, E. (1992). *Structured Systems Analysis and Design Method Application*. Prentice-Hall, Hertfordshire, UK.

Fenton, N. (1994). Software Measurement: A Necessary Scientific Basis. *IEEE Transactions on Software Engineering*, 20, 3, 199-206.

Fishbein, M., & Ajzen, I. (1975). *Belief, Attitude, Intention, and Behavior: An Introduction to Theory and Research*. Addison Wesley, Reading, Context MA.

Gane, C.,& Sarson, C.(1979). *Structured Systems Analysis: Tools and Techniques*. Prentice-Hall, Englewood New Jersey.

Gane, C. (1989). *Rapid System Development: Using Structured Techniques and Relational Technology*. Prentice-Hall, Englewood New Jersey.

Graham, I. (1994). *Object Oriented Methods*. Addison-Wesley Publishing Company, Wokingham, England.

Henderson-Sellers, B., & Edwards, J. M.(1990). The Object Oriented Systems Lifecycle. *Communications of the ACM*, 33, 9, 142-159.

Martin, J. & McClure, C. (1988). *Structured Techniques: The Basis For CASE*. Prentice Hall, Englewood Cliffs, N.J.

Orr, K.T., Gane, C., Yourdan, E., Chen, P. P., & Constantine, L. L. (1989, April). Methodology: The Experts Speak. *BYTE*, 221-233.

Orr, K. T. (1977). *Structured Systems Development*. Yourdan Press, New York..

Puhr, G. I., Nelson, H. J., & David, E. M. (1995). Teaching Object-Oriented Systems

Development: Challenges and Recommendations. *Object Oriented Systems*, 2.

Ross D. T., & Shoman, K.E. Jr.(1977). Structured Analysis for Requirements Definition. *IEEE Transactions on Software Engineering*, SE-3, 1.

Sanden, B. (1989). Entity Lifecycle Modeling and Structured Analysis in Real-Time Software Design—A Comparison. *Communications of the ACM*, 32, 12,. 1458-1466.

Sherif, C., W., Sherif, M.,& Nebergall, R. E. (1965). *Attitude and Attitude Change*. W. B. Saunders Company, Philadelphia and London.

Sherif, M. (1962, ed). *Intergroup Relations and Leadership*. John Wiley and Sons, Inc., New York and London.

Stevens, W. P., Myers, G. J., & Constantine, L.L. (1974). Structured Design. *IBM Systems Journal*, 13, 2.

Topper, A., Ouellete, D., & Jorgensen, P. (1994). *Structured Methods: Merging Models, Techniques*, and CASE. McGraw-Hill, Inc., NY.

Tung, Sho-Huan (1989). A Structured Method for Literate Programming. *Structured Programming*, 10, 2, 113-120.

Vessey, I., & Weber, R. (1986). Structured Tools and Conditional Logic: An Empirical Investigation. *Communications of the ACM*, 29, 1.

Yourdan, E. (1989). *Managing the Structured Techniques: Strategies for Software Development in the 1990's*. Yourdan Press/Prentice Hall, New York.

Yourdan, E. (1989). *Modern Structured Analysis*. Yourdan Press/Prentice Hall, New York.

Yourdan, E. (1975). *Techniques of Program Structure and Design*. Prentice Hall, Englewood, New Jersey.

Chapter III

Object Oriented Testing in Software Development

Samuel K. A. Agyemang
IBM Global Services

Object oriented technology is still growing and has not yet matured. Many articles have been written on object oriented software development processes, particularly in the area of testing. Most of the publications seem to agree with the fact that object oriented testing is a challenging aspect of the software development process. The main reason for this view seems to revolve around the fact that the objects and the code are inseparable and also, the idea of inheritance. Despite these views, the publications all seem to agree on one aspect, that object oriented when successfully tested leaves a better-maintained product compared to the traditional non-object oriented software. Object oriented software makes better maintainable software; it also has an added advantage over traditional software development because in the final analysis, it will cost less by shortening the development time as well as cutting down the cost of maintenance.

Object Oriented Testing

Object oriented software involves the methods to organize both information and the process that manipulates that information in accordance with the real world objects that the information describes.

The objects have attributes whose values define the state of the object and these also determine the value of the objects. (Kung, 1995) Object oriented software could be described to be just about objects. The concept behind object orientation is that it is closer to a person's perception of reality. Object orientation gives a new and powerful formula for developing computer software which makes it unique from the traditional form of software development. In a world where new products are emerging all the time, particularly in this Internet age, object orientation could help to improve the reliability and speed with which new software is developed. There could also be an added advantage of maintaining such software which is one of the problems in software development. There has already been a lot of interest generated about object oriented technology and the advantages it brings to the software development process which may be lacking in the traditional process. The powerful features of object orientation which are encapsulation, re-usability and inheritance also introduce problems for testing and maintenance, the anchor of a good software product. Most developers have tried to circumvent this problem by advocating the use of conventional testing tools for object oriented software. (Kung, 1995).

Object oriented development process provides some powerful and interesting features for software development (Hsia et al., 1998). It also brings to light some problems in the areas of quality of the software, particularly in the areas of testing and maintenance.

This will be the focus of this chapter, looking at some of the testing techniques and the problems of testing in determining if object oriented technology has any advantages over the traditional process. The chapter will look at aspects of testing in the object oriented technology, the issues involved and how they make object a quality product and the problems that may be encountered. Due to the growing importance of this technology, there has been a lot of testing strategies each trying to explain the advantages of object orientation. In this chapter, a critical view of some of the articles on the topic will be discussed to show the advantages object orientation has over traditional process. By the use of encapsulation, the designer could narrow the possible interdependencies with other components by way of interface without affecting the other units (Perry, 1990). Even though object oriented programming has some advantages over traditional, particularly by the use of the inheritance and encapsulation techniques, it also raises some problems of testing (Perry, 1990). The problem with inheritance and encapsulation may be that of accessibility. Since each class may inherit instance variables of its superclass, this could lead to readability problems in the code because of different definitions applied to classes in the hierarchy. Moreover, each class can also add to the list while the class cannot change the type of inherited instance (Taenzer et al., 1989).

Re-Usability and Testing

Object oriented technology has the advantage of re-usability. This makes it possible for a developer to tie new objects into existing ones and by so doing, avoid duplication of efforts. The reuse proposition has gained much currency because it makes it easier to construct a new application with few modifications as well as adaptations. The use of these techniques and properties renders the resulting software systems more reliable, easy to maintain as well as reuse. The likelihood of detecting an error and the objective of cutting costs and saving time rests with testing. The re-usability of the products makes sense because it can recoup the investment through effects of scale. After all, one of the most important goals of software development is to improve the quality. In the traditional software development, the theory and methodology provide foundation to access the quality of the product which is not so with object technology. Thus, testing becomes a problem with object oriented design. Testing is necessary in the development of a stable and robust system using object oriented technology.

The re-usability library is supposed to be made up of a set of well-tested class. The library contains the user documents, development components and class implementations. Since these have already been used, they have been tested, which at least is necessary on the grounds of being economical. One of the propositions for reuse is the Generic Development Process for Object Oriented Applications. This process comes in three design flavors of non-optimized phase, the generic phase and the component aspect. In combination these three describe the application development process with the sole aim to quicken the reuse at the very early stages. The process makes the assumption that there will be in the later stages, applications to which these generic ones will be automatically applicable. The developer again makes a judgement call as to the general usability of the product.

However, there is no indication that there is a single technique which can be relied upon completely. In fact, re-use is attractive if the developer can guarantee that the components will be correct to work smoothly with the systems that will rely on them, rather than harming them.

Inheritance in object oriented processes also illustrates flexibility and promotes re-use. In inheritance, the properties of one class are defined for all its subclasses. They in turn inherit its properties. This makes it possible for the software that implements the operations of the superclass to use its subclass. There could be an instance of an object class having more than one superclass (Kung, 1995). An example is a graduate teaching assistant who could be both a student and employee. Methods inherited from one superclass have to be retested in the context of the subclass since the superclass may not include every occurrence of the subclass. It makes it possible to reuse components with similar behavior. This is one of the best ways to divide a program into an economical set of classes. An example could be the automobile which as a superclass could include electric powered cars, gas-powered cars, buses, trucks and a host of others. This can help speed up the development process which will need only a few lines of code, thereby, culminating in lower cost (Siegel, 1996).

Re-use sometimes requires some prerequisites such as a competitive market. This is necessary because in a competitive market time is crucial to reduce cost. There is no doubt that developing a complete application from scratch is costly, so if there is any method that can be used to cut costs, it should be applied. Above all, there should be a need for a supportive corporate culture. To have a successful re-use, developers should be well compensated for their work and have a free hand and time to be able to build robust, efficient and re-usable components. The usefulness of a reusable component hinges on the quality of people who put them together. They should include people who have the skills and the ability to understand technical objects and be able to maintain quality reviews. The team should be headed by a leader who is focused and productive. In the absence of these factors, the development process is time consuming and involves many errors which can be costly. Therefore, for reuse to be successful organizations must have the collective vision to support reusable software. Object orientation is a promising technology for increasing the reuse of already used components (Schmidt, 1997). Object oriented components are becoming increasingly mainstream. This gives object orientation an advantage over the traditional software development. Software testing is a difficult process which demands preparation in the execution of tens of thousands of test cases and test data sets. This requires extensive support and the possibility of omitting certain parts.

Dynamic Testing

The method where an implementation is decided by the system since it is not known until during the runtime. Dynamic testing helps to locate faults which might be in the executable data. The tests are applied to the models and that helps to speed up the process and keep the formal models scrutinized properly for errors. The execution here is performed under typical circumstances to verify conformance. In the traditional method, the test detects errors which reflect on the implementation of each method. Thus, polymorphism makes it possible to use one name and protocol interchangeably with objects of different classes which may still remain in execution.

There is a widely held view that dynamic testing will successfully uncover errors. The system will choose what type of method to employ during the execution. The developer leaves the choice of method to the system as to which one to use based primarily on the type of object. The method goes through the compilation format to get rid of class interface incompatibles. The developer then paraphrases the code line by line to uncover errors in coding. There is a need for a tool to get this process done efficiently. In most cases, scripts are defined to aid this form of testing. Those scripts rely on what is referred to as grey-box testing which operates under a combination of functional and structural testing.

Dynamic testing demands that test cases be designed accompanied by a selection of test dates. This is, however, a very complex method which confirms that testing in object oriented technology is a major challenge. Although object oriented technology supports many kinds of fault prevention, testing still remains necessary to maximize operational reliability.

Cluster and Class Testing

Clusters are a collection of classes which relate to each other by way of functionality. Each one of these clusters is based on the behavior of the system. Cluster testing is less costly compared to class testing. Library clusters come about as a result of implementation issues. Most of the classes in the cluster have already been tested. Anytime a change is made to a previously tested software, there is the need to run the cluster test. There is, however, the tendency to pile on the clusters. Finally, they become too large that there will not be enough time to review the code. When this happens, the goal is defeated because it was supposed to cost less; but since errors may be detected in the final product, it is going to be expensive to fix those errors. However, this problem can be eliminated. This is done by doing class test and also a combination of cluster and class tests which may be automated. Cluster testing is comprised of three stages. The initial testing of the cluster is documented. The next stage is to review test plan. The final stage is the execution and recording of the results of the test. Within the cluster test plan, there are required tests. The functions to be tested must have been noted from the object oriented analysis and design stage. Included also is the list of configurations to be tested, the classes in the cluster, as well as the test cases (Murphy, et al., 1994). One such tool designed for cluster testing is Automated Class Exerciser (ACE). The cluster testing, when used efficiently, can lead to discovering very encouraging results. The use of tools like ACE can help developers to concentrate on specific test cases. This is an advantage over the traditional software development methods (Murphy et al., 1994). The rising cost of software development products, makes object orientation an advantage. Cluster and class testing used in object oriented software development make it easier to locate errors and fix them early to reduce costs. By the use of testing tools, developers can perform regression testing which is easier to review. These tools can be automated to speed up the testing process (Murphy et al., 1994). The object models that have been stored can be re-used for automated testing and cutting costs (Poston, 1994).

Integration Testing

Integration testing emphasizes fundamentals of behavior. Here classes are integrated and tested according to the test order, and the emphasis is on the function and the interactions between behavior (Kung et al., 1995). The testing is concerned with the behavior of the software and less concerned with the structure. In the traditional testing, the software is in imperative language with functional structure in view. However, this is not so with object orientation. In the imperative structural form, it is descriptive and in a control flow sequence, where theory based testing is the norm. What is being tested is known and covers all the metrics. In the object oriented programming, where the languages may be imperative, it is evident at the integration level. Where functionality is primary, the emphasis is on structure rather than behavior. The structure of the system becomes the primary motive and of less concern is the behavior. Testing therefore becomes problematic. The very idea of function is to make sure that the system functions correctly or properly. On the other hand, object oriented software is different from traditional structural software. Here the program is minimized, hence, there does not seem to be a well defined structure. This to some extent can be an advantage for object orientation because there is no structure upon which testing can be based (Jorgensen et al., 1994). The problem of testing in object orientation arises because of the erroneous attempt to apply traditional testing to object oriented software. Software testing may be primarily focused on what the program does. It is concerned with the structure of the program. When developers produce a software, it is the satisfaction of their clients as to how the program behaves; they could care less about its structure. If the customer is satisfied that the program is fulfilling his needs, the engineers would have done a good job. Objects by behavior show some form of integration, but not structure (Jorgensen et al., 1994)

This again can be a problem with regard to testing of object orientation because objects may look alike and jointly correct, but in their composition, there could be errors. In object oriented technology, this poses a problem since it uses encapsulation. By encapsulation, a designer hides the data structures and implementation details of the procedures. Access to this private data is by operation of the object (Kung,1995). The whole idea of encapsulation is to hide within and to be reusable because they have already been tested. Encapsulation gives an invocation of chain member function. However, unit testing cannot be proven to discover integration level problems. The use of encapsulation in integration testing becomes a problem since it seems to justify unit testing. If a superclass is modified, then there would be a need to retest all its inherited methods. However, it becomes a problem if after a subclass is added, we might have to be called to retest the methods that were inherited from it superclass. On the other hand, if the new subclass is an extension of the superclass and there is no interaction between, then there is no need for retesting. It must be noted that not all object oriented languages support multiple inheritance. In cases where they do, it only becomes an issue if the same component inherits along divergent paths (Perry, 1990). Integration testing can reveal a lot of errors which may not be detected in unit testing. These errors are visible during the interactive stages among classes. In object orientation, every class inherits an attribute from a superclass. This being the case, the initial methodology assumes that a class should necessarily call the initialization code of its superclass. But there have been problems concerning a lack of invocation from the superclass. When this occurs the result is initialization error.

There is also the integration of the black and white-box integration process which relies on fundamental pairs. The importance of this theory is that the use of the finite set from the blackbox theory is deficient, and therefore, there is the proposed heuristic whitebox technique. This testing is by implication the testing of the source code (Perry, 1990). Under this form of testing the statements and all aspects of the program like data flow paths must be tested in execution. These two forms of testing are intertwined. The weakness of the specification based testing is complemented by the program based testing (Perry, 1990). Specification based testing is about how specific criteria is met; it does not address the portions of the program that need to be executed in order to meet each of the specified parts. The program based testing does not tell us anything about the functional performance. A combination of both would be a perfect mix. In specification based testing, when a program is said to be adequately tested, it presupposes that all the functions are covered. However, one test which is adequate might not necessarily be adequate for the other. Equivalent programs could have different implementations. Thus, a test that executes one implementation could not be expected to execute all the other statements of the other implementation. Again, two programs which may look similar might require separate tests (Perry, 1990). The testing covers fundamental pair, which in mathematics is as good as that of all the equivalent ground terms. (Chen et al., 1998). On the surface the theory sounds plausible, but the problem is that it does not expose the errors in the program. To counter this deficiency is the proposition of a supplemental test made of several subtasks which are often combined into a methodological framework. In the object oriented methodology, the data and code are merged together, and this makes it easier to use since it is just messages being sent by way of interface. When the need to create a new class comes up, a subclass could be created and the inheritance theory permits re-use.

Quality Metrics

There has always been a problem as to how to measure the quality of a software product. The methods used in measuring the quality of software in the traditional way are a starting point which needs to be built upon in the object oriented process. This is because of the unique characteristics of object oriented technology. Software metrics can be used to identify where to allocate resources which become very important in decision making. Managers and developers need this reliable information in their decisions. Testing of systems is one such time consuming activity that needs to be identified so scarce resources can be used where needed most (Braude, 1998). There is the view that non-object product metrics does not satisfy assessment of the quality of object oriented software systems (Braude, 1998). However, metrics if they are to be reliable must be validated. This is necessary since there could be a measure seemingly correct, but might be of no value to the problem being evaluated.

Object orientation has an advantage of reuse, encapsulation and inheritance. There can be different instances within an organization which need to be taken into consideration, or the system could even be different from the original one for which the code was written. In addition to this, is the question of partial use of the re-use code. In the software development process, from analysis through design, there must be a conscious effort thoroughout to produce a quality product. The quality of the product has its genesis in this area of development which becomes the link between the developer and the final product. If the design is faulty, it is not going to be acceptable to the user. In the final analysis it is going to cost more at this stage for the product. There is always the likelihood that the cost of fixing the errors at the end stage of the final product will be about ten fold the cost at the design and analysis stage. The evaluation of object oriented software may be measured in terms of how reliable the product is and the less complex it is. There is also the need to be concerned as to how many more times the software could be used. The quality of the product will rest on how good the design was. Reliability then becomes the criteria upon which the quality is measured. This is not always the case with every software product.

Good software has to be user-friendly. Basically, it must be simple enough for the user to use with minimal problem. One of the advantages of object oriented software is re-usability. Object oriented techniques in general can be said to improve the software design process and facilitate modification and reuse in a way traditional does not. The economic advantage of re-use cannot be overemphasized. The ability to rely on quality re-usable products makes it faster and less costly to produce. It also gives developers confidence to know that there already exists tested products which can be of use. This is mainly with the design process, which may not be applicable to all object oriented software products. The fact that some of these factors may be in conflict is the reason why object oriented testing is a difficult proposition. These can be used as guidelines upon which a developer may build a quality software.

Validation and Verification Testing

In the object oriented process, testing could be divided into verification and validation. In validation, there is first the static analysis of the use cases and object model to find out if they are consistent. Finally, it is to check the completeness of the specification by inquiries from the customer. In the verification phase, we want to know if the engineers are building the correct system. This is necessary because fundamentals of failure arise from the fact that the software doesn't do what the users wanted. Coupled with this is the possibility that the developers might have gotten it wrong from the analysis stage and, therefore did not know exactly what the users wanted. Validation answers the question: Does this product meet the set of requirements for which it was made? The engineers conduct tests to ascertain whether the right objects are being developed to meet user requirements. The tests are necessary to observe what the reactions of this new object is going to be as well as the interactions and effect it might also have.

The verification process, on the other hand, tends to be more detailed and is conducted not at the end, but in the course of the development. Verification process is about functionality and this occurs during the execution of tests against the software. This process deals with later discovery at a point when the design or implementation fails. In the traditional development methodology, the testing process is not often integrated with the development process. There ha e been proposals for an integrated object oriented testing in all aspects of development. The emphasis is to be on the objects models from the domain analysis stage where they are refined to the next stage of the application analysis. By this stage the product would have been iteratively and incrementally tested. The errors would have been removed at the earliest possible time to minimize the cost. The author Shel Siegel quotes Barry Boehm who studied the relative cost of fixing these problems. He confirms that the relative cost is less at the earliest possible time than at the later stages. According to Boehm's account, it is about five times more costly at the design stage, ten times at the coding stage and between 40 to 1,000 times at the maintenance stage (Siegel, 1996).

The Iterative Process

This process help continuous improvement of the examination of the goals and evaluation of the level of achievement. Unlike the traditional method of software development, the object oriented process emphasizes the need for care during the analysis and design stages. In most cases it has been established that the failures at the requirement stage tend to be large in part affecting the quality of the product. The process reviews the previous objects and evaluate the reusability of the objects to complete the test for quality assurance. There are advantages of testing in object orientation using high level testing on formal specifications and usage profiles. The behavior of the software system is specified in object oriented format (Chan et al., 1998). The prototyping and implementing of object oriented programs can be made faster by using a conceptual clear object oriented style specification. With specification based testing, a new technique is thereby incorporated into the testing process. This could be combined with usage based testing to effectively complete the most widely used parts of a software system. However, these techniques are not unique to object oriented programs, they could be applied to traditional software development (Chang, et al. 1998). The idea behind this is that software development begins with a requirement specification. In usage based testing, the difference is in the underlying principles between traditional testing and object oriented testing. In the traditional software, tests could be generated through the usage of modules based on their probabilities. This is where object orientation differs from traditional software, since object orientation design depends on classes and objects. It does becomes difficult to develop a form of structure. The objects have operations and attributes which are a reflection of the state of the object (Chang, et al. 1998).

When a conclusion is drawn that a program has been adequately tested, then by implication, it has been covered according to the criteria selected (Perry, 1990). The idea here is to find out if the program meets its functional specifications. Sometimes this is done by the use of a tool. However, most of these tools cover mathematically designed subroutines. In another form of testing, the formal specification method is applied to avoid going through the details to collect implementation information. This gives the definition of class structure as well as perfect information on the behavior of the operation. At the end of the construction of the test scenario, test cases based on the data profile can be generated. An enhance state transition diagram (ESTD) can be derived from the formal specification system. The multilayer nature gives a tester a design between specification and usage and, thus, makes it possible for the user to view the design in an understandable way. The advantage is that it is possible to represent a class object in an ESTD then the whole system could be done in the same way. It becomes easier to also represent a single diagram drawn from a complex system. Testers relying on the state model could also check the execution programs in accordance with specification. The quality of the object oriented product should be able to address all the phases of the software cycle. While it could be said that object oriented development methods have increased the quality of software, there are still some issues with testing to determine the quality of the product. The articles reviewed while trying to explain how the object oriented process is a better form to use in software development, concedes that there are inherent problems too. For testing to be done on a program, the testers would have to define the objective of such a test. The reason is to ensure that a comprehensive test could done. However there is not one single algorithm that can be said to be feasible for any given requirement (Chen et al. ,1998). Most of these testing processes are impeded by issues arising from encapsulation and inheritance. The current testing processes all seem to lack the basis to efficiently perform the task necessary to produce a quality software. However, the process is an improvement on the traditional development process. One of the reasons why testing is considered problematic is because it is not integrated into the development infrastructure. If and when the two processes are integrated, the end result would be a better product. The approach would begin the testing process early so there would be early error detection, and this could be fixed quickly. The end result is likely to be a quality product (McGregor, 1994).

Conclusion

The object oriented testing process takes advantage of early testing in the development life cycle. This, therefore, could result in further improvements and also shorten the time spent to achieve the desired quality. However, the integrated testing approach is too visible in the object oriented technology. It gives an impression, sometimes erroneously, that more time is being directed toward testing. In the long run, it could shorten the amount of effort which is needed to be employed for a comprehensive testing process. In the software development process, testing is costly so any method to cut that is a step in the right direction. Irrespective of the method employed, integrated testing reduces the cost in the development process. It is difficult to predict the future of any software, but one thing is certain, the purported demise of the object oriented technology is not here yet. The fact that no one can safely say what kind of sophisticated system our users might want without the use of object technology in the process, that confirms that object oriented technology is here to stay. This becomes even more obvious with the Web development applications. In the traditional development process, the basic unit of testing is a subprogram; whereas, object oriented technology relies on a class. Even though traditional methods may be efficient, they cannot be applied to objects without some form of adaptation to object orientation. Areas which for a long time resisted object technology are no longer immune. Databases like Oracle 8 now support subobjects which have their own identities. These databases are now allowing the benefits of object orientation and sometimes applications. It is true that object orientation has made a lot of progress into the software development, it will continue for sometime to be just a fraction of the traditional market especially in the databases. Testing should be made an integral part of the software development process. Testing in object orientation, no matter how difficult can detect faults in the software and give some level of confidence.

References

Arnold, Thomas R, Fuson, William A (1994, Sept.) Testing "In A Perfect World" *Communications of the ACM*, 78-86.

Barbey, Stephane, Ammann, Manuel & Strohmeier , Alfred (1994). Open Issues in "Testing Object Oriented Software" *ECSQ '94* (European Conference on Software Quality), Basel, Switzerland (Abstract)

Barbey, Stephane, Strohmeier, Alfred (1994) "The Problematics of Testing Object Oriented Software" *SQM '94 Second Conference on Software Quality Management*, Edinburgh, Scotland, UK (Abstract)

Binder, Robert V. (1994 September) Design for Testability in Object-Oriented Systems *Communications of the ACM*, 87-101.

Binder, Robert V. (1995) Object Oriented Testing: Myth and Reality http://www.rbsc.com/pages/myths.html.

Binder, Robert V. (1996) The FREE Approach to Testing Object Oriented Software: An Overview. http: //www.rbsc.com/pages/FREE.html.

Chen, Huo Yan, Tse, T.H, Chan, F.T. & Chen, T.Y In Black and White: An Integrated Approach to Class Level Testing of Object-Oriented Programs. A*CM Transactions on Software Engineering and Methodology*, 250-295.

Erickson, Carl, Jorgensen, P.C. (1994, September). Object -Oriented Integration Testing *Communications of the ACM*, 30-38.

Jaaksi, Ari (1998 January). A Method for Your First Object-Oriented Project. The *Journal of Object-Oriented Programming*, 17-25.

Kung, David, Gao, Jerry, Hsia, Pei, Toyoshima, Yasufumi, Chen, Chris, Kim, Young Si & Song, Young-Kee (1995 October) Developing an Object-Oriented Software Testing and Maintenance Environment. *Communications of the ACM*, 75-86.

Liao, S.Y, Cheung, L. S & Liu, W.Y. (1999 January). An Object-Oriented System for the Reuse of Software Design Items. *The Journal of Object-Oriented Programming*, 22-28.

Lorenz, Mark (1993). *Object-Oriented Software Development A Practical*

Guide. Englewood Cliffs, New Jersey, 78-110.

McGregor, John D, Korson, Timothy D (1994 September) Integrated Object-Oriented Testing and Development Processes *Communications of the ACM*, 59-77.

McGregor, John D, Sykes, David A (1992) *Object-Oriented Software Development: Engineering Software for Reuse*: Van Nostrand, Reinhold, New York, 193-219.

Murphy, Gail C, Towsend, Paul, Wong Pok Sze (1994 September) Experiences with Cluster and Class Testing *Communications of the ACM*, 35-47.

Poston, Robert M (1994 September) Automated Testing from Object Models *Communications of the ACM*, 59 - 77.

Schmidt, Douglas C(1995 October) Using Design Patterns to Develop Reusable Object-Oriented Communication Software, *Communications of the ACM*, 65-74.

Siegel, Shel (1996) *Object Oriented Software Testing A Hierarchical Approach* John Wiley & Sons Inc. New York , 117-310.

Chapter IV

Technical and Market Viability of Object Database Technology

Jozsef T. Komlodi
American University, USA

Despite its decade long history, object database technology has never entered mainstream system development. In this work, I look at the background of the slow adoption, and the possible future outlook of this technology based on my personal experience and the published literature. Object databases represent a revolutionary new technology and provide superior storage facility for complex data structures and types. They also enable close language binding and a unified development process. It is a mature technology with advanced database management and development features and has several proven and robust deployment examples. Besides its current technical excellence, this technology is also demonstrating future potential through such emerging technologies as Java, Application servers, and XML. The past failure of object databases to proliferate the market was mainly due to unawareness, lack of skills, and the overwhelming existing investment in relational systems. As these factors are changing by the end of this century and new technology adoption is accelerating, object databases are looking forward to a slow but sure take off.

Technical and Market Viability of Object Database Technology

It might be a somewhat surprising fact that object databases have been around for as long as a decade. Since their appearance, market researchers and technology experts have been making confident projections that they would conquer the landscape of software industry. Indeed, information technology has gone through an amazing series of changes, but object database technology has yet to enter mainstream computing. Is this due to the overall weakness of this architecture, or is it rather the result of slow adoption of new technology?

By the second half of the 1990s, more and more new software projects selected object oriented (OO) technology as the basis for their development. This paradigm shift naturally drew increased deployment of OO analysis, design, and language tools. Objects became the basic unit of processing posing new demands on data storage requirements. The increased complexity of data structures and types also affected the architecture of modern databases. Aggressive changes in the business environment, such as globalization and deregulation, are demanding greater flexibility and complexity of supporting information systems. As a result, their underlying data pool also needs to reflect these architectural changes.

Once again, why has object database technology not entered mainstream enterprise development despite the favorable technical environment? Do object oriented database management systems (OODBMS) offer a different and improved technology and architecture, or are vendors only trying to take advantage of the increasing popularity of the OO paradigm? Is this technology mature and scalable enough for prime time? Will future technologies leverage object databases fostering their widespread application, or will they suffice with the relational model? These are the questions that I will attempt to address in this chapter. This review is based on both personal experience in OO development and the extensive body of OO literature.

Technical and Architectural Validity

The operational principles of today's OODBMSs were inherited from their early ancestors. Object databases were developed to handle complex, interrelated data structures. They were first used in computer-aided design (CAD) applications where relational databases could not provide the performance needed. Object databases provided persistent storage in a single user environment with high performance. These early systems could store objects, classes, associations, and methods. In the late 1980s, commercial vendors started developing independent OODBMS products. They added database capabilities to support multi-user, distributed applications. In the second half of the 1990s, the increasing popularity of OO languages has renewed the attention toward object databases. Next, I will look at the core technology of object databases, especially those basic architectural features that validate and differentiate OODBMSs. These technical improvements over relational technology will help to understand the very need for this technology in certain areas of information technology (IT).

Complex Data Relationships

The efficient handling of complex data relationships is one of the greatest advantages of object databases over their relational counterparts. This improvement was an important driving force in the adoption of OODBMSs for early users. Information access patterns differ from application to application. Standard business programs select a small subset out of a large amount of data for processing, just like a typical payroll system. Whereas, in other applications, such as in engineering programs, a larger amount of data is being manipulated by constantly navigating from data element to data element. For example, to inspect a motor we start from the motor object itself and navigate to its components using large sets of highly interrelated data. As the relational model does not support the automated handling of data relationships, data structures have to be dealt with explicitly. Relational database management systems (RDBMS) store relationships as data and not as structure. The conversion has to be done manually and it takes time. RDBMSs manage data relationships by foreign keys. At runtime, the system needs to scan two or more tables comparing foreign keys to recover relationships between data elements. This join process is a crucial bottleneck in relational technology. More than two or three joins in a retrieval execution may slow down processing unacceptably. On the other hand, object oriented database (OODB) technology allows the implicit storage of data relationships. As objects have unique identity, pointer-like data structures can represent relationships among object instances. Users simply declare data relationships and OODBs automatically generate and handle them. As the traversal of data links is direct (e.g., following a link,) there is no need to execute time-consuming join operations or looking up index tables. For highly complex data structures this method usually results in magnitudes faster information retrieval.

The classic example of storing a virtual car in a garage will simply and powerfully demonstrate the difference between OODBMSs and RDBMSs. Solving the task in an object oriented fashion, there is an object for the car and an object for the garage. It only takes one operation to accomplish the goal and park the car (in Java: garage.park(car).) Storing the same car in a "relational" garage requires much more work. All information must be disassembled into tables. It means the storing of each part of the car in its own table: wheels in one table, mirrors in another, etc. The next morning the car has to be reassembled again joining the parts together. This continuous transformation requires a great amount of extra program code and slows down processing. In object oriented systems the car and all its parts are objects. Since the database understands their relationships, the entire structure can be handled as a single unit. Data elements and their relationships can be stored and retrieved as they are; there is no need for dis- and reassembling. Because of this revolutionary different data storage approach, OODBMSs are more suitable for handling complex, interrelated data.

Complex Data Types

Besides the capability to handle highly structured data, object databases also provide extensible support for complex data types. If information nicely fits into simple data types such as names, id numbers, or account balances, than the fixed number of built-in data types of relational databases will provide sufficient support. However, an increasing number of applications process more complex data. These may have dynamically varying size, or contain nested or user-defined arbitrary structure. A good example might be the data used in web applications such as images, text, audio, and video. An important characteristic of OODBMSs is their extensible data type system. Developers can define additional data types and an object database will handle them equally with its built-in types. Applications do not have to translate the data types of the programming languages into the built-in data types of the database systems. They can store them in their native format easing and speeding up development.

Close Language Binding

In traditional relational systems there is a wall between the database and the application using it. The data is persistent (permanent) in the database and is transient (temporary) in the application's memory space. The program communicates with the database with read and write commands when the data is drawn from and written into the database. In object databases this separation does not exist. Applications manipulate both persistent and transient data the same way. Any kind of data can be persistent, and the same operations can be executed on persistent and transient data. Objects are retrieved identically regardless of location. A nice strategy to implement object persistence is "persistence by reachability." In this case, an object is persistent if it is reachable from another persistent object, and it will continue to exist in the database even when the application is terminated (e.g., the Java binding in the Objectstore database from Object Design.) The changes in persistent data are committed in transactions. While the OODB language interface offers mechanisms to define and open databases, commit or abort transactions, acquire locks, and accessing data within a database does not require any additional constructors. For example, if an object has not been retrieved from the database yet, the program does not need to do any additional operations. The underlying database system will automatically recognize the situation and retrieve the object.

According to Marry Loomis, object oriented programmers do not want to consider whether objects reside in the memory or on the hard drive, they simply want to work with objects. They do not want to deal with the issue whether an object has already been retrieved from the database. They want to use OO language structures and have the underlying system deal with the problem of persistence, whether objects are on the disk, in the cache, or in the memory (Kalman, 1994). As OODBMSs inherit the data model of OO programming languages and provide seamless integration, they can elegantly meet such needs of OO programmers.

Unified Development Process

Besides the benefits for programmers, close language binding also simplifies the lives of system analysts and designers. OODBMSs evolved to support OO languages and to take advantage of object orientation in the database too. OODBs follow the same concept like OO analysis, OO design, and OO languages allowing a unified conceptual approach during the entire development process. This unified approach simplifies development and eases communication between users, analysts, and programmers. In the case of relational databases objects have to be mapped to tables. It takes time to create the relational tables and views, and it is also hard to keep up the model with changes in the physical implementation. This results in applications that are difficult to maintain. Using OODBs, there is no need for semantic transformations as the same object model is used during the entire lifecycle. Designers do not have to translate an object model to a relational one. This unified approach provides higher quality systems that are easier to maintain.

Technical Maturity

Although object database technology may sound unfamiliar for several IT professionals, this is not a new technology. In fact, most of the object database vendors have been around for a decade now. They have been continuously improving and tuning their products. OODBMSs have already gone through four or five versions, and they are stable, robust and able to perform in the most challenging situations. Even though it is a mature technology, it is still very often mistakenly criticized for its immaturity and lack of advanced database management features. Thus, here I will highlight some of the characteristics that raise OODBMSs to the level of industrial strength enterprise computing.

The best and only way to demonstrate the robustness of a technology is to present real-life applications where it has already proven itself. This has to be the case for object databases too. Looking for the best example, I could easily find hundreds of the cases of successful deployment in business-critical missions. I came across several OODBMSs handling terrabytes of data for hundreds of concurrent users with very challenging performance requirements. In processing environments where the information stored was very complex and structured, such as telecommunication, finance, or web applications, object database solutions often provided fifty to eighty times better performance than relational database systems. In many cases the relational data model could not provide sufficient performance at all. However, the example that I eventually decided on will effectively present both scalability and reliability of object databases.

Next, I will take a brief look at the information system of the Chicago Stock Exchange (CHX.) It seems to be an especially relevant case as CHX competes by executing trades faster and less expensively. In the stock market, all transactions must be reliably maintained and processed. After careful consideration, CHX selected Versant's OODBMS as the basis for its next generation system. The implementation was structured into a three tiered system. It features a client tier, an application server tier, and an object server tier. The object server tier is based on two pairs of Versant fault tolerant servers. Performance can be increased during operation by adding object server nodes and rebalancing. Dynamic rebalancing is possible through the capability of the OODBMS to enable objects to be distributed regardless of address or physical location. (Most of the technical characteristics mentioned above will be explained in more detail later.)

CHX was impressed by the scalability of the Versant OODBMS: "Versant ODBMS scales well; we can very easily add new servers to absorb growth. Versant also provides better performance because it caches objects on the client as well as the server, where relational systems only cache data on the server" ("Chicago Stock", n.d.). According to John Kerin: "Relational would have imposed too much overhead" (Baer, 1999). On the whole, the OODBMS of the Chicago Stock Exchange has achieved its business and development goals. Further more, during the stock market's dramatic loss and gain in October of 1997, the system showed excellent resistance. As Kerin says: "On Tuesday, October 28, 1997 when the CHX moved $1.6 billion worth of stocks and experienced three times its normal systems load, the Versant ODBMS performed superbly keeping up with the unprecedented volume."

Besides the robustness and the maturity of the core technology, regarding advance development and second storage management features object databases are also catching up with and even advancing relational technology. Next, I will give a list of these improved features based on three leading products: Versant's object database,

Jazmine from Computer Associates, and ObjectStore from Object Design. Advanced development tools include graphical database designer, drag-and-drop interfaces, component wizard, support for Java, ActiveX, Hypertext Markup Language (HTML), Visual Basic, and C++. System integration features include support for OLE DB, Open Database Connectivity (ODBC), Common Object Request Broker Architecture (CORBA), Distributed Component Object Model (DCOM), DB2, Oracle, Structured Query Language (SQL) classes, and web serving application programming interfaces like Netscape's and Microsoft's standards. Second storage management features include transparent fail-over, online incremental backup, two-phase commit, long transactions, asynchronous replication, versioning, on-line schema evolution and disk space management.

Due to the limited length of this chapter, I will not explain these features in greater detail, but I believe that this impressive list by itself may picture the current capabilities and comfort of object database technology.

Future Use

To anticipate the future potential of an underlying, supporting technology such as databases, one has to look at the possible future trends in IT. The question is whether the general direction of technical evolution points toward the increased use of the services of the technology examined. Next, I will look at those emerging technologies that are likely to have wide acceptance in the near and more distant future and have the potential to leverage and foster object database technology.

Java

Object oriented languages have been around for three decades. They have always promised a better organization and management of programming code as opposed to structural languages. Despite this substantial advantage, languages such as C++, or Smalltalk, have never managed to get into the mainstream of enterprise computing. However, in the second half of the 1990s this situation started to change radically. This change was mainly due to the introduction of Sun's OO language: Java. This language quickly became a web-related buzzword, and by the end of this decade it is also gaining substantial support in real-life enterprise applications.

Java is a modern programming language. It promises to offer services in most of the areas that are required in today's application development projects. First of all, Java is an elegant object oriented language. It was designed learning from the positive and negative features of already existing languages. Other advanced characteristics include: free availability, platform independence, web awareness, wide industry support, enormous marketing and research assistance (from vendors such as IBM, HP, Oracle, Netscape), and support for middleware technologies (COBRA, Enterprise Java Beans (EJB), Extensible Markup Language (XML)). Utilizing its appealing architecture and ease of use, several new software development projects are being implemented entirely in Java. As this language continues to mature, it will have a tremendous opportunity to eventually become the C of the 21st century.

There will be a growing need for object databases as Java continues to grow in acceptance. As described earlier, the problem of mapping Java objects to relational databases is a considerable one. Although it can be done, well-documented studies have shown that the program code itself mapping objects into relational database structures might consume 40-60% of development and maintenance resources. It is hard to envision companies continuing to do it, especially as more and more of them become familiar with OO programming. Further more, the unified object oriented approach that object databases provide will also be a main consideration for developers using OO programming and design methods. Today, the majority of already existing data is stored in relational databases and is manipulated by structural languages. However, as OO languages continue to gain acceptance this situation will gradually change.

Data and Workload Distribution

Distributed computing is one of the greatest promises in the near future of information technology. It is a revolutionary new architecture, where the network itself behaves as the computer, and information and processing power is spread across worldwide networks. OODBMSs were constructed in the early days of the distributed computing era; thus, they are able to take advantage of the available parallel computing power. Relational databases provide only limited support for workload and information distribution. All the processing happens on a central server including data buffering and join and select operation execution. OODBMSs do not have the same problem. They were designed to take advantage of distributed computer power and make use of multiple servers and clients to handle information storage and processing. Rather than having one huge database spread across a disk farm, as it is the case with a RDBMS, an OODBMS can have sections of the database (clusters of objects) distributed across many (hundreds or thousands in the Objectivity/DB architecture) servers. In an OO system objects might be located on the client or on a local server or somewhere on the network. They can be dynamically moved to the location where they are most needed, reducing retrieval time. This is accomplished using object identity to locate and identify objects.

Besides the distribution of data, OODBMSs also allow the distribution of workload. Most of the currently available object databases support the execution of object methods (e.g., Jazmine from Computer Associates.) Objects request the services from each other and the thread of execution goes from object to object and from database to database. This is the service of OODBMSs and transparent to programmers. Consequently, by moving objects from server to server or to client caches, the associated workload can also be reallocated. Moreover, the client side of OODB applications can be tuned for the nature of the task. In OODBMSs there is an in-memory database at each client, which frees developers from having to implement data chases by hand. By moving collections and sets of objects into client caches the execution of queries can also be done at the clients.

Object databases usually support COBRA and DCOM interfaces, thus they are able to provide object broker services. Applications located anywhere on the network can request services from objects residing on OODBMSs. As distributed computing gains more acceptance, the inherently more distributed nature of object database will become a significant advantage.

Application Servers

For the last two years application servers have received a great amount of attention. Most of the software companies that have products in the middle tier are either developing or planning to develop application servers. Application servers already have a half-a-billion dollar market and, according to analysts (Ricciuti, 1998), in the coming four to five years this will increase to $4 billion.

Enterprises are beginning to use application servers to integrate Web applications and existing systems together for e-commerce and other web-based applications. They simplify and speed up the task of linking new web systems and legacy systems. An application server is somewhat like a Web server in that it services clients running browsers by executing business logic (usually written in C++ or Java), and accessing back-end databases or other applications (such as PeopleSoft, SAP.) They run in the middle tier and handle the application logic and connectivity that previously was handled by fat clients. This is the logic that determines how a business system should behave.

Most of the application server products are written in modern OO programming languages such as C++ or Java. The business logic running on application servers is also developed in these languages and usually takes advantage of middleware technologies such as COBRA, EJB, and DCOM. As application servers heavily use objects and object-related technologies, their support by OODBs seem to be a logical consequence. Several application servers use OODBs for object caching and storing. Providing an object cache within a single application server can have significant performance benefits, as objects do not need to be reloaded each time someone wants to perform an operation on them. Caching across application servers can further increase performance by minimizing routing of requests to the optimal server. It also improves availability of services by increasing redundancy of information (especially for read-only data), resulting in increased performance and scalability.

The strategic relationship made in February 1999 between Object Design, Inc. (an object database company) and BEA (an application server company), reflects well the support opportunities that OODBMSs can provide to application servers. According to Scott Dietzen, the chief technology officer of BEA's WebXpress division, 'ObjectStores' architectures are especially well-suited for our customers who are deploying Java applications across a cluster of BEA WebLogic [application] servers. ObjectStores' ability to maintain a consistent, in-memory cache on every server results in excellent performance, scalability, and reliability, which are critical considerations in deploying EJB components (Walsh, 1999).

XML

XML is a universal format for data interchange. It was developed by the World Wide Web Consortium (W3C) organization and accepted as a standard in February 1998. Technically speaking, it is a meta-language that provides rules for document definition. It can solve one of the biggest problems in enterprise computing: data integration. XML gives the possibility of presenting data in such a meaningful manner that allows independent systems to understand and process it. XML is easily portable, is described in ASCII, and can be transmitted using standard protocols like Hypertext Transfer Protocol (HTTP). In an XML document, every data element comes with identifying meta information and the nesting of elements can convey data structure. AS XML is self-describing, its processing does not require custom code. Applications can be written generically to interpret XML documents.

According to the Gartner Group (Object Design, Inc., n.d.), a typical enterprise devotes 35-40% of its programming budget to developing programs that transfer data between different databases and applications. XML helps to ease this problem by integrating data between data sources. The traditional method of data sharing is the generation of custom code to facilitate interchange of information. This custom code grows quickly with the integration of additional system elements. The alternative is to use XML as the universal interchange format.

XML will be the most important new technology for the Web since HTML. Its impact will be broad and widespread. It is already beginning to be used to describe data in various vertical and horizontal industries. Banking and finance are using it to present transaction and financial information. Education is using it to define course content for distance learning and web based training. E-commerce is starting to use it to define catalog content, billing information, orders, and other pieces of data involved in an online transaction. It will change how Web pages are constructed since it describes content whereas HTML describes the page layout.

Early efforts addressing server side XML processing were mainly implemented by a simple isolated XML interface in front of a relational database. However, this solution is not sufficient in most of the cases. Relational data structures do not offer flexible enough storage facility due to the inherently hierarchical nature of XML data. If the full

XML tree-like data structure needs to be stored, the object oriented model hands down a better storage format than the relational, and OODBMSs will show significant speed advantages.

According to Tim Bray, coauthor of the XML specification, and based on his experience with XML's precursor Standard Generalized Markup Language (SGML), structured documents are not easily stored in relational databases:

> "You can do it, but it requires a whole lot of ad-hockey and kludgeware. In the world of XML, sometimes this won't be a problem, because a certain proportion of XML is going to be used to interchange metadata, purchase orders, and remote procedure calls, which are naturally tabular and will work just fine. But there will be another proportion [of XML documents] that does have document-style structures and causes such problems. How big are the relative proportions going to be? Nobody knows" (Walsh, 1999).

Steve Muensh , an XML evangelist at Oracle, thinks XML documents will be just transitory and only exist for the transition time over the network: "This is data they already have in their enterprise relational databases and this is data which customers have no intention of representing natively as a set of XML documents on the file systems" (Walsh, 1999).

On the other hand (as OODBMS vendors see it) to leverage the full benefits of XML in the middle tire, besides simple information transmission, storage, caching, querying, and manipulation of native XML data are also required. This greater integration provides a unified view of XML data, and its hierarchical nature is preserved. As a result, no slower operation is involved (like joins) at retrieval time to reconstruct data. Furthermore, even if XML is only going to be a transient format, native caches still make sense for commonly accessed XML documents or pieces of XML trees.

XML technology has huge potentials and the relational data model is not the best way of storing XML documents. However, I would not underestimate the marketing power of relational database vendors. They may put substantial resources into advertisement insisting that all is needed is a faster machine and it will work.

World Wide Web

The wide variety of data types used in web pages, the complex management of hyperlinks, and the overall organization of web site structures limit the scalability of solutions relying on file structures or relational databases. Objects compose the majority of information presented on the Web. Image files, audio files, hyperlinks, text, pieces of Java code and other information that comprise a Web page are all rich data type objects. Although an object-relational database may provide a sufficient solution for storing rich data, most of the web systems also incorporate a significant amount of highly structured information. Web applications not only store information of different types, but this information is also highly interrelated and linked together. The next piece of information a user wants is frequently related to the last piece they "touched". Object databases are a natural match for storing this kind of information. The reason why OODBMSs did well in telecommunication network management applications and in financial trading desks is that both of these application areas have information that is highly interrelated, navigated from piece to piece and time critical. The excellence of OODBMSs in these areas ensures a superior architecture over relational databases for web applications.

I looked at XML as one of the technologies that may foster the wide spread of OODBMSs. However, as this technology may play an extremely important role for the Internet, it deserves a second look. One of the most interesting and powerful potentials of XML is its ability to define the contents of web pages and web interfaces. XML will change the web and allow more autonomous services to be created. In the next two years, more and more sites will use XML to define the content of sites so that automated search tools can more easily search it. This will make applications like e-commerce more feasible and will essentially create electronic marketplaces where programs do the searching, bartering and procuring on the behalf of web users. Though we are only in the early days of this e-commerce market, it is already apparent that XML will be the biggest thing to affect the Internet and web development since HTML. As I described it earlier, for the manipulation and storage of XML formatted data, OODBMSs give a better solution than relational technology.

The majority of Web content is stored in native file systems. These file systems have never been optimized for concurrency or performance in a multi-user environment. For example, a request for a document on a large web site may require as many as 5000 disk sector reads before the system gets to the location of the appropriate file. These I/O operations consume the most time in the entire computing environment. The usual solution to these problems is to install more hardware. An alternative software solution, on the other hand, can provide an in-memory cache for the fast location and retrieval of information objects. Using object oriented databases, their hash tables can offer a cache to maintain directory listings. These systems have been optimized for managing of vast amount of complex type data with high performance in large distributed systems. Empirical tests (Versant, n.d.) showed that a minimum of a 30-time throughput increase can be achieved using OODBMSs.

The importance of web technologies in the future is not a question any more. The question is how much object database technology will be able to leverage the mass deployment of the Internet. Even though Web information handling it provides better solutions than the relational model, as I pointed out earlier, superior technology does not always assure a winning position.

Costs and Limitations

It is not too difficult to realize the great potentials that OODBMSs have in general, and especially in certain areas of information technology. However, one might ask the question: So why has OO database technology not become a mainstream storage facility yet?

The biggest problem is unawareness. Most application developers and project managers have either never heard of, or ever considered using object databases instead of traditional relational products. Besides this, the slow adoption of new technology in general and the exotic nature of this solution has been a major slowing factor. Despite its long history, object technology is still not a widely used paradigm. Developers do not know how to program or think in an object oriented manner. Due to the lack of programming, analysis, design, and database administrator skills, OO database technology also raises a considerable educational challenge for enterprises. It requires a substantial commitment to training and to the proper use of the OO concept.

The overwhelming installation base of RDBMSs and the huge amount of legacy data stored in them is another major discouraging factor. Even when OO languages are used, they manipulate legacy data. Enterprises stay with relational technology to "leverage" the existing investments (software, hardware, training, expertise) they have in their relational databases.

The strategy that relational vendors use to target the object technology market is also a slowing factor of the adoption of object databases. Relational vendors developed a hybrid technology to support OO features by relational databases. Although object-relational (OR) databases can present some object oriented behavior, they do not provide a satisfactory solution in most of the cases. In OR architectures OO data structures are decomposed into constituent parts and stored either in columns in tables or in linked external binary files. This solution has several disadvantages. First of all, where join operations are involved during retrieval performance suffers eliminating the manipulation of complex interrelated data. Besides this major problem, the support for close language binding, client-side caching and object distribution may cause considerable technical challenges. Although I mentioned only some of the possible drawbacks of OR technology, even this limited list clearly shows that a pure object database approach better facilitates most of the current and future storage requirements. Even though it is not the best solution, as vendors make OO features more sophisticated, hardware gets more powerful, and OR companies put an increased amount of effort into marketing, this technology will very likely continue to be the biggest competition for object database products.

These factors mentioned above are largely business or human not technology reasons for the slow adoption of OODBMSs. However, looking at the history of information technology in the 1990s, one has to admit that superior technology does not always assure a winning market situation.

Future Directions

The appearance of object databases was triggered by a technical need that relational technology could not fulfill. CAD applications required storage facilities that could effectively and efficiently handle complex, interrelated data structures. Due to its very nature, relational technology was not and is still not a good solution for this purpose. At the beginning of its history, object database technology provided services in a very limited area of computing. However, as object technology became more popular and the World Wide Web moved into the focus of information technology, the relevance of object databases became obvious in much broader means. Object databases fit very well with OO languages as they provide close language binding and a semantically unified model throughout the entire development lifecycle. OODBMSs also provide more efficient storage and manipulation of complex data structures and types. This ability has gained significance by the increase of the complexity of computerized industry processes and by the growing importance of web integration. As a result of the anticipated potentials of object database technology, in the late 1980s and early 1990s this industry raised vast market expectations. Market watchers expected OODBMS vendors to grow by a 60-100 percentage yearly as their technology matures. There were still important features missing form leading products such as scalability, improved database management capabilities, integrated development environment etc. As improvements would be made in these areas analysts expected vendors to radically gain market share.

This has not happened. Even though object database technology has more than a decade of history by now, it never entered mainstream enterprise development. OODBMS products can demonstrate proven technology with applications in all areas of industry such as banking, healthcare, manufacturing, telecommunication, and software. They provide magnitudes better performance and scalability than their relational counterparts, widely used standards, query capabilities, rapid and flexible development environments, and advanced second storage management features. In short, object databases provide a competitive alternative for relational technology. However, due to human and business factors, this technology is by far not the typical choice. The revolutionary new way of thinking, small vulnerable vendors, and the huge investment in relational technology are all discouraging factors. Until present times, object database technology has had a slow and difficult growth. As we enter the 21st century the question is whether this growth will slow down even more or will get accelerated by new technology trends.

Several trends emerged in information technology in the last two years that may provide additional momentum for object databases. New software projects are more and more likely to use OO programming languages such as Java and C++. The complex data types of web and e-commerce applications, and the highly hierarchical structure of XML documents ask for a different kind of storage facility. Object oriented application servers and distributed object systems may also increasingly benefit from the services of OODBMSs. Besides new technologies, awareness is also gradually increasing as a new generation of skilled information technology workers is entering the workforce. Even tough the technology environment never looked more promising, now the future projections are much more moderate. Market watchers learned that this is a complex technology that is hard to understand and promote. Its adoption is slower than more obvious technologies due to nontechnical factors. Several object database vendors admitted that currently OODBMSs only have a highly technical niche market. To help this situation vendors will have to change their marketing attitude and open up new markets for their products. According to IDC's Olofson: "The challenge for ODBMS vendors is to change their ways of doing business away from highly technical end-users and toward ISVs and system integrators. They may have to develop more of [a] consulting business or align themselves with others who already offer extensive services." (Mendel, 1999)

Looking at the last 8 years of historical market data of OO database vendors an average of 30% growth rate can be seen. This increase has reached the expansion rate in other fields of computing. Future projections from market research firms show a 40% growth for the next five-year term. Even though this is not an exceptionally high expectation, OODBMS vendors will have to work very hard to fulfill it.

References

Baer, T. (1999, Jan 18). Object Databases. *Computerworld*, 33, 66.

Kalman, D. M. (1994, December). Object Database Essentials: HP's Dr. Mary Loomis Explains the Fundamentals of Object Database Technology [48 paragraphs]. DBMS ONLINE [On-line serial]. Available WWW: Hostname: www.dbmsmag.com File: int9412.html.

Mendel, B. (1999, March). XML Buoys Databases for Corporate Markets. *Infoworld*, 21(13), 38-39.

Object Designs, Inc. (n.d.). Server-Side XML: Taming the Tower of Babel. Object Design, Inc. Available WWW: Hostname: www.odi.com Directory: ODILIVE/FRAMEWORK File: main.asp?sKey=HOME.

Ricciuti, M. (1998, August). Application Server Eludes Definition [34 paragraphs]. CNET [On-line serial], Available WWW: Hostname: News.com Directory: News/Item File: 0,4,25616,00.html?st.ne.ni.rel.

Versant Corporation. (n.d.). Chicago Stock Exchange. Versant Corporation. Available: WWW: Host: www.versant.com:82 Directory: us/finance File: ficustomer1A.html.

Versant Corporation. (n.d.). Software Solutions to Internet Performance Problems. Versant Corporation. Available WWW: Hostname: www.versant.com Directory: cgi-bin/vwscgi/whitepaperapp File: NEWTASK?REQNUM= 2&RESOURCENAME=INTERNET _PERF.

Walsh, J. (1999, January). XML Poses Data-architecture Debate [27 paragraphs]. Info World Electric [On-line serial], Available WWW: Hostname: www.infoworld.com Directory: cgi-bin File: displayStory.pl?/features/990125xml.html.

Chapter V

Software Reuse and Object Technology

Jane Fedorowicz
Bentley College, USA

Denis Lee
Suffolk University, USA

Introduction

Companies are increasingly requiring that new information systems development projects employ object oriented (OO) analysis, design and programming approaches. The hottest new Web tools and languages have object capabilities built into them. Much of the movement toward the OO paradigm for systems development is based on claims of pioneers and vendors that adoption will lead to better and faster designs, more maintainable systems, and most audibly, reusable software. A typical set of attributions appears in CACM: "OO technology promotes a better understanding of requirements and results in more modifiable and maintainable applications, providing other benefits such as reusability, extensibility, robustness, reliability, and scalability. OO technology promotes better teamwork, good communication among team members, and a way to engineer reliable software systems and applications" (Fayad and Tsai, 1995).

However, to paraphrase Brown and Wallman (1998), object technology is neither necessary nor sufficient for reuse, or what they call component based software engineering. Reuse may be theoretically easier in an OO environment, but it is frequently cited in non-OO projects as well. Notably, 80% of the 120 large companies responding to a survey by the Cutter Information Group cited reuse as a driving reason for adopting object technologies (Radding, 1998).

Definitions of reuse vary depending on the nature of the reused component. This study adopts the following definition: "Software reuse is the process of building or assembling software systems from predefined software components that are designed for reuse." (McClure, 1997, p. 3). Under this definition, reusable components may be objects or program source code, reflecting a commonly held view of reuse. However, reuse programs may also incorporate software specifications, project plans, frameworks, or other software project deliverables. While focusing on the synergies expected from the reuse of objects, this study also examines other aspects of OO and reuse as they influence today's software practices.

Background

Several theoretical reuse frameworks have been proposed in the literature, including the very comprehensive effort in Kim and Stohr (1998). However, reuse has only recently begun to be investigated and defined in a field research setting. Several case studies have been published illustrating the benefits and costs of reuse programs and approaches. In one study, significant development time and monetary savings were chronicled at Schwab for their e-trade system, which also resulted in improved user response time, a key competitive advantage within their industry. Schwab's success was predicated on adopting a single object language, Java (Levin, 1998).

Reuse proponents frequently point to the Software Engineering Lab at NASA as a leading success story for reuse. Reuse rates from 75% to 96% are reported for their projects, with the caveat that cost to develop code for reuse is higher than the cost to develop code without reuse as a stated goal. However, total development costs and error rates have dropped dramatically with reuse (Basili and Caldiera, 1995). Other studies at companies like Travelers' PC Claims unit, IBM, MBA Technologies, and 20th Century Fox have shown similar patterns of benefits (Fichman and Kemerer, 1998; Radding, 1998; Ross et al., 1996; Rothenberger and Hershauer, 1999).

Many of these case studies are primarily illustrative in nature. However, a couple of them augment the case history with an analysis of the activities noted at the site. Rothenberger and Hershauer tested a software reuse measure based on lines of code in three kinds of component software at one site. They computed an overall reuse rate of 67.4%, surface structure 0.4%, 57.0% reuse in the middle structure, and 95.9% reuse of the deep structure.

In the most comprehensive field study of all, Fichman and Kemerer examined 15 projects at eight IBM sites. To their surprise, they found IBM's current reuse practice to be informal and ad hoc, rarely extending beyond project team confines. They also found that many organization-centric reuse activities (such as formal reuse programs and centralized libraries) had been disbanded due to low participation and overall staffing reductions. They propose a reuse model comprising four dimensions; wherein, a suitable combination of organizational model, production model, incentives and control, and funding and cost management need to be synchronized to support a successful and systematic reuse strategy.

In a predecessor project to the current study (Fedorowicz and Villeneuve, 1999), we analyzed surveys from over 200 OO practitioners to ascertain their level of experience with OO tools and techniques, and also to assess their perceptions of the usefulness and benefits of OO. Many vendors' claims were upheld by professionals using the tools, yet not always to the extent that the vendors anticipated. In particular, OO techniques were perceived as hard to learn, and do not give a novice an anticipated edge in acquiring expertise. Overall, however, respondents preferred to use OO for application development, as well as to support team-based activities, such as client communications, project team communications, and new team member familiarization. Professional users expected that OO would require a greater time investment at the beginning of SDLC, with time savings accruing at the latter stages of a project's implementation and use.

The most favorable preferences and benefits were reported by those respondents who have used OO the most. Those with OO experience, who have worked on the largest projects, and who have employed OO in the most SDLC steps had the most positive responses to the survey. Those who adopted formal methodologies and development environments also expressed more favorable opinions than those who work without them. Thus, in its users' eyes, OO appears to exceed expectations once the professional has invested considerable time in learning the techniques and applying the tools needed to develop systems effectively within the OO paradigm.

These results enumerate the many perceived benefits of OO within individual development projects. However, there are many potential cross-project, or organization-wide advantages of adopting OO technologies that may prove to be even more significant to a company. The current study will build upon the project orientation of this study, while expanding the focus to encompass organization-wide implications of object technology.

Of particular relevance in the prior study, respondents reported expectations that objects they have worked with are or will be shareable and reusable. This opinion was stronger when OO was used in a greater number of Systems Development Life Cycle steps, when project size was larger, and when the respondent had greater OO experience. In other words, the more OO was used, the greater the expectation for resulting reuse practices. These findings bear out many of the relationships proposed by the Kim and Stohr software reuse framework and illustrated by the case studies described earlier. Their significance motivates the need for a more in-depth survey to explicate more precisely the characteristics of reuse in practice, at both the project and organizational level. The current study, outlined in the next section, includes descriptive analyses of the adoption and diffusion of OO and reuse technologies and identifies some of their project and organizational benefits.

The Study

Practitioners with extensive systems development experience were surveyed to measure more precisely their experience with OO tools and techniques and to relate the benefits (and costs) that accrue due to OO adoption. In addition, the survey focuses on reuse, the most highly hailed of all OO benefits. A major goal of this study is to identify what is being reused, by whom, whether reused objects are developed in-house or purchased from an outside clearinghouse, and under what circumstances they can be reused. The study will also identify the added costs of producing reusable code (vs. traditional, application specific code), where in the Systems Development Life Cycle extra time or effort is required to successfully produce a reusable end product, and under what circumstances reusable objects are actually reused.

A three page questionnaire was developed based in part on the earlier OO survey, several widely used MIS surveys on usefulness and user satisfaction (e.g., Delone and McLean, 1992), and from practitioner writings on reuse (e.g., McClure, 1997). It was pretested in an object oriented design course taken by advanced M.S. in Computer Information Systems students. The final, slightly modified questionnaire was distributed in July, 1997 to about 1,000 systems developers. The majority of the mailing list was obtained from *PC Week,* and comprised experienced systems developers. A smaller number of respondents were from a mailing list of reuse specialists who had been participants in reuse conferences and trade associations. A total of 190 usable surveys were returned. This paper contains a descriptive analysis of the data.

Preliminary Results

Tables 1 and 2 give demographic data for the respondents and their companies. Respondents have considerable OO and reuse experience. They are seasoned IS practitioners. They are employed by a range of companies, spanning many industries as well as small and large organizations. Twelve percent report the existence of a formal Reuse Program at their company, 5 percent used to have one, but it has been disbanded (as was the situation at IBM as noted by Fichman and Kemerer), and another 4 percent describe various other approaches to a formal program.

Respondents were asked to estimate the extent of OO and reuse adoption within their organizations. Table 3 summarizes these responses. While 16 percent reported no OO efforts within the past year, 20 percent perceived that most or all of their company's application

Table 1: Respondent Demographics

Respondent Demographics	Mean Value
OO experience	3 years
Reuse experience	3.6 years
Years in computer industry	15 years
Years in current position	5
Percent male	91%
Age	40

Table 2: Company Size and Experience with Reuse Programs

Company Data		**Percent**
Number of employees		
	<100	24%
	100-999	20%
	1000-9,999	29%
	>10,000	28%
Percent with Reuse Program		12%
Percent without Reuse Program		80%
Percent that used to have a program but don't need it anymore.		2%
Percent that used to have a program but it didn't work and was disbanded.		3%
Other Reuse Program response		4%

Table 3: Companies' Exposure to Objects and Reuse

Organizational effort in the past year (choose one only)	**Number of companies reporting that this percent of applications developed were OO**	**Number of companies reporting that this percent of applications developed contained reusable components**	**Number of companies reporting that this percent of components were developed expressly for reuse**
None	30 (16%)	16 (8%)	40 (21%)
< 25%	72 (38%)	65 (36%)	81 (43%)
25-50%	34 (19%)	37 (19%)	21 (11%)
50-75%	10 (5%)	21 (11%)	16 (8%)
75-99%	15 (8%)	13 (7%)	5 (3%)
All	13 (7%)	17 (9%)	2 (1%)
Don't know	16 (8%)	21 (11%)	24 (13%)

development efforts were object oriented. Only 8 percent perceived that their company did not reuse components in the past year, while 27 percent reported that over half or all applications contained reused components. However, efforts to design components expressly for reuse were not as prevalent. Twenty-one percent reported no components were developed for reuse, although this does not preclude components from being purchased from a component vendor or other source (as indicated in Table 4). Twelve percent reported that half to

Table 4: Sources of Reusable components

Source	Percent	Correlation with % of applications containing reusable components	Correlation with % of components developed for reuse
Percent of reusable components developed in-house using special tools and environments	12%	.01	.18**
Percent of reusable components developed in-house using programming languages	49%	.24***	.17**
Percent of reusable components purchased individually	9%	.17**	-.04
Percent obtained as shareware or in the purchase price of a development environment	12%	-.16	-.04
Percent of components purchased in an object "library" or "package"	11%	-.05	-.04
Percent obtained as shareware	1%	-.07	-.01
Other sources (contracted, etc.)	4%	.01	.05

all of their in-house development of components were intended to be reused.

Source of components was correlated with percent of components developed for reuse in Table 4. The results support the contention that in those companies where components are specifically designed for reuse, a higher percentage of reusable components are produced in-house, while those purchasing components do not necessarily design their software for reuse. Specifically, those companies reporting the highest percentages of components being developed for reuse (in Table 3) were more likely to indicate in-house development of components using programming languages (p= 0.05) or specialized tools and environments (p=0.05). Correlations with percentage of applications containing reusable components show that for most of these applications, developers build their own components (p=0.01) or purchase them individually (p=0.05). This suggests that reused components tend to be application-specific rather than generic building blocks or of unknown reliability.

OO and reuse activities are more likely to involve development of new applications than existing ones. As seen in Table 5, each of the

Table 5: Adoption of technologies for New vs. Existing Applications

	Percent of new applications employing this technology	**Percent of existing applications employing this technology**
Reuse	51%	19%
Objects	51%	11%

Table 6: Top Five Categories of Reused Items at Respondents' Organizations

Reused Items	**Percentage of Respondents**
Code	62%
Data Objects	57%
Programming objects	55%
Subroutines	54%
Software Design	37%

technology practices was employed in just over half of new applications with equal frequency. However, modifications to existing applications involved reuse only 19% of the time, and objects only 11% of the time, confirming that newer projects are more likely to take advantage of these practices than those that are being retrofit.

The top five categories of reused items are indicated in Table 6. Overall, only four categories of reusable components were reported by more than half the respondents, including code (62%), data objects (57%), programming objects (55%) and subroutines (54%). It is clear that code segments of various kinds are perceived to be the most highly reused components, far exceeding development methodologies, tools and frameworks in organizational reuse programs.

Respondents perceived many benefits extant from their company's reuse activities. Table 7 summarizes their perceptions of the reasons reuse is practiced in their organizations, which represents their response on a 5-point scale with 1 representing "agree" and 5 "disagree". In addition, correlation analysis of this set of reasons with the length of personal and organizational reuse experience is included in the table. Where results are significant, the correlations demonstrate that more organizational experience with reuse increases the respondents' level of agreement with many of the reasons companies practice reuse. However, individual respondents with higher personal levels of experience are not more likely to have higher expectations of benefits than their less experienced counterparts. This argues in

Table 7: Respondents Perceptions of Their Companies' Reuse Benefits

Reason for Practicing Reuse	Mean Response	Correlation with respondent's reuse experience	Correlation with % of applications containing reusable components	Correlation with % of components developed for reuse
Increase software productivity	1.70	-.07	-.25***	-.24***
Shorten software development time	1.68	-.08	-.23***	-.16**
Improve software interoperability	2.08	.03	-.18**	-.18**
Develop software with fewer people	2.40	-.05	-.04	.02
Move personnel more easily from project to project	2.77	-.01	-.05	-.04
Reduce software development costs	2.01	-.12	-.18**	-.07
Reduce software maintenance costs	1.87	-.04	-.12	-.19**
Produce more standardized software	1.94	.03	.08	-.08
Produce better quality software	1.79	-01	-.17**	-.28***
Provide a powerful competitive advantage	2.14	-.02	-.17**	-.22***

support of the contention that many of the benefits of reuse are recognized to accrue to organizations rather than to individual projects or tasks.

Respondents from organizations with higher levels of reuse practice were more likely to attest to project-level benefits, including increased software productivity, shorter development time and better quality software. Experience also correlates with higher expectations for organizational-level benefits of improved software interoperability and providing a competitive advantage. Either the benefits play out in practice, or the level of buy-in of reuse-oriented organizations positively biases their employees' perceptions of the value of reuse.

Interestingly, software development cost reduction is significantly correlated with a higher percentage of applications employing reusable components, but not when more components are specifically developed for reuse. Also, lower software maintenance costs are expected when higher percentages of components are designed to be reused. Adopting existing components is seen as shortening development time, and spending the extra effort to produce reusable components is seen as paying off later on when the system is to be maintained.

Conclusions and Future Trends

Like the Fedorowicz and Villeneuve study of OO benefits, more reuse experience was associated with significantly higher perceived reuse benefits overall; however, it is organizational rather than personal experience that leads to higher benefit expectations. This study shows that the benefits of reuse play out at both the individual project level and the organizational level and suggests that efforts to promote reuse and to share components among projects are worthy of carefully planned organization-wide investment. Like OO, increased experience with reuse raises perceptions of decreasing maintenance costs, but only when a significant conscious effort is made to develop reusable components.

Although the benefits of reuse were readily discernible in the results, the adoption and diffusion rate of reusable components were not as high as expected, nor were the findings on experience-related benefits. For example, while producing standardized software is a benefit rated highly by many respondents, the results show that those with extensive reuse experience do not report higher standardization expectations than those with less experience. One explanation may be the frequent shift of development tools relied on by software developers. In the past few years, the programming language of choice in the OO world shifted from specialized OO languages like Smalltalk to generic, but not entirely object-based C++, and now to the "purer", more shareable Java. These frequent changes make it difficult to standardize on a single development languages, and may produce situations in which components that should have common elements were developed with different tools over time. As companies (like Schwab) recognize the reuse benefits of a common software platform, we may see a rise in reusable component development efforts, as well as in increase in overall diffusion rates.

The majority of reused components were developed in-house, most frequently using programming languages. A smaller number were purchased from external sources, perhaps because of a lack of fit or a lack of confidence in the quality of externally developed components.

As more and more organizations garner experience with both OO technologies and reuse, the benefits achieved by experienced developers joined with a significant pool of readily available, reusable components should lead to increasingly cheaper and shorter development cycles. Success is more likely to occur in companies where project teams and project managers are rewarded or recognized for their reuse activities.

In addition, as the software industry continues to provide OO-based development tools that operate seamlessly over the Web, we should see an increasing supply of certified high-quality reusable components for sale from independent developers. Adopters or purchasers of these components will need to rely on third party certification processes to assure the reliability and usability of the purchased components. Without some outside assurance, this market opportunity remains limited. The OMG, with its CORBA standard, is a good start toward attesting to the shareability of object-based components. Other assurance standards will be needed to convince reticent developers of the quality of other functions offered by external component sources.

Future Research

The analysis in this paper gives a brief introduction to our understanding of the adoption and diffusion of OO and reuse in practice. Further analysis of the data collected in this study should help researchers and practitioners better understand how and when to rely on object-oriented and reuse techniques by establishing patterns of adoption, use and benefit achievement. The study examines the issue of object reuse at both the individual project and organizational levels which will enable the establishment of guidelines on best practices for systems development and maintenance, as well as projecting future trends in the marketing and sharing of objects and other reusable components.

Clearinghouses for code, whether internal libraries or independent vendors, are just now appearing in the marketplace. Additional research and analysis will lead to prescriptions for critical success factors for providing such services and suggest cultural changes that must accompany technical change in practice in order to truly achieve widespread reuse.

References

Basili, V. R. and Caldiera, G. (1995). "Improve Software Quality by Reusing Knowledge and Experience", *Sloan Management Review*, 37(1), 55-64.

Brown, A. W. and Wallnau, K.C. (1998). "The Current State of CBSE", *IEEE Software*, September-October, 37-46.

Delone, W. H. and McLean, E.R. (1992). "Information Systems Success: The Quest for the Dependent Variable", *Information Systems Research*, March, 60-95.

Fayad, M.E. and Tsai, W.-T. (1995). Introduction to section on object-oriented experiences, *Communications of the ACM*, 38 (10), 50-53.

Fedorowicz, J. and Villeneuve, A.O. (1999). "Surveying Object Technology Usage and Benefits: A Test of Conventional Wisdom", *Information and Management*, 35(6), 345-356.

Fichman, R.G. and Kemerer, C.F. (1998). "A Project Team-centric Approach to Systematic Software Reuse", University of Pittsburgh Katz Graduate School of Business Working Paper No. 757, June.

Kim, Yongbeom and Stohr, E.A. (1998). "Software Reuse: Survey and Research Directions", *Journal of Management Information Systems*, 14(48, 113-147.

Levin, R. (1997)."Java Boosts Reuse", *InformationWeek*, 701, September 21, p. 82.

McClure, Carma (1997). *Software Reuse Techniques: Adding Reuse to the System Development Process*, Prentice-Hall, New Jersey.

Radding, A. (1998). "Hidden Costs of Code Reuse", *InformationWeek*, 708, November 9.

Ross, J. W., Cynthia Mathis Beath and Dale L. Goodhue (1996). "Develop Long-term Competitiveness through IT Assets", *Sloan Management Review*,38(1), . 31-42.

Rothenberger, M.A. and J.C. Hershauer (1999). "A Software Reuse Measure: Monitoring an Enterprise-level Model Driven Development Process", *Information and Management*, 35(5), 283-293.

Chapter VI

Reuse in Object Oriented Modeling: An Empirical Study of Experienced and Novice Analysts

Gretchen Irwin
University of Auckland, NZ

Chamini Wasalathantry
Ernst & Young, NZ

Introduction

Object Oriented (OO) technology and software reuse are widely believed to be key ingredients to improving systems development productivity and quality (Meyer 1989; Cox 1990). Software reuse is broadly defined as the application of existing systems development artifacts to new development projects. OO technology supports reuse in a number of ways. For example, at the programming level, reuse is supported through built-in components (classes) and specialization of the class hierarchy. At the analysis and design levels, OO pattern handbooks provide reusable solution templates to known modeling and design problems (Gamma et al. 1995; Fowler 1996). The systematic use of these and other artifacts can, at least in theory, reduce the time taken to develop new systems by leveraging the knowledge gained from prior projects.

While the claims of the benefits of software reuse and OO technology have been widespread, the empirical evidence has been inconsistent and somewhat lacking. Many case studies report substantial productivity gains and quality improvements from code reuse (e.g.,

Banker and Kauffman 1991; Lim 1994). Other studies, however, show that OO programmers primarily engage in low levels of reuse such as code scavenging (Lange and Moher 1989; Rosson and Carroll 1996; Fichman and Kemerer 1997), or that reuse is a cognitively demanding and often error-prone activity (Maiden and Sutcliffe 1992; Kim and Lerch 1997). Furthermore, many researchers and practitioners argue that the reuse of upstream artifacts such as analysis and design models can have a significantly higher payoff than the reuse of downstream artifacts such as programming components (Boehm and Papaccio 1988; Biggerstaff and Richter 1989). However, there is very little empirical research on the reuse of upstream software artifacts (an exception is Maiden and Sutcliffe 1992).

This chapter begins to address the lack of empirical research on the reuse of OO analysis and design artifacts. We investigated the cognitive costs and benefits of reusing a given (source) OO analysis model for a new (target) modeling task. The cognitive costs include the time and effort the analyst invests in understanding the source task, identifying the similarities between the source and target, and adapting the source solution to the target solution (Biggerstaff and Richter 1989; Curtis 1989). The cognitive benefits, presumably, include reduced time and effort to construct the target solution.

Our primary research question is to explore the effect of reuse on the OO modeling process. Given the abundance of research on expert-novice differences in modeling, design, and programming (e.g., see Detienne 1997), we are also interested in whether reuse has a different effect for novice versus experienced OO analysts. We conducted a verbal protocol study where novice and experienced OO analysts were asked to solve the same target problem. Some analysts were given a source problem and OO solution to reuse (the reuse condition); others were not (the control condition).

As expected, we found that novices in the reuse condition spent additional effort on problem understanding due to the reusable artifact. However, the effort spent on understanding the source example and mapping between it and the target problem did not "pay off" in terms of reduced effort in constructing the target solution. In addition, novices in the reuse condition evaluated their solutions less thoroughly than did the control subjects. Experienced OO analysts in the reuse condition spent less effort on problem understanding than did their counterpart in the control group. The source example seemed to facilitate the experienced analysts' problem understanding rather than adding an extra burden to it. However, as with the novices, there was no noticeable reduction in the effort spent on constructing the solution between reuse and control subjects. These findings, along with the results of other empirical studies, suggest that the cognitive benefits to software reuse are still poorly understood. We suggest several avenues for future research on the cognitive aspects of reuse, particularly the reuse of OO analysis and design artifacts. We need to learn more about how and where the reuse of upstream artifacts can be effective. A better understanding of these issues will foster the design of tools that effectively support novice and experienced developers in their reuse efforts.

The rest of the chapter is organized as follows. The following section sets the context for the study by reviewing empirical studies of OO modeling and software reuse. The third section describes the study we conducted and the fourth section presents the results. The chapter concludes with a discussion of the limitations of the study and the implications for researchers, educators, and practitioners.

Background

> Such is the software engineer's plight: time and time again composing a new variation that elaborates on the same basic theme: 'Neither ever quite the same, nor ever quite another.' (Meyer, 1989, p. 3)

Experienced software engineers do not solve every problem "from scratch." They find successful solutions to known problems and use the solutions again and again, adapting them as necessary to new contexts (Curtis 1989). The goal of software reuse is to extend and formalize the "natural" form of reuse practiced intuitively by experts. The vision of software reuse is that software engineers will systematically retrieve and apply robust, quality software development artifacts throughout the development life cycle, and that this practice will lead to order-of-magnitude improvements in development productivity and quality (Biggerstaff and Richter 1989).

The benefits of software reuse can be achieved with or without OO technology. However, there are many aspects to object orientation that make it particularly conducive to reuse. At the programming level, object orientation promotes the creation of encapsulated objects with well-defined interfaces. Programmers can reuse these objects in a "black-box" manner without having to understand the details of how things work within the object. OO programming environments also promote reuse through inheritance. Inheritance is the mechanism that allows a new class to share the definition of an existing class and to extend that definition by adding specialized characteristics and behaviors.

While the reuse of programming artifacts can be beneficial, many researchers and practitioners believe that more significant gains are possible from the reuse of analysis and design artifacts (Biggerstaff and Richter 1989). This belief stems from the time-intensive nature of analysis and design and the high cost of correcting errors made during these upstream development activities (Boehm and Papaccio 1988). OO analysis and design reuse is particularly promising because of the tight integration between the problem domain and the solution domain — many problem domains can be "naturally" represented in terms of interacting objects that map directly onto implementation constructs (Rosson and Alpert 1990).

Over the last decade, several types of reusable analysis and design artifact have emerged from the OO community. Design frameworks, for example, provide skeletal designs for certain well-defined domains, such as the Model-View-Controller framework for user interface design in Smalltalk-80 (Deutsch 1989). The framework consists of a set of closely related abstract and concrete classes that are specialized and instantiated for specific applications. More recently, Fowler (1996) and Gamma et al. (1995) have documented dozens of reusable OO analysis and design patterns. Each pattern represents an abstract solution to a recurring problem, and unlike a design framework is not programming language-dependent.

The arguments and activity in support of OO analysis, design, and code reuse are appealing. However, the empirical evidence is somewhat mixed. The following section reviews empirical studies of software reuse by individuals to assess what we know about the cognitive costs and benefits of reuse. Given the scarce number of studies on OO analysis and design reuse, we then review empirical studies of the OO modeling process to better understand how reuse might be expected to influence the process.

Empirical Studies of Software Reuse

Many case studies have reported strong positive outcomes from software reuse. For example, Hewlett-Packard observed 24-51% reductions in software defects and 40-57% increases in programmer productivity across several projects (Lim 1994). First Boston Corporation achieved an order of magnitude improvement in programming productivity one year after the implementation of an integrated CASE tool and reuse program (Banker and Kauffman, 1991).

On the other hand, there is also considerable evidence that the vision of widespread, systematic software reuse remains elusive in practice. For example, in the First Boston case cited above, over 60% of the reuse derived from programmers reusing their own code although the reuse library contained many reusable components authored by other programmers. Fichman and Kemerer (1997) examined four case sites that had adopted OO technology to encourage and improve software reuse. Reuse in these sites was limited to the reuse of low-level objects such as strings and containers or to salvaging code for a system rewrite. Other studies of OO programmers have observed "code scavenging" (copying, pasting, and editing code from one application to another) as the dominant form of reuse (Lange and Moher 1989; Detienne 1991). While these types of reuse can certainly be useful, they fall considerably short of the productivity and quality gains that are promoted with OO technology.

One of the obstacles to reuse is that it is a cognitively demanding activity. The reuse process consists of retrieving, understanding, mapping, and modifying (Gick and Holyoak 1980; Biggerstaff and Richter 1989). Individuals will be unlikely to reuse unless they perceive that the cognitive effort and time required to locate, understand, and apply an existing artifact is less than the effort and time required to create a new artifact "from scratch" (Prieto-Diaz 1989). In addition, there may be cultural and attitudinal obstacles such as the reluctance of programmers to reuse artifacts they themselves did not create (the NIH or Not Invented Here syndrome), or the belief that reuse is akin to copying (Hoadley et al., 1996).

Several studies have experimentally examined the reuse of programming, design, and systems analysis artifacts, albeit not in an OO-specific context. These studies shed some light on the specific processes that can make reuse a difficult endeavor. For example, Woodfield et al. (1987) showed that programmers performed poorly when asked to evaluate the reusability of given abstract data types. They consistently underestimated the effort needed to adapt an existing abstract data type to a new situation. In some sense, this finding is not surprising, as software engineers are notoriously poor at effort estimation (Boehm and Papaccio, 1988; Brooks, 1990).

Another problematic aspect of reuse is analogical mapping. Analogical mapping is the identification of appropriate similarities between the reusable artifact (the *source*) and the current problem (the *target*) (Gick and Holyoak 1980). Successful mapping requires that the source and target domains are understood and appropriately compared. The difficulty of analogical mapping depends, in part, on the similarity between and the familiarity of the source and target domains (Gentner, 1983). In Kim and Lerch's (1997) study, subjects were given an OO program to reuse in solving a new problem. For one group (the control group), the target task was nearly the same as the source problem. Reuse in this condition was expected to be easy and successful, and in fact, all subjects in this condition successfully reused the given program. In the other group, the source and target tasks had the same entities and objectives but differed in terms of the entity roles and relations. Only one third of these subjects succeeded in reusing the source program. They attempted and failed to map the source solution directly to the target solution and succeeded only after they retrieved or constructed an intermediate representation to "bridge" the cognitive distance between the source and target representations.

In Maiden and Sutcliffe's (1992) study, experienced and novice analysts were given a structured analysis artifact to reuse on a new modeling problem. In this case, the source artifacts were structurally similar to the target problem. Most of their subjects attempted reuse and the solutions of the reusers were more complete than the solutions of the control subjects. However, novices tended to "lazily copy" from the source example rather than carefully applying and modifying the source to suit the requirements of the target problem.

The studies by Kim & Lerch (1997) and Maiden & Sutcliffe (1992) suggest that the extent and type of source-target similarity is an important issue for successful analogical mapping and subsequent reuse. In Kim & Lerch's study, the source representation had to be transformed to an "intermediate" representation before it could be applied to the target problem. Very few subjects were able to make this transformation. In the Maiden & Sutcliffe study, an intermediate representation did not appear to be needed, and subjects recognized the analogy between source and target. However, the high degree of similarity in this case seemed to promote sloppy reuse among novices.

Empirical Studies of OO Modeling

There is an abundance of empirical research on conceptual modeling and software design that provides a foundation for understanding how reuse may fit into the OO modeling process. Research in this area focuses primarily on the modeling or design activities, difficulties, and decomposition strategies used by experienced and novice designers.

Design activities focus on what individuals do as they work on a design task. For OO design tasks, several consistent results have been observed for novices. For example, novices tend to focus first on problem domain entities and then on class identification, which is consistent with the approaches prescribed in many OO analysis and design texts (e.g., Jacobson 1992). Novices have difficulty translating domain entities into a stable set of classes, and they postpone consideration of functional details such as method specification until much later in the modeling process (Pennington et al., 1995; Detienne, 1997). Novices also tend to have difficulty with core OO concepts such as inheritance and distributed functionality (message passing). Inheritance is often used inappropriately to capture composition relationships and distributed functionality is inappropriately replaced by something akin to a "main" procedure in structured programming languages (Rosson and Carroll, 1990; Detienne, 1997). Presumably, reuse could help novices with one or more of these difficulties, particularly since learning by example is an important and often-used strategy for them (Anderson and Thompson, 1989).

Empirical studies of experienced OO designers show that they transition easily from the problem domain to the solution domain and spend most of their time working with solution domain constructs (Pennington et al., 1995). They evaluate their solutions extensively primarily through mental simulation (Srinivasan and Te'eni, 1995). As mentioned earlier, expert designers use solutions from their own experience as a natural part of their problem-solving process. The reuse challenge for experienced designers is, thus, considerably different than that for novices. The reuse of OO analysis and design artifacts may be most likely to aid the experienced designer when he or she is working in an unfamiliar domain.

Design strategies can be described in terms of what drives the overall structure of the solution and how the problem is decomposed into subproblems. The overall structure of the solution can be function-centered, object-centered, or procedure-centered (Detienne, 1997). The use of one structuring method over another seems to depend both on the designer's expertise (e.g., novices tend to use a procedure-centered plan) and the type of problem (e.g., problems with a strong data emphasis and complex hierarchical structure lend themselves to an object-centered approach) (Detienne, 1997; Pennington et al, 1995). Several types of decomposition strategy have also been observed, including top-down decomposition (Jeffries et al., 1981) and opportunistic design (Visser 1990). In Pennington et al's (1995) study, the experienced procedural designers displayed clear patterns of opportunistic behavior (i.e., jumping between levels of abstraction), and the experienced OO subjects showed a somewhat less opportunistic strategy. However, we are aware of no studies that investigate whether and how software reuse influences the design strategies employed by experienced or novice analysts.

Summary

What does prior research tell us about the expected effect of reuse on the OO modeling process? We know that reuse can present cognitive challenges, particularly if the source solution is far removed from the target problem (Kim and Lerch 1997). In any case, additional cognitive effort must be expended to understand the source solution and map between the source and target domains. If mapping between the source and target domains is successful, we would expect that solving the target problem will be easier than solving "from scratch." This was the case for the control group in the Kim and Lerch (1997) study. However, mapping between the source and target may also lead to "lazy copying" and less rigorous evaluation of the target solution. This was the case for novices in the Maiden and Sutcliffe (1992) study. And finally, it is unclear whether or how reuse influences the overall design strategy used by novices or experts.

An Exploratory Study

We conducted an experimental study to investigate the impact of reuse on the OO modeling process. Since the primary emphasis was on modeling *processes* rather than modeling *outcomes*, we relied heavily on concurrent verbal protocols (Ericsson and Simon, 1993). This technique elicits a sequential trace of individual problem-solving behavior by asking each subject to "think aloud" as he or she solves a problem. Sessions are audio- or videotaped and later transcribed for analysis. Concurrent verbal protocols provide a high degree of data richness and have been used in many studies of design and data modeling (Detienne 1991; Pennington et al., 1995; Srinivasan and Te'eni, 1995; Kim and Lerch, 1997).

In our study, participants were assigned to either a reuse or a control condition. Reuse subjects were given an example problem and OO model solution (the *source*) to review, followed by the problem to be solved (the *target*). They were told they could reuse the given example in any way they saw fit if they thought it would be helpful (Gick and Holyoak, 1983). The source problem was highly similar to the target problem and the source solution was designed to be highly reusable. Control subjects were not given an example to reuse.

Eight subjects participated in the study. Three subjects were experienced OO analysts/designers who were recruited from a Smalltalk Users Group. They had between four and ten years of professional OO development experience. The remaining five subjects were novice OO designers. At the time of the study, they were nearing the completion of a sixteen-week course on OO development. The course was largely project-based and included the analysis, design, and implementation of a prototype system in Smalltalk. Prior to this course, the novices had not been exposed to OO technology, although all had completed at least one programming course (typically in Pascal or COBOL). Participants were randomly assigned to one of the experimental conditions, as shown below.

The target task was to construct an OO model for a hospital's activity-based costing system. The OO solution had to include a class structure diagram showing classes, relationships, attributes, and methods. In the reuse condition, the source example consisted of a problem description and completed OO model for a service organization's value-chain analysis system. For both tasks, the primary system objective was to allocate organizational resources to activities in order to track the costs of each activity. While there were several minor differences between the source and target solutions, both consisted of three main subproblems: resources, activities, and allocations.

Table 1. Experimental Design

Experience Level	Reuse Condition	Control Condition
OO Novice	R1, R2, and R3	C1 and C2
OO Experienced	R4 and R5	C3

Protocol Analysis

When data collection was completed, the videotaped sessions were transcribed and parsed into "thought fragments" called protocol segments or statements (see Ericsson and Simon (1993) for details of the process followed). Protocol segments that reflected verbatim reading of the target problem description or questions to the researcher were excluded from further analysis. Each remaining protocol segment was then coded according to a predefined coding plan.

Coding proceeded in two phases. In the first phase, each protocol segment was assigned one of the following modeling *activity codes*: (1) problem understanding (U); (2) solution development or solving (S); (3) solution evaluation (E); or (4) planning or monitoring (M). Each activity code is described briefly below.

A *problem understanding* (U) code was assigned to protocol segments where the subject was focused on the problem domain. This included rereading the task description to acquire information or clarify questions about the domain, identifying high-level requirements, defining the system boundaries, or reasoning about the problem domain (Sutcliffe and Maiden, 1992; Pennington et al., 1995). For subjects in the reuse condition, this code also included analogical mapping activities, where the subjects was exploring the source problem and solution or identifying the parallels between the source and target problem domains.

A *solution development* or solving (S) code was assigned to segments where the participant was constructing part of the OO model. For example, a solving code was assigned when the subject listed potential classes, drew part of the OO diagram, specified attribute or method details, corrected previous errors, or specified relationship cardinalities (Pennington et al. 1995). In the reuse condition, this code was also assigned if the subject was constructing the target solution while referencing the source solution.

An *evaluation* code was assigned to segments where the subject was assessing either the completeness or correctness of his/her solution. Evaluation activity included proposing alternative solutions for consideration, providing the rationale for a chosen alternative, testing a solution through mental simulation, and/or checking for missing or unmet requirements in the solution (Srinivasan and Te'eni, 1995). In the reuse condition, an evaluation code was also assigned where the subject was assessing the correctness or completeness of the source solution by comparing it to the source solution.

A *monitoring* code was assigned to segments where the subject was reflecting on the overall problem-solving process, planning the problem-solving strategy, or deciding to change direction during the session (Sutcliffe and Maiden, 1992). For subjects in the reuse condition, this code was also assigned where the protocol segment reflected an awareness of being influenced by the source example or an explicit strategy to reuse the example.

In the second phase of coding, we examined the solving codes in more detail to determine the overall problem-solving strategy used by each participant. A level of *abstraction* code was assigned to each protocol segment that was previously assigned a solving code. The level of abstraction codes were similar to codes used in prior studies (Srinivasan and Te'eni 1995) and are defined below.

Level 1: Specification of intra-class properties (i.e., attributes and methods). This is considered to be the lowest level of abstraction since it pertains to the most detailed aspects of the solution.

Level 2: Class identification.

Level 3: Specification of generalization and recursive relationships.

Level 4: Specification of association relationships. For the purposes of this study, an association relationship is considered to be the highest level of abstraction because it involves relating two separate parts of the solution and recognizing that the relationship itself has attributes and methods.

Each participant's protocol was coded independently by the two authors after training and practice sessions. The average level of coding agreement on the activity codes between the two authors was 89% (ranging from 85-94%). On the level of abstraction codes, the average agreement was 90% (ranging from 80-94%). These agreement rates reflect a respectable level of inter-rater reliability, comparable or better than those reported in other studies (Sutcliffe and Maiden 1992).

Two types of analysis were performed on the coded protocols to examine the similarities and differences in problem-solving activities and processes within and across groups. First, for each protocol, the number of segments in each activity category was tallied and then divided by the total number of segments in that protocol. The resulting percentages give a rough estimate of the time or cognitive effort devoted to each activity and are consistent with measures of time or effort used in prior studies (Pennington et al. 1995).[1] Second, we created a transition graph for each participant that plots the level of abstraction codes over the duration of the protocol. These transition graphs show the solution development process in detail, emphasizing the shifts between higher and lower levels of abstraction over time (Srinivasan and Te'eni 1995).

Results

The results of the study are organized into two sections. First, we discuss the impact of the reusable example on OO modeling for novices. Second, we discuss the influence of the example on modeling for experienced OO analysts.

The Effect of Reuse on Novice OO Modeling

Table 2 shows the proportion of the protocol spent on each modeling activity for each of the five OO novices. Figure 1 compares the average effort devoted to each activity for the reuse and control groups.

As Table 2 and Figure 1 show, novices in the reuse condition differed from novices in the control group in several ways. The reuse subjects, on average, spent more effort on problem understanding (40% versus 31%) and less effort on evaluation (17% versus 30%). However, the two groups spent roughly the same effort on solution development (31% versus 29%). Each of these observations is discussed in turn.

We expected the novices in the reuse condition to devote more effort to problem understanding because they had to contend with the source example in addition to the target problem description. We examined the protocol segments for reuse subjects and found that, on

Table 2. Distribution of Protocol Segments across Activities for Novices.

	Problem Understanding	Solution Development	Evaluation	Monitoring	Total
Reuse Condition					
N01 (R1)	46%	22%	23%	10%	100%
N05 (R2)	42%	25%	17%	16%	100%
N33 (R3)	32%	47%	12%	9%	100%
Control Condition					
N04 (C1)	31%	27%	31%	12%	100%
N21 (C2)	32%	31%	30%	7%	100%

Figure 1. Percent of Protocol Spent on Modeling Activities for Novices

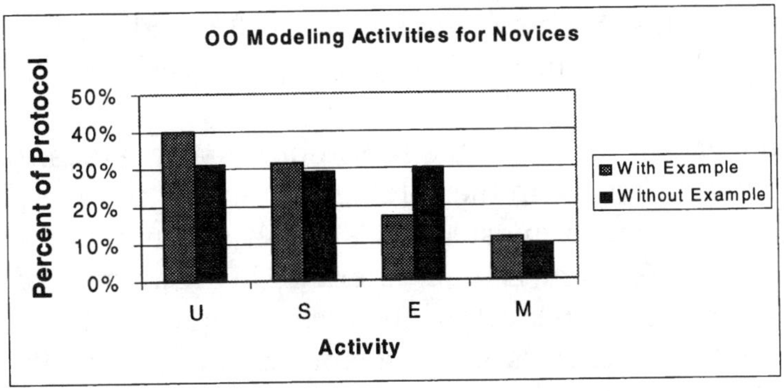

average, sixteen percent of the understanding segments involved understanding or mapping from the given example (16%, 6%, and 26% for R1, R2, and R3, respectively). Typical statements in this category include:

R1 [while working on part of her OO diagram, stops and looks at the example problem description]: "So in this one, we are overall trying to manage an organization's cost... so that's the same."
R2 [while working on part of his OO diagram, stops and looks at the example solution]: "So here they have Allocation [class] to connect employees to activities."
R3 [after reading part of the target problem description]: "It does seem similar to that example, with tracking the cost of things."

We expected that the effort novices devoted to understanding and mapping from the source problem would "pay off" by making the construction of their OO models easier. However, as shown in Figure 1, there was little difference in the amount of solution development activity between reuse subjects and control subjects. On average, 18% of the subjects' solution development (S) statements involved reuse (18%, 28%, and 9% for R1, R2, and R3, respectively). While the novices did attempt to apply portions of the source solution, these attempts did not reduce the overall effort devoted to constructing the solution.

Figure 2 further illustrates this point. The figure shows transition graphs for two novices, one in the reuse condition (R2) and one in the control condition (C1). Each transition graph shows the level of abstraction and the sub-problem of focus for each solving statement over the duration of the session. As stated earlier, levels of abstraction range from level 1, intra-class properties, to level 4, interclass association relationships. Each solving statement focused on one of three main subproblems, which are labeled A, B, and C, respectively, in Figure 2.

Even if we consider only the subproblems where reuse occurred, there is little difference in the solving activity for reuse and control subjects. For instance, most of R2's reuse statements focused on subproblem A. Yet there is little difference in the amount of effort or the transitions between levels of abstraction for subproblem A across R2, C1, and C2. In all cases, subproblem A is revisited multiple times

Figure 2. Transitions between Levels of Abstraction for Novices R2 (Reuse Condition) and C1 (Control Condition).

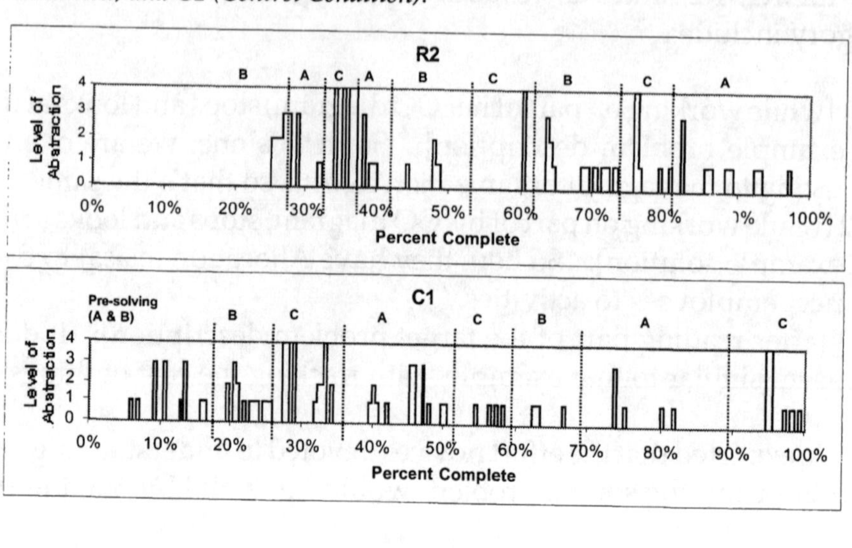

during the session and generally the higher levels of abstraction are addressed before the lower levels.

The third observation about novices in the reuse versus the control condition is that the latter subjects evaluated their solutions more often than did novices in the reuse condition. We reexamined the evaluation statements for all novices and classified each statement depending on whether the emphasis was on solution completeness or correctness. Completion statements focused on whether an issue or problem had been addressed in the solution (i.e., Is it done?), regardless of whether it was addressed well. These statements often depicted the subject ticking items on a mental checklist, as in the following excerpts:

"Activities, we've got that" (R1).

"OK, we have employee-related costs covered" (C1).

Correctness statements, on the other hand, focused on whether an issue or problem was solved correctly (i.e., Is it right?). For instance, subjects might evaluate a proposed solution by stating the rationale or modeling heuristic underlying the solution, or by mentally simulating how the solution would work at runtime. The following excerpts illustrate these types of correctness-centered evaluation:

"The physician's bonus is important, but then I don't think it's important enough to generate another class" (R2).

"Billable activity should be a class because of the different variables" (C2).

"Oh, percent of time can't be there because we don't have that related to an activity" (R1).

"An activity should be able to compute its cost... because it knows all its sub-activities, and it knows every sub-activity's cost according to what employees are assigned to it, and every one of those employees knows its cost, right?" (C2).

In the reuse condition, 38% of the novices' evaluation statements were completeness-oriented, and almost a third of these statements checked the target solution by comparing it to the source solution rather than to the target problem requirements. The remaining 62% of the evaluation statements focused on correctness. The control subjects spent less effort on completeness-checking (20% on average) and more on assessing the correctness of their solutions (80% on average). Thus, the novices with a reusable example performed a less-rigorous evaluation of the target solution than did the control subjects. It is interesting, however, that the reuse subjects' early evaluation statements were similar in nature to the control subjects. In both situations, subjects used OO modeling heuristics to propose and assess alternative solutions. The control subjects sustained this type of evaluation throughout the session. Reuse subjects, however, often turned to the example when they couldn't decide how to proceed; from then on, most evaluation statements involved comparing the target solution to the source solution or superficial checking of completeness.

A final point about the modeling process for novices in the reuse and control conditions pertains to their overall modeling strategies. We found no evidence that the reusable example changed the way novices approached or decomposed the problem. The example was used in an ad-hoc manner rather than as a consistent guide or resource. The modeling strategy varied across individuals. R3, for instance, worked in a mostly bottom-up fashion. He began at the lower levels of abstraction (identifying attributes and classes) and let these details drive the formation of the higher-level structure. C2 and R2, on the other hand, tended to postpone many of the lowest-level details until the latter part of the session. All novices, however, moved from subproblem to subproblem and within each subproblem, transitioned between multiple levels of abstraction. All novices visited the more difficult subproblems (A and C in Figure 2) more than once during the session.

The Effect of Reuse on Expert OO Modeling

Table 3 and Figure 3 show the distribution of experienced analysts' verbalizations across the four activity categories (problem understanding, solution development, evaluation, and monitoring).

The first observation from Table 3 and Figure 3 is that the expert in the control condition spent more effort understanding the problem requirements than did the reuse subjects (31% for C3, versus 16% and 22% for R4 and R5, respectively). The effect of the example on problem understanding in this situation is interesting, particularly since it is the opposite of what was observed for the novices. The example seemed to facilitate the experienced analysts' problem understanding rather than to increase the understanding workload (as it did for the novices). For instance, R4 read a portion of the target problem about tracking the time an employee spends on various activities. He immediately recalled a partial solution from the source example and began

Table 3. Distribution of Protocol Segments across Activities for Experienced Analysts.

	Problem Understanding	Solution Development	Evaluation	Monitoring	Total
Reuse Condition					
E35 (R4)	16%	28%	33%	23%	100%
E37 (R5)	22%	33%	19%	26%	100%
Control Condition					
E38 (C3)	31%	36%	22%	11%	100%

Figure 3. Percent of Protocol Spent on Modeling Activities for Experienced OO Analysts.

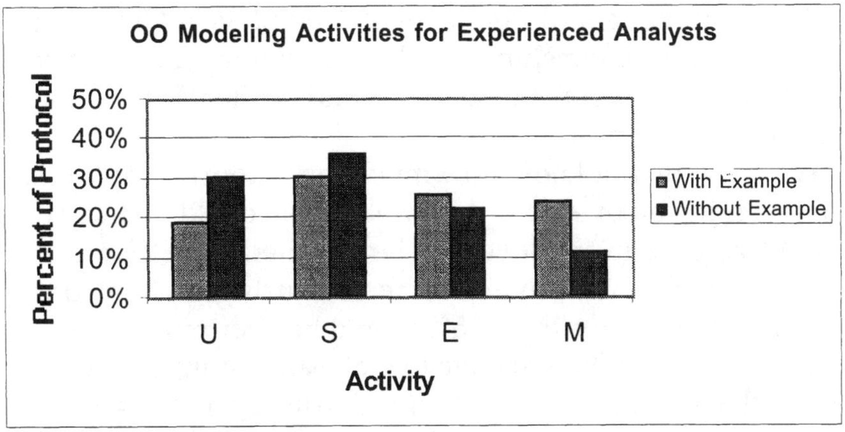

evaluating its applicability to the target task. He transitioned from reading to evaluating and solving, with very few understanding statements interspersed. The control subject, reading the same part of the target problem, said, "So let me re-read this, so we will be estimating time, hum." At several other points in the protocol he verbalizes other understanding statements about this area, such as:

"So employees and their costs are allocated to the activities they perform."

"[re-reading] By allocating employees' time to activities they perform, the employee related cost, yeah, yeah. These allocations also allow the clinic to determine where... Yeah, obviously, it's a time allocation thing."

"The employee is based solely on this notion of the cost, employees have costs, spend time - so there's the time allocation thing, working on activities."

The given example also helped the reuse subjects define the problem boundaries. The example may have indirectly provided information to the reuse subjects about how much detail was needed in the solution. More of the understanding protocol segments for the control subject (C3) were focused on exploring what was or was not within the scope, thinking more deeply about, and clarifying issues about the problem than for the reuse subjects as illustrated by the following statements. Not coincidentally, C3 also had the most thorough and detailed solution complete with code specification for methods.

> "So why are benefits different for each employee? Hum, well, is there some relationship that relates an employee to a benefit cost? I suppose it depends on what kind of offer that the clinic made to the employee."
>
> "Well, you do not know how much these hourly employees are working on overtime. And well, if you could do like you could, assume an employee can be allocated more than 100% of his time? So if you have one of these hourly guys they could work 125% and the extra 25% would be overtime."
>
> "So I guess I'm going to have to make an assumption at this point that the sources of data collection are... and I'm going to make an assumption that an activity is a sequence of different tasks."

Figure 3 also shows that the control subject had more solving activity than the reuse subjects did. This may be partially related to the prior point about the reuse subjects using the example to help define the boundaries of their solution. The control subject developed his OO model to a far greater level of detail than was required for the task or attempted by the other participants. This subject in fact wrote the Smalltalk code for each of his methods; whereas, other participants specified the names of the methods and commented on what they would do (but not how they would do it). One of the reuse subjects commented at one point, after specifying a method name, "And I could write the code for that, but, I don't think it's required for this." If C3's detailed method specification statements are excluded, the nature and amount of solving activity was similar across all experienced OO analysts.

One other difference between the reuse and control subjects is shown in Figure 3. The experienced OO analysts in the reuse condition engaged in more monitoring activity than the control subject (23% and 26% for the reuse subjects versus 11% for C3). An examination of the monitoring statements for the three analysts showed no consistent differences in the nature of these statements. The monitoring statements in all protocols consisted primarily of planning the overall modeling strategy. The difference seems to be in the time or effort spent on monitoring rather than on the nature of these activities. It is possible that R4 and R5 devoted more effort to these activities because they spent less effort on understanding and, thus, had more time available for other activities.

Figure 4 shows the transitions between levels of abstraction for two experienced OO analysts, one in the reuse condition (R4) and the one in the control condition (C3). As with the novices, these graphs chart only the solving activity (S-coded statements) for each subject. The graphs also show which of the three main subproblems (A, B, or C) the subject worked on at a particular time.

Both reuse subjects, R4 and R5, had fairly consistent problem-solving strategies (R4's is shown in Figure 4). Both participants did

Figure 4. Transitions between Levels of Abstraction for Experienced OO Analysts R4 (Reuse Condition) and C3 (Control Condition).

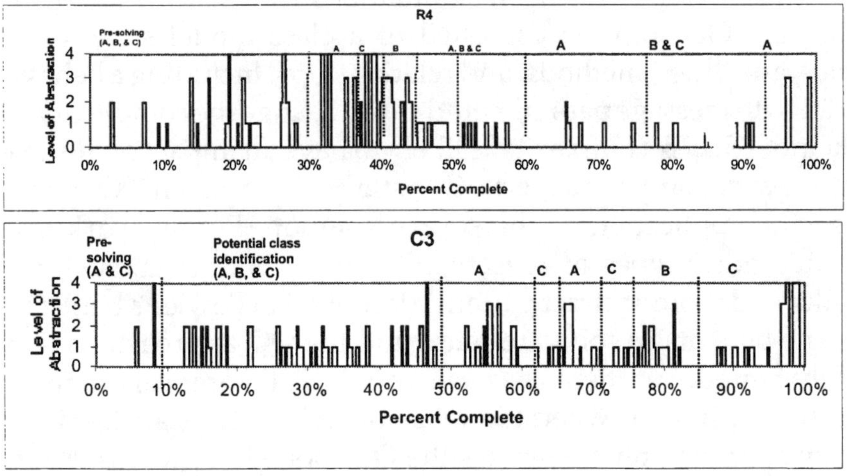

some preliminary solving as they read the target problem (as did many of the novices described earlier). After this, the strategy was generally top-down, where first the overall structure of the solution was constructed, followed by specification of the attributes and methods.

C3's strategy was somewhat different. He stated early on that he would do several "passes" through the problem. His first pass consisted primarily of class identification (see Figure 4). Roughly halfway through the session, he began the second pass where he solved each subproblem in detail. There is no evidence from the protocols to suggest that reuse accounted for this difference in strategy.

Limitations, Implications, and Future Directions

The aim of the study was to explore the effect of a reusable example the cognitive processes of OO modeling. Before discussing the implications of our findings, several limitations of the study deserve mention. First, as with many protocol studies, the small sample size limits the generalizability of our findings. While our sample size of eight is not unusual for this type of study (Jeffries et al. 1981; Lange and Moher 1989; Pennington et al. 1995; Srinivasan and Te'eni 1995), we had only three experienced OO analysts, and only one of these analysts was in the control condition. Thus, caution must be used in generalizing the findings to other analysts with different types of prior experience and exposure to OO technology. Clearly more studies are needed with larger samples and subjects with different background.

Studies of reuse in other task situations are also warranted. In this study, the OO solution consisted of a class model showing class names, attributes, methods, and relationships. Including a behavioral model with message passing could easily change the complexity of the task. Indeed, task complexity is likely to have an impact of the level of reuse - particularly for experts. Our study also used an OO model for a specific application as the source solution. Future work should examine other types of reusable OO analysis artifact, such as the smaller and more abstract patterns described in Fowler's book (1996).

The benefits of software reuse and the OO approach have been widely touted, but there has been very little theoretical or empirical research on how or when the reuse of OO analysis artifacts can be effective, or how reuse changes the OO modeling process. We were particularly interested in the cognitive costs and benefits of reuse. From prior research, we expected the primary cost to be the additional effort needed to understand the source example and map between the source and target domains. We expected the primary benefit to be the ease of constructing the target solution with reuse. In our study of eight novice and experienced OO analysts, we found the following:

1. Novices in the reuse condition spent more effort on problem understanding than did the novices in the control condition.
2. Experienced analysts in the reuse condition spent less effort on problem understanding than did the control subject. The given example seemed to facilitate their understanding of the target problem and moved them more quickly into constructing and evaluating their solutions.
3. The reusable example had no effect on the effort spent constructing the target solution. This observation held for both novice and experienced analysts.
4. Consistent with Maiden and Sutcliffe's (1992) study, the novices in the reuse condition were less rigorous in evaluating their solutions than were their counterparts in the control condition.

There are several implications of these findings for future research and educators. First, the lack of support for the "pay off" to reuse requires further investigation. There are several plausible explanations for the lack of difference in solving activity between reuse and control subjects. One is that not enough effort was invested in the up-front reuse activities of source-target understanding and mapping. If the subject's understanding of source-target analogy was weak, then solving by analogy may also be problematic and time-consuming. Alternatively, the analogy may be correct and subjects may still have difficulty applying the analogy to solve the target problem. This may be the case particularly for novices who have difficulty moving from the problem domain to the solution domain in OO design tasks (Pennington et al. 1995). Finally, there may be an issue of "critical mass" - the effort spent on understanding a reusable artifact may not pay off unless a large portion of the artifact is actually reused in the target solution. This may have been the case for our experienced analysts, who reused less of the given example than did the novices.

A second issue for future research is the impact of reuse on solution evaluation. The results of our study along with those of Maiden and Sutcliffe's (1992) study suggest a hidden cost to reuse for novices. If novices are able to recognize the similarity between the source and target problems, they may adopt a problem-solving strategy that involves superficially copying the source solution and ignoring the original target problem requirements. This strategy results in limited and superficial evaluation of the target solution. In cases where the source solution must be modified or adapted to the target problem, this "lazy" reuse may actually lead to worse solutions than if the target problem were solved from scratch. This has implications particularly for educators. For educators, attention must be paid to how reuse is encouraged and taught. Novices must be encouraged to explore the applicability of a reusable artifact and to identify areas where the reusable artifact is only partially reusable.

The third and final issue for future research is what we can learn from experienced analysts' reuse. In our study, the given example helped the experienced analysts to understand the target problem - they spent less effort on problem understanding activities than did the control subject. This may be a hidden benefit to reuse that deserves further exploration. Further investigation of how experts comprehend analogies may help to foster more effective problem solving behaviors in novices.

Endnote

[1] As Pennington et al (1995) also note, time and effort are not the same thing. We do not have time-stamps associated with each protocol segment, as time stamped data is also problematic. For instance, pauses would be extremely difficult to code in a meaningful way.

References

Anderson, J. R. and R. Thompson (1989). Use of Analogy in a Production System Architecture. *Similarity and Analogical Reasoning*. S. Vosniadou and A. Ortony. Cambridge, Mass., Cambridge University Press: 267-297.

Banker, R. D. and R. J. Kauffman (1991). "Reuse and Productivity in Integrated Computer-Aided Software Engineering: An Empirical Study." *Management Information Systems Quarterly* 15(3): 375-401.

Biggerstaff, T. J. and C. Richter (1989). Reusability Framework, Assessment, and Directions. *Software Reusability, Volume 1*, Concepts and Models. T. J. Biggerstaff and A. J. Perlis. New York, ACM Press: 1-18.

Boehm, B. W. and P. N. Papaccio (1988). "Understanding and Controlling Software Costs." *IEEE Transactions on Software Engineering* 14(10): 1462-1477.

Brooks, F. P. (1990). No Silver Bullet: Essence and Accidents of Software Engineering. *Software State-of-the-Art: Selected Papers*. T. D. Marco and T. Lister. NY, Dorset House: 14-29.

Cox, B. (1990). "Planning the Software Industrial Revolution." *IEEE Software* November: 25-33.

Curtis, B. (1989). Cognitive Issues in Reusing Software Artifacts. *Software Reusability, Volume II: Applications and Experience*. T. J. Biggerstaff and A. J. Perlis. Reading, Massachusetts, Addison-Wesley: 269-287.

Detienne, F. (1991). Reasoning from a Schema and From an Analog in *Software Code Reuse. Empirical Studies of Programmers: Fourth Workshop*. J. Koenemann-Belliveau, T. Moher and S. P. Robertson. Norwood, NJ, Ablex: 5-22.

Detienne, F. (1997). "Assessing the Cognitive Consequences of the Object-Oriented Approach: A Survey of Empirical Research on Object-Oriented Design by Individuals and Teams." *Interacting with Computers* 9: 47-72.

Deutsch, L. P. (1989). Design Reuse and Frameworks in the Smalltalk-80 System. *Software Reusability: Volume II, Applications and Experience*. T. J. Biggerstaff and A. J. Perlis. Reading, Mass., Addison-Wesley Publishing: 57-71.

Ericsson, K. A. and H. A. Simon (1993). *Protocol Analysis: Verbal Reports as Data*. Cambridge, Mass., MIT Press.

Fichman, R. G. and C. F. Kemerer (1997). "Object Technology and Reuse: Lessons from Early Adopters." *IEEE Computer* 30(10): 47—59.

Fowler, M. (1996). *Analysis Patterns: Reusable Object Models*. Reading, Mass., Addison-Wesley Publishing.

Gamma, E., R. Helm, et al. (1995). *Design Patterns: Elements of Reusable Object-Oriented Software*. Reading, Massachusetts, Addison-Wesley.

Gentner, D. (1983). "Structure-Mapping: A Theoretical Framework for Analogy." *Cognitive Science* 7: 155-170.

Gick, M. L. and K. J. Holyoak (1980). "Analogical Problem Solving." *Cognitive Psychology* 12: 306-355.

Gick, M. L. and K. J. Holyoak (1983). "Schema Induction and Analogical Transfer." *Cognitive Psychology* 15: 1-38.

Hoadley, C., M. Linn, et al. (1996). When, Why and How Do Novice Programmers Reuse Code? *Empirical Studies of Programmers, Sixth Workshop*. W. D. Gray and D. A. Boehm-Davis. Norwood, NJ, Ablex Publishing Company: 109-130.

Jacobson, I. (1992). *Object-Oriented Software Engineering: A Use Case Driven Approach*. Wokingham, England, Addison-Wesley Publishing.

Jeffries, R., A. Turner, et al. (1981). The Processes Involved in Designing Software. *Cognitive Skills and their Acquisition*. J. Anderson. New Jersey, Lawrence Erlbaum Associates, Publishers: 255-283.

Kim, J. and F. J. Lerch (1997). "Why Is Programming (Sometimes) So Difficult? Programming as Scientific Discovery in Multiple Problem Spaces." *Information Systems Research* 8(1): 25-50.

Lange, B. M. and T. G. Moher (1989). Some Strategies of Reuse in an Object-Oriented Programming Environment. *Computer-Human Interaction '89*, ACM.

Lim, W. C. (1994). "Effects of Reuse on Quality, Productivity, and Economics." *Software* 11(5): 23-30.

Maiden, N. and A. Sutcliffe (1992). "Exploiting Reusable Specification Through Analogy." *Communications of the ACM* 35(4): 55-64.

Meyer, B. (1989). Reusability: The Case for Object-Oriented Design. *Software Reusability: Volume II, Applications and Experience*. T. J. Biggerstaff and A. J. Perlis. Reading, Mass., Addison-Wesley Publishing: 1-33.

Pennington, N., A. Lee, et al. (1995). "Cognitive Activities and Levels of Abstraction in Procedural and Object-Oriented Design." *Human-Computer Interaction* 10: 171-226.

Prieto-Diaz, R. (1989). Classification of Reusable Modules. *Software Reusability, Volume I: Concepts and Models*. T. J. Biggerstaff and A. J. Perlis. Reading, Massachusetts, Addison-Wesley: 99-123.

Puhr, G. I. (1995). Analogical Reasoning and Reuse in Object-Oriented Analysis. *Accounting and Information Systems*. PhD Dissertation, Boulder, University of Colorado.

Rosson, M. B. and S. R. Alpert (1990). "The Cognitive Consequences of

Object-Oriented Design." *Human-Computer Interaction* 5: 345-379.

Rosson, M. B. and J. M. Carroll (1990). "Climbing the Smalltalk Mountain." *SIGCHI Bulletin* 21(3): 76-79.

Rosson, M. B. and J. M. Carroll (1996). "The Reuse of Uses in Smalltalk Programming." *ACM Transactions on Computer-Human Interaction* 3(3): 219-253.

Srinivasan, A. and D. Te'eni (1995). "Modeling as Constrained Problem Solving: An Empirical Study of the Data Modeling Process." *Management Science* 41(3): 419-434.

Sutcliffe, A. and N. Maiden (1992). "Analysing the Novice Analyst: Cognitive Models in Software Engineering." *International Journal of Man-Machine Studies* 36: 719-740.

Visser, W. (1990). "More or Less Following a Plan During Design: Opportunistic Deviations in Specification." *International Journal of Man-Machine Studies* 33: 247-278.

Woodfield, S., D. Embley, et al. (1987). "Can Programmers Reuse Software?" *IEEE Software* July: 52-59.

Chapter VII

How to Transform Legacy Systems into Object Oriented Systems

Hernán Cobo
Universidad Nacional del Centro De la Pcia. de Bs. Argentina

Virginia Mauco
Universidad Nacional del Centro De la Pcia. de Bs. Argentina

Introduction

The OO paradigm is the predominant software trend of the 1990s. According to the literature, it provides a unifying model for various phases of development, facilitates system integration, allows prototyping, encourages software reuse, eases system maintenance and provides support for extensibility (Meyer, 1997). An OO system is best developed starting with OO analysis. However, some times this may be difficult because of the existence of so many systems developed 20 or more years ago, which are still used. These systems are called legacy and may be defined as large software systems people do not know how to cope with, but they are vital to organizations (Bennett, 1995). Hence, the decision on how to manage them is crucial because they may represent years of accumulated experience and knowledge. Besides, the software may be the only place where organizations business rules exist.

Maintenance costs are a major issue with software (Pressman, 1992). Legacy systems maintenance is a difficult task because it is typical that during the maintenance process the structure and the documentation of the system deteriorate, making the maintenance progressively harder. It is essential to record the understanding of the system before it is forgotten and to structure it in such a way that it can be easily accumulated and retrieved. The development of new architectures and the improvements in programming methods and languages, have caused a need to reverse engineer and reengineer existing program code in order to get as much value as possible from legacy systems while exploiting the latest technology.

This chapter describes a project whose aim is to develop a tool to transform legacy systems in order to simplify and improve their maintenance and understanding, taking benefit from OO technology. To achieve this, it is necessary to capture and recover all the knowledge extracted from imperative programs and store it in a higher level structure, which can be analyzed and manipulated. From this structure objects and classes are recognized and extracted to rewrite the program in an OO language. Besides preserving the original functionality, the new code generated should be structured, legible, modular, reusable, and more easily maintainable. The only source of information is programs imperative source code, and its quality has a great influence on the quality of the recovered objects. To minimize this influence, programs are first syntactically restructured and modularized. As part of this research, a prototype has been developed which implements the algorithms to restructure, modularize and extract objects automatically. Human intervention is allowed in order to improve the results.

Background

There has been a lot of work done to improve the quality of legacy code because it has a great impact on legacy systems comprehension, maintenance and evolution. All these efforts may be referred to as software reengineering activities (Arnold, 1994). Reengineering generally includes some form of reverse engineering to achieve a more abstract description, followed by some form of forward engineering or restructuring (Chikofsky & Cross, 1994).

Two different techniques, which are the basis to be used in many reengineering tools, have been defined for translating source code. Program translation via transliteration and refinement is the standard approach. The alternative approach is called translation via abstraction and re-implementation. In this process, the source program is first analyzed in order to obtain a programming-language-independent abstract description of the computation being performed. Following this abstract description, the program is then re-implemented in the target language. The central feature of this approach is the abstraction step as it allows the translator to benefit from a global understanding of what the source program does (Waters, 1994).

From the definition above, it follows that there are two principal issues to be considered in translating a program via abstraction and implementation. One of them is the definition of a repository to represent data and knowledge extracted from the program and the implementation of the processes to capture and store them in the repository besides the processes to recover this information from the repository. The other issue to be taken into account is the definition of the reengineering transformations that will be done based on the information stored in the repository.

The internal representations chosen for a software system play a critical role in the reengineering process because they may constrain the types of transformations to be applied to programs, and a specific transformation may require the representation to have determinate features. Each representation is most adequate in specific contexts (Ottenstein & Ottenstein, 1984). Abstract syntax trees, for example, are a good starting point for thinking about the translation of an input string (Aho, Sethi & Ullman, 1986). They are suitable when the only concerns are edition and the generation of straightforward code. Another representation called program dependence graph was originally defined as an intermediate program representation well suited for compiler optimizations (Ferrante, Ottenstein & Warren, 1987). But later work showed the advantages of using this representation in software engineering (Binkley, Horwitz & Reps, 1995; Cobo & Mauco, 1996; Horwitz & Reps, 1992b; Horwitz, Reps & Binkley, 1990a). A program dependence graph can support editing, translating, debugging and program metrics; it is open to incremental data flow update and it is ideal to compute slices (Ottenstein & Ottenstein, 1984).

There exist several works aimed at improving software quality and understanding to support many maintenance and reengineering activities, by means of transformations defined over the information about a program stored in the repository. Some of them are based on trying to understand or improve a program by automatically recognizing instances of known code patterns, named plans or clichés, and organizing them hierarchically to build a description of the program

(Bush, 1985; Fiutem, Tonella, Antonio & Merlo, 1996; Rich & Wills, 1994; Quilici, 1994). The definition and updating of a library of clichés complete enough, the existence of idiosyncratic code, and the application to programs of a determinate domain can be mentioned as some disadvantages of this approach.

Restructuring is one of the oldest and most refined reengineering techniques (Arnold, 1994). Many algorithms have been defined to restructure programs by introducing new variables in them (Böhm & Jacopini, 1966; Linger, Mills & Witt, 1979). These algorithms work with any arbitrary program, but they always change program topology, even in structured programs.

Program modularization consists of decomposing a monolithic program or module and replacing it with a functionally equivalent collection of smaller modules (Pressman, 1992). Different strategies have been defined to extract functions from programs and they analyze functions as candidates for reuse or to rewrite the program, in a modular way according to the goals of each work (Burd, Munro & Wezeman, 1996; Cimitile, De Lucia & Munro, 1995; Lanubile & Visaggio, 1997). Many of these works employ program slicing, a program decomposition method well suited for isolating functionality in a program. It is a technique for restricting the behavior of a program to some specified subset of interest, which automatically decomposes a program by analyzing its data and control flow (Weiser, 1984).

Migrating imperative to OO code has been receiving considerable attention during the last years. The migration from imperative programs to OO ones points to construct a hierarchy of classes that perform the same computations as the original procedures. Each class encapsulates a data object and a number of methods for processing that data object. Several techniques have been proposed to identify object-like features in imperative programs (Cremer, 1998; George & Carter, 1996; Jin, Mah & Shin, 1997; Liu & Wilde, 1990; Livadas & Roy, 1992). Other approaches were specially designed to programs written in a specific programming language, like Fortran (Ong & Tsai, 1993; Subramaniam & Byrne, 1996) or Cobol (Beziven, Lennon & Nguyen, 1995; Sneed, 1996). All these works agree in that transforming an imperative program into an OO one is a difficult task which cannot be completely automated. The automated techniques are only able to identify potential objects and their feasibility can only be assessed by human intervention.

Studying the Problem

In most cases, source code is the only documentation available of legacy systems. For this reason and before object generation, source code features influence was carefully analyzed. Therefore, to obtain an OO system from a legacy system different ways to improve code, such as restructuring and modularization, were studied first to get a clear and adequate partition of the integral system.

Another of the most important problems is to design a repository to store and to manipulate legacy systems in order to improve and update them according to the last technologies.

Alternative of Intermediate Representations

Many intermediate representations have been defined to store information about a program. Some of them are oriented to reflect a program's control structure; others, are centered in a program's hierarchy, and finally there are some more specific which are not based on any of the previously mentioned ones.

Control-oriented representations.

They cover the needs for representing any control structure since they are based on atomic actions such as conditional and unconditional jumps. Another important feature of these representations is that they make easier a program's control flow extraction. One of the most popular is the Three-Address Code (Aho et al., 1986).

Hierarchy-oriented representations.

They propose top-level structures with important semantic information in order to deduce the control aspects of each one. On the other hand, they represent a program's hierarchical structure in a very natural way. One of the most used is the Abstract Syntax Tree (Aho et al., 1986).

Restructuring

A structured program is a compound program constructed from a fixed basis set {sequence, if-then-else, whiledo} (Linger et al., 1979).

Code restructuring algorithms can be split into two groups:

a) The restructuring process implies the modification of the original program, adding one or more control variables which allow structured code simulation.

b) The restructuring process involves the recognition and replacement of unstructured code portions by structured clichés.

Among the ones belonging to the group a), Böhm and Jacopini's (Böhm & Jacopini, 1966) and Linger, Mills and Witt's algorithms (Linger et al., 1979) can be mentioned. Both algorithms always modify the program's general structure.

Some problems of the algorithms classified within group b), as Bush's algorithm (Bush, 1985), are the definition and update of the cliché library in order to contain as many cases as possible, the existence of non recognizable code and the limitation of their application to programs of a given domain.

Modularization

Interleaving is a source of difficulties when trying to understand a program (Rugaber, Stirewalt & Wills, 1995). It makes it difficult to accomplish a variety of tasks such as extracting reusable components, localizing the effects of maintenance changes and migrating to OO languages.

For this reason, it would be desirable to maintain the interleaving degree of the incoming code at a minimal level. Otherwise, techniques to detect and eliminate it would have to be applied.

A way to improve the comprehensibility and maintainability of a legacy system is modularization (Cimitile et al., 1995). In particular, there are three goals that modularity tries to achieve in practice: capability of decomposing a complex system, of composing it from existing modules and understanding the system in pieces. To accomplish modular composability, decomposability and understanding, a system should be divided in modules with high cohesion and low coupling (Pressman, 1992).

Normally, modularization algorithms use program slicing to break large programs into manageable pieces functionally equivalents.

Program slicing is a technique for restricting the behavior of a program to some specified subset of interest (Weiser, 1984). A slice S(v,n), of a program P, on variable v, or a set of variables, at statement n yields the portions of the program that contributed to the value of v just before statement n is executed. S(v,n) is called a slicing criterion.

Slices can be computed automatically by analyzing data and control flow. A program slice has the added advantage of being an executable program.

If a program is represented by its program dependence graph, the slicing problem is simply a node-reachability problem; thus, slices may be computed in linear time (Horwitz et al., 1990a).

Different types of slices have been defined. One of them is the output-restricted slice, which is a slice without output statements. Output statements are as windows into the current state of computation which do not contribute to the realization of the state (Gallagher & Lyle, 1991).

Object Extraction

In a conventional programming language, an "object" can be identified as a collection of routines, types, and/or data items (Liu & Wilde, 1990). The routines will implement the methods associated with the object, the types will structure the data it encapsulates or processes and the data items will represent the actual instances of the class.

The candidate "objects" will be a list of three sets:

Candidate Object = (F, T, D) where F is the set of routines, T is the set of types and D the set of data items. Anyone of these sets can be empty.

The goal is to find a useful partial classification of routines, types and data items, meaningful in the context of the program and its real world domain.

A large part of the information for this classification can be obtained analyzing the relationships among the components of the program, but carefully selected heuristic or human intervention will be needed to eliminate casual or without sense relationships.

Ideally, sets from different objects should not overlap, and then a routine, type or data item should not appear in more than an object. However, it is not required that objects be completely disjoint since object identification methods should capture those situations in which efficiency considerations forced the programmer to transgress good design principles.

In addition, the definition given above does not distinguish clearly between the concepts object class and object. In some cases, it can be easier to find first the class and then its instances and in others, inside out. Therefore, it is more convenient to try both together.

The two approaches to find objects seem to be useful. The first one is based on persistent and global data and establishes links with the routines that manipulate it. The second one is based on data types and establishes relationships among these types and the routines that use them as formal parameters or return values. A detailed description of two methods to implement these approaches can be found in Lui & Wilde (1990).

A Solution to Reengineer Legacy Systems into OO Systems

As part of this project two structures have been defined to store legacy systems in a form independent from their syntax and attempting to obtain more abstract information to accomplish global transformations to the system.

One of them, called Intermediate Language (IL), was specially designed to allow the tool to be used with programs written in different imperative languages. An advantage of this structure is that the algorithms designed to enhance code quality are independent from the original source code. It also allows rewriting the improved programs in a language different from the original one. The languages considered were Pascal, Cobol, C and Fortran. The other structure is the Extended Program Dependence Graph (EPDG), which is an extension defined over the Program Dependence Graph (Ferrante et al., 1987). It was designed to store and manipulate in an easy way the information represented in the IL.

The reengineering process is decomposed in three steps: code restructuring, modularization and object extraction. All these topics are treated below.

Figure 1 shows a diagram with the general structure of the whole project.

Intermediate Language

Using the most useful features of the two alternative representations described before and considering the issues concerning this project, the IL was defined. The IL maintains two different views of the control structure of a program. It gives a global view, by means of block statements, and it also maintains all the primitive statements with control flow level of detail to allow regenerating automatically the original code. In consequence, it represents a tree structure that shows a hierarchical view of the program in which the leaves compose a directed graph that reproduces the original control structure.

A detailed study of the selected languages helped to obtain a set of statement-types that shared the analyzed languages. Such statements were represented in IL in different ways. Some of these statements maintain a one-to-one correspondence with their representation in IL. They were built grouping the common characteristics in the chosen languages.

Another more complex functionality needed more than one IL statement to be represented. Therefore, it was necessary to create another type of statement with a higher abstraction level (block statement) to include all the atomic statements, so as not to lose referring information to the original ones. This kind of statement was also used to characterize statements that were not common factors in the four languages considered, but that could be built composing other simpler ones.

Besides, proper IL primitive statements were defined to represent

Figure 1. General structure of the whole project.

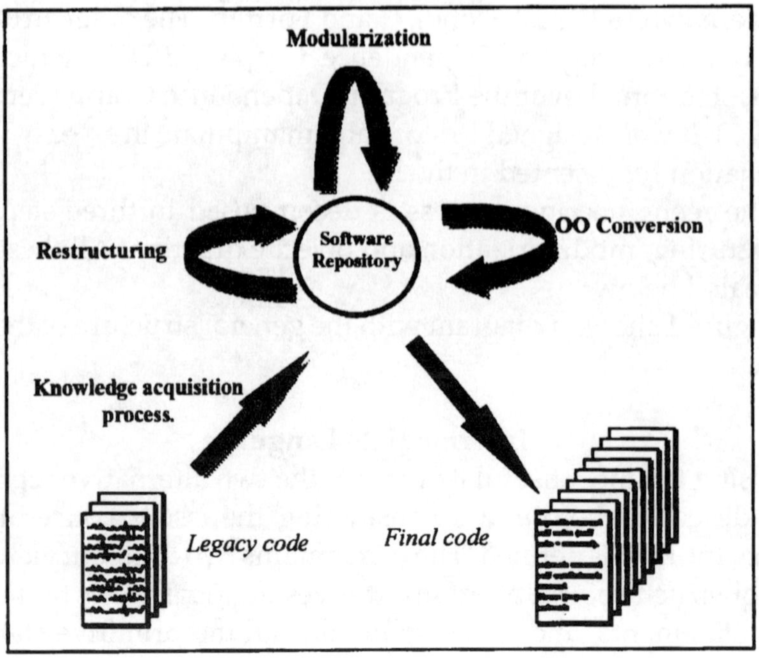

control structures like conditional and unconditional jumps and labels.

Finally, a statement form called particular was created to represent the uncommon statements but which could be composed by relationships among the already defined ones. In summary, the IL statements are classified in two levels: one lower and indivisible in which the simplest statements of basic functionality are represented

Figure 2. A small Pascal program and its IL and labeled graph representations.

Source Program

```
Procedure Ppal( )

begin
  while a < 10 do
     begin
        x := x*10;
        a := a + 1
     end;
  b := x
end.
```

Intermediate Language

```
statement(1,block_stat(subroutine,[2],[3,8]),"Procedure Ppal ()",-1)
statement(2,subroutine(ident("Ppal"),[]),"",1)
statement(3,block_stat(ciclo,[4,7],[5,6]),"while a < 10 do\n",-1)
statement(4,cond(relational(less, ident("a"),number("10")),
          internal_label(5),internal_label(8)),"",3)
statement(5,assig([operator(mult, ident("x"),number("10"))],
          [ident("x")]),"x := x * 10;\n",-1)
statement(6,assig([operator(add, ident("a") number("1"))],
          ident("a")]),"a := a + 1;\n",-1)
statement(7,go(internal_label(4)),"",3)
statement(8,assig([ident("x")],[ident("b")])," b := x \n",-1)
statement(9,max_statement(pascal),"",-1)
```

Code Represented as a Labeled Graph

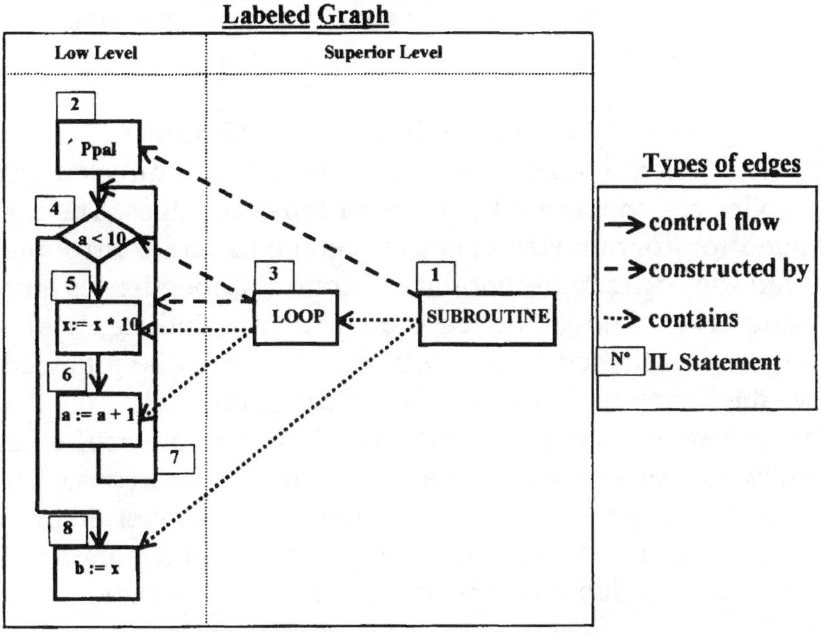

and another of higher abstraction for the more complex functionality statements.

Figure 2 shows a small program written in Pascal and its representation in IL. As can be seen clearly, the abstraction level represented by the block statements SUBROUTINE and LOOP contains the low-level statements that form the program's control flow.

A system in IL is represented in different abstraction levels. The low-level statements are linked mutually to form the control structure of the represented program; for this task they have control primitives already mentioned. The higher level statements reference the primitive and simple statements. Furthermore, they are used to refer to the statements that are contained in block structures such as loops, conditionals, and so on. It is also important to emphasize that these types of statements do not form part of the control flow.

There are primitive statements in some languages that involve more than one conceptual action. In this case, a block statement of IL is used which includes all the corresponding IL primitive statements to accomplish the equivalent task. For example, a block statement that contains two primitives, the first one to write and the other to advance, represents the statement written in Pascal.

All these statements are in a structure that stores them. Each statement has an identification number, the original statement text in the source program and a number used by primitive statements to refer to the block statement in which they are contained.

Extended Program Dependence Graph

The EPDG is the other structure defined. It is a directed graph whose nodes are connected by different types of edges. The nodes correspond to program statements (assignments and control predicates), and the edges represent data or control dependences among these statements. The set of these dependences induces a partial ordering on the statements in a program that must be followed to preserve the functionality of the original program.

The dependences are of two types. Data dependences emerge between two statements when a variable that appears in one of them could have a wrong value if the two statements are inverted in their execution. Control dependences hold between a statement and the predicate whose value controls immediately the execution of that statement.

Control dependence edges are labeled T or F, and the source of an edge of this type is always the Entry node or a predicate node. Data dependence edges are labeled with the name of the variable that origin them.

One of the most important characteristics of the EPDG is that it exposes potential parallelism. This means that two nodes n1 and n2 may be executed simultaneously unless a dependence between them exists.

The EPDG can be considered divided into two components: the control dependence subgraph and the data dependence subgraph. The control dependence subgraph contains information about control dependences that exist among the statements in the program. It is built from the program control flow graph and the post-dominator tree (Ferrante et al. 1987). Each node n of this subgraph has a level number that represents the length of the path from the initial node of the subgraph to the node n. The addition of the level for each node allows one to determine quickly and simply if a program is or is not structured. Moreover, it contributes to simplify the transformations defined to transform an unstructured program into a structured one (Cobo & Mauco, 1996). The data dependence subgraph contains the information concerned with data definitions and uses in a program. It is constructed using a variant of data flow equations (Aho et al., 1986) and a list of used and defined variables for each node. In the original program dependence graph, a final use node is included for each variable v to represent the final value of v when the program finishes. But frequently, a same variable may be used in a program to store different and independent computations. To reflect this fact, the EPDG contains one final use node for each different use of the same variable.

A program written in IL is represented with a set of EPDG's; one of which corresponds to the main program and the rest to each one of its subroutines. To construct it, a control flow graph and a post-dominator tree are generated for the main program and for each subroutine. Each program statement is represented with a node in the corresponding control flow graph, with the exception of jump statements (go to) that generate edges, and subroutine call statements that are represented with a node and a call edge whose destination is the control flow graph of the corresponding subroutine.

During this construction process jumps are solved in such a way

Figure 3. A System Extended Program Dependence Graph

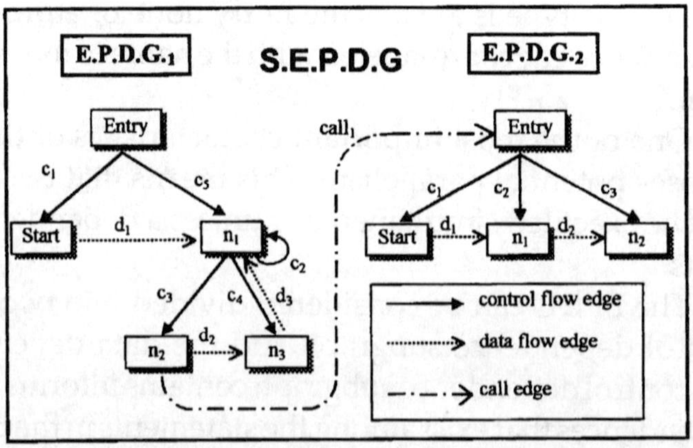

that they do not exceed the boundaries of each subroutine. In this way, the only one possible relationship between any pair of control flow graphs is through the edge that represents the subroutine call.

Thus, a set of EPDG's linked through call edges is obtained which is called System EPDG. In each EPDG, each node represents an IL statement and it is control dependent on nodes of the EPDG to which it belongs. The determination of the level of each node of an EPDG is independently computed for each EPDG. Figure 3 contains a very simple System EPDG.

Restructuring Step

The Restructuring Step turns an arbitrary unstructured program into a functionally equivalent structured one. As stated before, a program is structured if it is built only combining sequence, selection and iteration control structures.

An EPDG is structured if it is built from the composition of the control structures just mentioned. In a structured EPDG each node is control-dependent on only one of the nodes of the immediate superior level. This implies that the subgraph induced by control dependences is a tree. Therefore, a program is structured if it can be represented with a set of structured EPDG's. To determine that a program is not structured it will be necessary and sufficient to find a control edge that destroys the tree structure of at least one of the EPDG'S that constitute its representation.

The restructuring process analyzes each EPDG separately to determine if there are control dependences that break the tree structure. If one is found, the restructuring algorithm defined in (Cobo & Mauco, 1996) is applied to the corresponding EPDG. It is important to emphasize that this algorithm does not modify the EPDG subgraphs which were already structured. Furthermore, as it is only applied to unstructured EPDG'S, the program subroutines already structured preserve their original structure.

Modularization Step

The Modularization Step decomposes a monolithic structured program into a functionally equivalent collection of smaller modules, combining program slicing techniques and a set of criteria like cohesion, coupling, fan-in, fan-out, factoring, and so on.

A variant of output-restricted slice was defined to capture all relevant computations involving a given variable. Thus, it does not depend on statement numbers as the original slice definition. Besides, this variant takes as reference the final use nodes to compute one slice for each computation. Following this definition, a slice is constructed for each different use of each variable in the program.

A lattice ordered by set inclusion is then created to determine the relationships between the computed slices (Gallagher & Lyle, 1991). The lattice is a graph, where each node represents a slice and each edge the relationship "is included in." This structure is called Slices Inclusion Graph (SIG). Each node stands for a candidate module, and a node included in more than one slice expresses code reusability. The leaves of the SIG are called maximal slices, and they represent the more relevant system's computation since they are the program's outputs. The other nodes are partial results, but essential to compute the maximal ones.

The SIG represents a program decomposition into modules. At a glance, maximal slices should be modules, since generally program's outputs are the externally visible manifestation of functionality (Bieman & Ott, 1994). On the other hand, nodes further from the leaves have less possibility of being modules. However, to evaluate if each slice is a worthwhile module a deeper analysis for each slice is required. The analysis comprises the two stages explained below.

Decomposition.

The program slicing technique, allows a statement *s* to be included in more than one slice which expresses that *s* is required to compute different variables. Therefore, an analysis should be made to ensure that the repetitive execution of a statement does not change the original functionality.

The concept of duplicated statement is then introduced to define a statement whose repetitive execution does not produce side effects. Thus, each statement is labeled as duplicated or non-duplicated. With this classification, a study of each node of the lattice is done. The aim is to detect and remove from the graph those slices reused more than once with at least a non-duplicated statement. Hence, it can be assured that non-duplicated statements are executed only once.

Applying the program slicing technique for each variable in the program allows to obtain a maximal program decomposition. Nevertheless, some computations do not give new information. So, it is interesting to detect and remove this kind of slices.

Another concept, called complement, is used (Gallagher & Lyle, 1991). The complement *c* of a slice *s* is constructed by removing the statements of *s* from the original program. Since *c* must be executable, there will be certain crucial statements that are necessary in both the slice and the complement. The complement is computed for each node of the SIG. If the original program and the complement are the same then the slice is removed from the graph.

Although the program slicing technique obtains a good system decomposition, sometimes code duplication is presented as a drawback. There are certain portions of code that are not an independent slice but are duplicated in more than one slice. Generally, those sets of statements are partial computations of the same variable, which occasionally have a semantic meaning in the application domain. Therefore, an analysis should be made to detect and extract them as modules.

The concept of reused statement is then introduced to define a statement that belongs to more than one slice and is not an independent slice. Each slice is represented with a characteristic vector. This vector is the implementation of the characteristic function. Sets of reused statements are obtained applying intersection, union, complement and difference operations between the characteristic vectors.

Each set is completed to form a slice and then the SIG is regenerated to include the new slices.

Composition.

The SIG is at the maximal decomposition level. Each slice represents a candidate module that must be analyzed considering some criteria before its implementation.

The algorithm ensures that the slices obtained have high cohesion and low coupling, since they compute a single output (Ott & Thuss, 1989).

Other criteria are evaluated for each node of the SIG like fan-in, fan-out, lines of code, tokens count (Pressman, 1992). If a slice does not verify the criteria, it is removed from the SIG. Once the analysis is finished, the program is rewritten in IL, and it is ready to be translated to the desired source language.

Different systems, languages and users may have distinct criteria to define a good module.

The prototype takes this into account giving the possibility to specify some variables like optimal number of statements for a module.

OO Conversion Step

Since the concept of OO programming increases maintainability and reusability of systems, the last step, called OO Conversion Step, aims at turning a structured and modular imperative system into an OO one. Potential classes are identified (including the instance variables and methods), using two complementary methods based on an analysis of global variables and data types (Liu & Wilde, 1990).

Both methods were studied and analyzed to find their advantages and disadvantages. This suggested that the better way to obtain objects from structured and modularized imperative systems is combining these methods. In this combination, global variables, which show the existence of a class instance, and data types, which represent in a primitive form the object classes in the imperative languages, should be taken into account. The more complex part is the definition of such combination in order to get the better results. It was also concluded that if only source code is going to be considered, a better way for locating potential objects different from the previously mentioned ones does not exist.

First of all, the global based method is applied. The instance variables of each one of the classes that emerge by this method are the globals that remain grouped. Next, the types based method is applied without taking into account the routines assigned to the classes computed by the previous method. The instance variables of each one of the classes defined by this method are the fields, if a record is being considered. In any other case, as the class is a specialization of some existing class (for example, the Array class), it has no instance variables. In either case, the methods of each class are the routines assigned to it.

However, it is probable that some routines and global variables remain without being assigned to any object. The routines are those that neither use nor modify global variables directly and have no parameters. The global variables are those which are neither used nor modified directly in any routine but are real parameters of user-defined routines.

Then the system class is identified. It is the class which has among its methods the routine that was the main program in the imperative source code. Nevertheless, if the routine that was the main program does not appear among the methods of any class, the class system is created. In both cases an instance variable for each class determined by the global method is added to its instance variables. It also added one instance variable for each global variable remaining unassigned. Its methods are increased with the unassigned routines.

In addition, the instance variable parent is added to each one of the identified classes, with the exception of the system class. It is a reference to an instance of the system class. An alternative would have been that the system class was accessed by other classes through inheritance. However, this option might be only viable if multiple inheritance was available—if this was not the case, such inheritance link might produce conflicts with other possible parents. For this reason, to reach the stated objectives and though it was less convenient, a client link was selected in place of the inheritance link.

Since the system class is the one which contains among its methods the routine that was the main program in the source code, it activates the program's execution.

The greatest present inconvenience is inheritance detection within the extracted objects.

There are two ways of using a class: inheriting from it or being its client. None of the aspects of objects technology cause so much discussion as when and how to use inheritance (Meyer, 1997). Besides, during the development of this work the existence of a third relationship was found: different implementations of the same object. This is due to the fact that in imperative programming there is a tendency to distribute a form of data (object) according to its persistence (dynamic structures, files, tables and so on). It is not possible to detect syntactically if one of these three relationships is present, or if none of them holds.

Furthermore, in (Benedusi, Ibba, Naddei & Natale, 1993) it is assured that the similarity among routine names and/or data structures is not reliable. There can exist "false homonymous" that accomplish completely different functions (or implement different data structures), and also "unknown synonyms " can have the same internal structure and accomplish exactly the same function. As a rule, the structural similarity (combining aspects of data and control flow) is not necessarily connected with functional similarity. The checkups of functional similarity are accomplished with the intervention of human experts. Perhaps the case that could be detected with greater safety is that of different implementations of the same object, if one corresponds to objects stored in a principal memory structure and the other, to objects stored in a secondary memory structure.

After a study of many cases and alternatives of imperative code for objects with and without inheritance it was concluded that the following elements might syntactically be analyzed:

Attribute names, Attribute types, Functions and procedures in which attributes appear as parameters and Modules functionality. It can also be asserted that none of these elements is reliable to detect inheritance automatically from source code of a structured and modularized program because syntactic similarity does not have to mean semantic similarity.

Future Trends

The development of an interactive reengineering toolkit would be really helpful because in legacy systems, source code constitutes a rich domain of structural as well as flow information. This toolkit would have to automatically construct visual representations from source code and it would have to allow manipulating and modifying the code directly in the visual environment. Thus, the software engineer would be allowed to graphically view source code at a higher degree of abstraction. Besides, it would be interesting to let the user select any desired level of granularity to view source code. All these facilities would produce a significant positive effect on program comprehension and understanding. In particular, the tool should assist the user during the restructuring step and most importantly during modularization and OO conversion. It would be of great help if the tool gave assistance to let the user modify the program once the OO program is derived. The structure of OO software is based on classes and their relationships; thus, OO source code modification can be seen as modifications of class structures and of the relationships among these classes. A standard OO design notation, like UML (Rational Software Corporation, 1997), can be used to represent the static structure of classes, attributes and methods, and the relationships between them such as inheritance.

Conclusions

To allow existing software to benefit from advances in OO methods, the software should be redesigned and reimplemented using an OO approach. This work has presented a three-step tool for deriving an OO program from unstructured, non-OO source code. The tool is a prototype and, although its application shows that it works, its complete development is a challenging task and some steps need to be enhanced. The resulting program is only a "first-cut" object representation which should be subsequently improved in order to obtain a more suitable OO model.

Subjectivity is involved in any modeling activity, and any mapping strategy from an imperative system to an OO one will require user assistance. User participation is sometimes necessary to work up conflicts and supply domain knowledge so that the resulting objects are more meaningful. The user is also required to assign a meaning name to the isolated functions.

This tool is an aid that enables the user to make decisions more easily by extracting information from imperative systems and by limiting the choices the designer would have to make, but it is not a substitute for the developer. Another benefit of the tool comes from its simplicity. It does not require knowledge of the application domain such as a large cliché library.

Although the use of the prototype in a set of case studies has preserved the functionality, a formal demonstration is still under analysis. But it can be assured that the extracted objects possess similarity with those objects that might have been built through an OO design.

Acknowledgments

The authors would like to thank Carlota Rodríguez, María del Carmen Romero, Edith Tejerina, Marcos Moreno and Ariel Zoia for their contributions to this work.

References

Aho, A. V., Sethi, R. & Ullman, J. D. (1986). *Compilers: Principles, techniques and tools*. USA: Addison-Wesley Publishing Company.

Arnold, R. S. (1994). "A road map guide to software reengineering technology." In R. S. Arnold (Ed), *Software reengineering* (2nd ed), Los Alamitos, California: IEEE Computer Society Press, 3-22.

Benedusi, P., Ibba, R., Naddei, R. & Natale, D. (1993). "Structure-based clustering of components for software reuse." Paper presented at the IEEE Conference on Software Maintenance, Montreal, Canad, 210-215.

Bennett, K. (1995). "Legacy systems: Coping with success." *IEEE Software*, 12, 19-23.

Beziven, J., Lennon, Y. & Nguyen, C. (1995). "From Cobol to OMT: A reengineering workbench based on semantic networks." Paper presented at the International Conference TOOLS USA, 137-152.

Bieman, J. & Ott, L. (1994). " Measuring functional cohesion." *IEEE Transactions on Software Engineering*, 20, 644-657.

Binkley, D., Horwitz, S. & Reps, T. (1995). "Program integration for languages with procedure calls." *ACM Transactions on Software Engineering and Methodology*, 4, 3-35.

Böhm, C. & Jacopini, G. (1966). "Flow diagrams, Turing machines and languages with only two formation rules." *Communications of the ACM*, 9, 366-371.

Burd, E., Munro, M. & Wezeman, C. (1996). "Extracting reusable modules from legacy code: Considering the issues of module granularity." Paper presented at the IEEE Working Conference on Reverse Engineering, Monterey, California., 189-196.

Bush, E. (1985). "The automatic restructuring of Cobol." Paper presented at the IEEE Conference on Software Maintenance, 35-41.

Cimitile, A., De Lucia, A. & Munro, M. (1995). "Identifying reusable functions using specification driven program slicing: A case study." Paper presented at the IEEE International Conference on Software Maintenance, Nice, France, 124-133.

Cobo, H. & Mauco, V. (1996). *Un algoritmo para reestructurar programas procedurales*. [An algorithm to restructure imperative programs]. Bogotá, Colombia: Memorias de la XXII Conferencia Latinoamericana de Informática, 979-990.

Cremer, K. (1998). "A tool for supporting the re-design of legacy applications." Paper presented at the IEEE Second Euromicro Conference on Software Maintenance and Reengineering, Florence, Italy, 142-148.

Chikofsky, E. J. & Cross, J. H. (1994). "Reverse engineering and design recovery: A taxonomy." In R. S. Arnold (Ed), *Software Reengineering* (2nd ed), Los Alamitos, California: IEEE Computer Society Press, 55-58..

Ferrante, J., Ottenstein, K. & Warren, J. (1987). "The program dependence graph and its use in optimization." *ACM Transactions on Programming Languages and Systems*, 9, 319-349.

Fiutem, R., Tonella, P., Antonio, G. & Merlo, E. (1996). "A cliché-based environment to support architectural reverse engineering." Paper presented at the IEEE International Conference on Software Maintenance, Monterey, California, 319-328.

Gallagher, K. & Lyle, J. (1991). "Using program slicing in software maintenance." *IEEE Transactions on Software Engineering*, 17, 751-813.

George, J. & Carter, B. (1996). "A strategy for mapping from function-oriented software models to OO software models." *ACM Software Engineering Notes*, 21, 56-63.

Horwitz, S., Reps, T. & Binkley, D. (1990a). "Interprocedural slicing using dependence graphs." *ACM Transactions on Programming Languages and Systems*, 12, 26-60.

Horwitz, S. & Reps, T. (1992b). "The use of program dependence graphs in software engineering." Paper presented at the IEEE 14th International Conference on Software Engineering.

Jin, Y., Mah, P. & Shin, G. (1997). "Deriving an object model from procedural programs." Paper presented at the 25th International Conference TOOLS Pacific. Australia, 233-241.

Lanubile, G. & Visaggio, G. (1997). "Extracting reusable functions by flow graph-based program slicing." *IEEE Transactions on Software Engineering*, 23, 246-259.

Linger, R., Mills, H. & Witt B. (1979). *Structured programming: Theory and practice*. Cambridge, Mass.: Addison-Wesley Publishing Company.

Liu, S. & Wilde, N. (1990). "Identifying objects in a conventional procedural language: An example of data design recovery." Paper presented at the IEEE Conference on Software Maintenance, San Diego, Califirnia. (pp. 266-271)

Livadas, P. & Roy, P. (1992). "Program dependence analysis." Paper presented at the IEEE Conference on Software Maintenance, 356-365.

Meyer, B. (1997). *OO software construction* (2nd ed). New Jersey: Prentice Hall PTR.

Ong, C. & Tsai, W. (1993). "Class and object extraction from imperative code." *Journal of OO Programming*, 58-68.

Ott, L. & Thuss, J. (1989). "The relationship between slices and module cohesion." Paper presented at the IEEE International Conference on Software Engineering, 198-204.

Ottenstein, K., & Ottenstein, L. (1984). "The program dependence graph in a software development environment." *ACM SIGPLAN Notices*, 19, 177-184.

Pressman, R. S. (1992). *Software engineering: A practitioner's approach* (3rd ed). Singapore: McGraw Hill International Editions.

Quilici, A. (1994). "A memory-based approach to recognizing programming plans." *Comunications of the ACM*, 37, 84-93.

Rational Software Corporation (1997). *The Unified Modeling Language*. Version 1. 1. Available: http: / / www.rational.com

Rich, C. & Wills, L. (1994). "Recognizing a program's design." In R. S. Arnold (Ed), *Software Reengineering* (2nd ed), (pp. 534-541). Los Alamitos, California: IEEE Computer Society Press.

Rugaber, S., Stirewalt, K. & Wills, L. (1995). "Detecting interleaving." Paper presented at the IEEE Working Conference on Reverse Engineering, Toronto, Canadá, 265-274.

Sneed, H. (1996). "OO COBOL recycling." Paper presented at the

IEEE Working Conference on Reverse Engineering, Monterey, California, 169-178.

Subramaniam, G.V. & Byrne, E. J. (1996). "Deriving an object model from legacy Fortran code." Paper presented at the IEEE International Conference on Software Maintenance, Monterey, California, 3-12.

Waters, R. C. (1994). "Program translation via abstraction and reimplementation." In R. S. Arnold (Ed), *Software Reengineering* (2nd ed), Los Alamitos, California: IEEE Computer Society Press, 390-411.

Weiser, M. (1984). "Program slicing." *IEEE Transactions on Software Engineering*, 10, 352-357.

Chapter VIII

Challenges and Issues to Consider When Upgrading Legacy Applications

Gerold E. Cameron
American University, USA

This chapter will focus on the challenges and issues an organization faces when trying to integrate or migrate their legacy applications with more advanced client/server information systems. These applications present a challenge when an organization attempts to integrate its legacy applications with newer technologies due to the rigid binding of the client to the legacy application server. FAIME, is an object oriented methodology that provides the tools to address application interoperation and plug-and-play. These tools open closed legacy applications through legacy applications decomposition and produce executable objects that bridge different operating systems, communication infrastructures, and databases. To convert a COBOL legacy application to an object-oriented application, a complete restructuring of the legacy program is needed. Objects and their inheritance structure must be identified, data usage and data flow must be analyzed, and instructions must be allocated to objects. Dynamic Object Oriented Programming allows parts of an application design that are represented by objects, to be modified dynamically. Integrating or migrating legacy applications with newer more advanced client/server architectures can be a very expensive and time-consuming undertaking.

Challenges and Issues to Consider

Legacy systems present a fundamental challenge to organizations which use them. These systems, for the most part were developed by a previous generation of developers, hence, the word Legacy. These applications were designed according to requirements and an implementation approach that existed earlier in the organization's life cycle. They were then introduced into computer environments different from those originally planned. Because legacy software systems are so vital to an organization's continuing existence, they are not retrieved or redesigned without compelling reasons. Major changes necessitate a significant investment in new technology, with a substantial risk that the new systems may fail to deliver the required services. Hence, organizations maintain functionality, correct defects, and upgrade legacy systems to be competitive in today's ever changing business environment (Schneidewind, N. & Ebert, C., 1998).

Integrating Challenges

There are several challenges a organization may face when trying to integrate their legacy applications with information systems designed to benefit from advanced client/server architectures, graphical user interfaces, and the World Wide Web (see figure 1). One such challenge is that of the High Level Language Application Programming Interface (HLLAPI) or the Enhanced High Level Language Application Programming Interface (EHLLAPI). This challenge is addressed by using Legacy Object Modeling. An enterprise object model maps information stored in industry standard relational databases to an object representation. A legacy object model maps information from a legacy application to an object representation in a similar fashion. Many of these legacy applications use a High Level Language Application Programming Interface (HLLAPI) or Enhanced High Level Language Application Programming Interface (EHLLAPI) which require a connection with mainframe CICS applications. These applications present a challenge when an organization attempts to

Figure 1. Legacy applications are being integrated with the existing client/server systems.

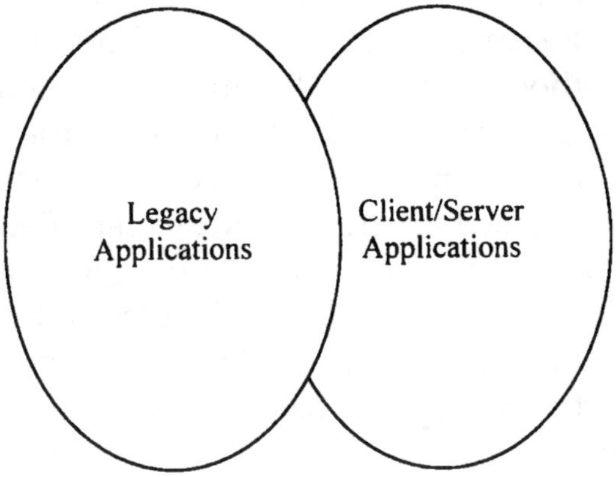

integrate its legacy applications with newer technologies because of the rigid binding of the HLLAPI client to the legacy application server. Any changes to the host application will result in an unstable client. The legacy object modeling approach overcomes this limitation by abstracting the legacy application's data and behavior in the form of a collection of objects (Noffsinger, W.B., Niedbalski, R., & Blanks, M., 1998).

Another such challenge is that of application wrappers. Object oriented wrappers have been presented as a way to enable legacy applications and object-oriented application to work together. However, object wrappers do not always solve the interoperability problem for COBOL legacy applications. A legacy COBOL application can be described as procedure-oriented with maybe several legacy programs working together. The main difference between legacy and object oriented applications is in their method of operation. Legacy application is a linear block of code with a sequence of PERFORM and CALL statements, while the object-oriented application is a fluid, data oriented collection of classes. It creates object instances and directs messages to their methods. A wrapper is a code that provides an interface for one program to access the functionality of another program. An object that encapsulates a COBOL legacy application, transforming its functional interface to an object interface is an object oriented wrapper, or object wrapper as it is often called. A procedural wrapper is a program that reconciles a COBOL legacy application's functional interface to an object interface. A combination wrapper is, on the other hand, a program that instantiates one or more objects, all of which reconcile a COBOL legacy application functional interface to an object interface. The *Year 2000* problem is easily solved with a procedural wrapper because the object-oriented program has a corrected number of methods and a small number of shared data items. To convert a COBOL legacy application to an object-oriented application, a complete restructuring of the legacy program is needed. Objects and their inheritance structure must be identified, data usage and data flow must be analyzed, and instructions allocated to objects. Many organizations can not afford the high costs and risks that are associated with this transition because of limited financial resources. Therefore, interoperable legacy and object-oriented applications are highly recommended (Flint, E.S., 1997).

OO COBOL is an Object Oriented Language (Arranga, E.C. & Coyle, F.P., 1997). Object Oriented COBOL supports typed, untyped, dynamic, static, persistent, simple, temporary, factory (class), system and exception objects, as well as Binary Large Objects (Blobs). OO COBOL has greatly benefited from other OO languages such as Smalltalk, C++, and Eiffel, but OO COBOL is neither a new concept nor one that has been created because Object Oriented languages are in style now. OO COBOL has been in development since November 1989 when the Codasyl COBOL committee, OO and other COBOL experts gathered to discuss how to best objectify COBOL. They concluded that OO COBOL is in many ways a more powerful and capable object-oriented programming language than many of the other OO languages. Important characteristics of OO COBOL are:

- Classes, which contain factory and object definitions;
- Factory objects, which contain data and methods;
- Object instances, which contain data and methods;
- Language constructs reuses (for class reuse), interface (to present different hierarchical interfaces), and prototype (for rapid application development);
- Multiple and single inheritance;
- Polymorphism;
- Automatic garbage collections;
- Data items as objects;
- Complete compatibility with previous COBOL standards;

- Named objects that may be retrieved in subsequent application executions;
- A class library;
- Parameterized classes;
- Object handles (as opposed to object pointers) to safeguard encapsulation; and
- Collection classes.

On the practical side, the learning curve for OO COBOL is considerably less than for other OO languages . It takes as little as 12 weeks to become proficient in OO COBOL programming, in contrast , it takes about 40-plus weeks to learn Smalltalk and about 80-plus weeks for C++. OO COBOL above all other languages will keep the information systems of businesses running well into the twenty-first century (Arranga, E.C. & Coyle, F.P., 1997).

Next, is the issue of the relationship of the legacy applications and the businesses they support. Discussions about legacy systems and data often center around the maintenance of old codes as well as making an existing system survive an upgrade of hardware, operating system, or database vendor. The important issue with legacy applications is that they are deeply embedded in the operations of a business. Dynamic Object Oriented Programming allows parts of an application design as far as it is represented by objects, to be modified dynamically. Integration efforts are often based on an architecture which dedicates one or more systems to be repositories of extracted legacy data as integrated objects that reside in an Integrated Object Database (IODB). By creating the legacy data as objects whose definitions are not subject to change, and by creating the IOB as a dynamic object system whose definition is fluid, data integration issues are able to be viewed as object mapping. A crucial component of dynamic OOP is its ability to rapidly construct domain specific languages in order to simplify programming the domain level problem. First, the implementation language is extended in domain-specific ways. Next, an entirely separate domain specific language is built in order to develop the target application. The separation of data modeling from data implementation that the use of a domain-specific language provides is crucial in managing complexity (Robertson, P., 1997).

Additionally, there is the challenge of application interoperability. FAIME, is an object-oriented methodology that provides the tools to address application interoperation and plug-and-play. The objective of application interoperation is to make two independently developed applications work with each other. The goal of application plug-and-play is to make an application interoperate with multiple competing applications that have similar functions. The interoperation problem can be approached by modeling a legacy application as an object oriented application. These tools open closed legacy applications through legacy applications decomposition and produce executable objects that bridge different operating systems, communication infrastructures, and databases. FAIME allows users to focus on the resolution of data semantics and business processes differences which are the concerns of consequence regarding interoperation. FAIME also provides tools to overcome accidental obstacles and to capture analysis knowledge for reuse in plug-and-play. It is designed specifically to accommodate legacy applications and has been successfully implemented in producing enterprise applications (Chu, B., Long, J., & Matthews, M., 1998).

Furthermore, there is the challenge of reengineering user interfaces using the Abstract User Interface Description Language (AUIDL). Many legacy systems, especially those in data processing, have a character-based user interface. Reengineering these interfaces would make them more user friendly and also prolong the life of the systems in which they are embedded. AUIDL is a language designed to provide an abstract representation of the original character based interface. Inference converts the character-based, or basic, AUIDL specifications into graphical AUIDL specifications that use graphical constructs to describe objects, screens, and screen sequences that the user can perceive. Developers can automatically produce a new graphical interface from the graphical AUIDL specifications using standard code-generation techniques. Integrating the new interface into the original systems has not proven to be much of a problem with the use of Easel Corporation's Easel. This is an application that allows one to develop GUIs that run on desktop computers under Windows, OS/2, or DOS, and also which communicate with IBM mainframe applications through an Easel 3270 emulator. AUIDL lets the developer represent structure with object orientation's inheritance and describe behavior with Milner's process algebra. Interface structure captures the possible relations among interface entities while behavior describes the interface dynamic aspects. Although AUIDL and other tools were applied to a specific environment they are portable (Melro, E., Gagne, P., Girard, J., Kontogiannis, K., Hendren, L., Panangaden, P. & De Mori, R., 1995).

Migration Issues

There are also several migration challenges that an organization will face when it tries to replace its legacy applications (see figure 2). Some of an organization's mainframes are probably going to be available well into the next century. But pressure is on to migrate as many of the legacy applications to distributed client/server architectures as possible. Few IT departments would try a Big Bang conversion of all their applications at the same time. Rather, most IT managers pursue a more cautious phased-in migration approach. Leading IT managers who have been through this process were asked to prioritize their applications for migration and their responses are summarized as follows:

- Avoid Big Bang conversions: Practice on small, nonstrategic systems or packaged applications (Dyno Nobel Inc.; Salt Lake City, UT).
- Begin the major migration process in earnest with customer-related, revenue-generating applications (Jain, S., CTO Trecom Business Systems; Edison, NJ).
- Concentrate on business functions instead of data (Couperus, J., Senior Consultant Control Data; Minneapolis, MN).
- Don't count on major cost savings: You may be exchanging expensive systems for expensive operations (Reed, D., Analyst

Figure 2. Legacy applications are being migrated into the Client/Server architecture.

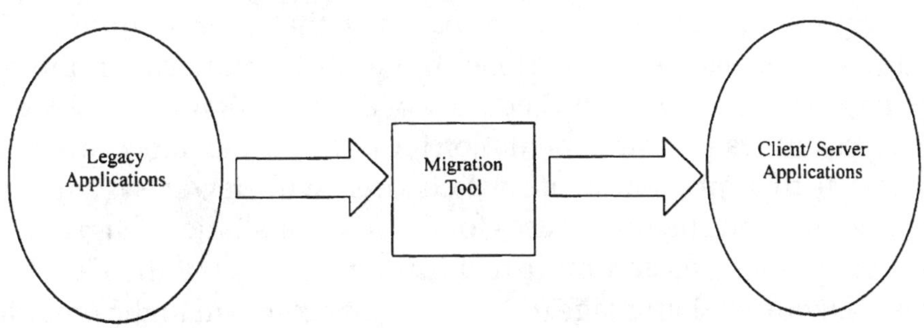

Texas Instruments; Houston, TX).
- Shoot for major decreases in maintenance and modifications times
- Allow three to five years (Hess, M., Vice President Gartner Group; Stamford, CT).

The most controversial aspect of downsizing is whether it reduces costs. That still remains an issue, but a new study suggests that the picture may not be as gloomy as many believe. As part of its strategic analysis of the benefits of migrating to client/server, Texas Instruments consulted a variety of companies that had already made the transition. The companies included vendors such as Ameritech, Apple, Hewlett-Packard, Intel, Kodak, Motorola, and Sun. Prior to migrating to client/server, these companies were spending on average 6% of their annual income on computing costs, including IT. (IT budgets range from 40 to 70 % of total computing costs.) After migrating, that figure decreased to 3% to 4% of revenues, according to Dick Reed, a bench-marking analyst at Texas Instruments. Reed says that, among 10 companies that successfully migrated to client/server, none reported IT cost increases, some realized minor costs savings, and a few reported significant reductions in IT expenses (Simpson, D., 1995).

Telephone giant GTE faced a migrating challenge when their legacy telecommunications applications was replaced using Distributed Object Management and Activation for Integrated Networks (DOMAIN). In this approach, one is able to model all applications in an enriched, CORBA-like Interface Definition Language (IDL). Based on the IDL model, tools have been developed to generate code automatically for database schema, a server skeleton and major portions of the graphical user interface. HTML and Java Script were chosen as the main languages for implementing the domain user interface because they make it easy to develop prototypes and produce computer-generated screens based on the model definition. The legacy system was treated as a black box and only its network and core business processes were studied. On e of the most significant obstacles to successful system implementation is the user's reluctance to change. To lessen this problem a site was chosen with fewer systems and smaller user and customer bases for the first installation. Migration of the legacy data was accomplished through the use of the DOMAIN Object Definition Language (ODL) files that conform to the metadata extracted from IDL. Next, Informix High Performance Loader (HPL) files are generated from the ODL files and loaded into the database. This method allowed the migration of 10 million objects (75 million database records) in three months during live operations. Domain successfully replaced the largest GTE legacy system in less than 18 months by bringing together people, software, and hardware combined with advanced software techniques with practical solutions to achieve a common goal shared by user, developers, and managers (Bollig, S. & Xiao, D., 1998).

Another issue is that of reengineering object-oriented legacy applications. The object oriented reengineering lifecycle consists of five general phases:

- Model capture: documenting and understanding the design of a legacy system.
- Problem detection: identifying violations of flexibility and quality criteria.
- Problem analysis: selecting a software structure that solves a design defect.
- Reorganization: selecting the optima; transformation of the legacy system.
- Change propagation: ensuring the transition between different versions.

Prior to reengineering a legacy system, it is necessary to understand its architecture and the relationships between its components. Model capture often presents a major hurdle and is the domain of choice for the application of browsers and reverse-engineering tools. Finding flexibility problems in legacy systems requires not only a specification of the criteria that the new, reengineered software must fulfill, but also a definition of the differences in these criteria. When possible defects in the legacy system are found, developers must analyze them, compare them with problems about unmet requirements, and understand how they affect the software. The reorganization stage consists of determining and applying the proper combination of operations to transform the legacy system to the target structures chosen during problem analysis. Change propagation is made by establishing the revised system throughout a corporate software environment, especially by mapping persistent objects to the new software structures. To ensure the continuity of the process, the results of the reengineering project must be documented. The reorganization of object oriented legacy applications does not differ markedly from more traditional reengineering concerns excepts for two noticeable characteristics :

1. The same basic technology that was used in the legacy software is applied in the target software but extended with advanced design concepts, such as frameworks. On the other hand, traditional reengineering aims dictate, at salvaging applications written in PL/1 and using hierarchical databases in a completely different environment based on Delphi and the World Wide Web.
2. Several iterations of reengineering might be needed before achieving a system with a desired degree of generality and adaptability. Object oriented reengineering is, therefore, largely a generalization process (Casais, E., 1998).

Migrating legacy systems towards object oriented platform can also be achieved by using design metrics (Cimitile, A., De Lucia, A., Di Luca, G.A., & Fasolino, A.R., 1999). The decomposition of a legacy system is the beginning for an incremental migration strategy: each object can be re-implemented independently using new object oriented technologies; old components can be used in their original form until the new equivalent objects show an acceptable level of reliability. Identifying objects in legacy systems is a particular case of the problem in clustering system components into modules (Canfora, G., Cimitile, A. & Muaro, M., 1993). The legacy systems are first decomposed into objects. Then the identification of objects begin centered around persistent data stores, such as files or tables in the database, while program and routines are candidates for implementing the object methods.

The next step is the association of the methods to the objects, which is accomplished by optimizing selected object-oriented design metrics (Chidamber, S. R. & Kemerer, C.F. 1994). In particular, it is done while trying to minimize the coupling between the objects. This decision was developed to avoid object-oriented decomposition of a legacy system from being detrimental to the design, requiring subsequent maintenance of the reengineered system. This approach was applied to a complex large system of the health service department of a municipality. The system analyzed had evolved over the past twenty years to support particular needs of managing pharmaceutical products. The study is still in progress, but analysis of the persistent data stores and identification of the potential objects have already been conducted along with the association of methods to data stores at the program level. The system studied runs on a mainframe, with the TP monitor CICS from IBM, two types of DBMS, hierarchical (IMS) and relational (DB2), and a proprietary industrial macro-set. The system is composed of 799 COBOL and 2 ASSEMBLER programs (about 40.5 MB, 550KLOC), 260 copybooks (about 1.3MB, 16 KLOC), 339 screen maps (about 4.5 MB, 100 KLOC), 275 files PSB (about 900 MB, 16 KLOC). The external functions of the system are controlled by 93 JCL jobs. An early analysis of the source code and the scarce available documentation indicated that the system had been historically developed from the hierarchical database IMS, which was the only database having data defining the objects of the application domain. At the time, relational database tables were not studied because only about 74 programs had embedded SQL code. Report generation is produced in COBOL by exporting the relevant data from the IMS database to VSAM files. These files were analyzed to identify data stores corresponding to the application domain objects. The files were then associated to segments of the IMS database using synonym and homonym analysis. As a result, 294 logical files, 310 physical files, and 76 IMS segments were identified and reduced to 143 data stores after the resolution of synonyms and the elimination of printer files (Cimitile, A., De Lucia, A., Di Luca, G.A., & Fasolino, A.R., 1999). This noticeable decrease was due to a large number of printer files and synonyms, which resulted from exporting the same IMS database segments into different files. Identification of the object methods was done using the same weights and the same threshold value as in the first pilot project. The association of interactive programs to the corresponding objects was immediate, due to fact that these programs utilized simple data input or updating operations, and in most cases benefited from predominant access to the corresponding data stores. In contrast, the percentage of programs with exclusive or predominant access were very low for programs containing embedded SQL code. This is mainly due to two factors: 1. The models of the data of the two databases (relational and hierarchical) are very different and, therefore, there was no correspondence between the relational tables and segments of the hierarchical database; 2. And the same program imports/exports conceptually non-homogenous data (Cimitile, A., De Lucia, A., Di Luca, G.A., & Fasolino, A.R., 1999). The next step in this pilot project will be the application of dominance analysis to the approximately 450 programs.

Discussion

The challenges or issues that one might come across when integrating or migrating legacy applications with newer more advanced client/server architectures can be a very expensive and time-consuming undertaking. Should one reengineer the organization to fit its new client/server applications or use objects and components to custom build the applications necessary for the enterprise? Based upon this research, I do not suggest the integration legacy applications with an organization's current information systems unless all other possibilities have been exhausted. If your legacy systems still enable your organization to remain competitive, and you are also able to expand, it is recommended to leave these applications in place. On the other hand, if the enterprise needs to become more competitive, it might consider focusing internally first on reengineering the business processes and work flows that are part of the legacy applications. I recently witnessed first hand DB-2 legacy applications being replaced with a newer Unix based client/server application named Colleague at the American University. The old legacy system no longer met the needs and objectives of the university. The migration process consisted of four phases. First, the Benefactor system was put in operation in 1998, then the General Ledger system, next the Student system, and finally the Human Resources system. The implementation for the entire system took about eight to ten months to complete. The Colleague interface is a Windows- based graphical user interface. Planning information and costs figures were not available for this discussion since the system so far has not delivered as anticipated. There are numerous bugs that were expected, being discovered on a daily basis with no immediate fix. It is sometimes very frustrating, because I am responsible for overseeing the process of capturing the information and images for graduate and undergraduate admissions and financial aid materials submitted to the Office Enrollment Services for review. It appears that the decision of whether to keep the DB-2 legacy system was not well thought out. It also appears that the guidelines as prescribed in the literature and in practice regarding implementing new information systems were not followed or ignored. Even if object oriented technology was used to replace the legacy system it might still run into problems because the implementation process as recommended in the industry and literature applies also to OO technology.

References

Arranga, E.C. & Coyle, F.P. (1997, March) Cobol: Perception and Reality. *Computer*, 30 126-128.

Bollig, S. & Xiao, D. (1998, June). Throwing off the shackles of a legacy system. *Computer*, 31 (6), 104-109.

Canfora, G., Cimitile, A. & Munro, M. (1993).A reverse engineering method for identifying reusable abstract data types. In: Proceedings of the first IEEE Working Conference on Reverse Engineering, Baltimore, Maryland, *IEEE Computer Soc. Press*, (Silver Sand, MD) 73-82.

Casais, E. (1998, January). Re-engineering object-oriented legacy systems. *Journal of Object Oriented Programming*, 10 (8), 45-52.

Chidamber, S. R. & Kemerer, C.F. (1994). A metrics suite for object oriented design. *IEEE Transactions on Software Engineering*, 20 (6), 476-493.

Chu, B., Long, J., & Matthews, M. (1998, September). FAIME: an object-oriented methodology for applications plug and play. *Journal of Object Oriented Programming*, 11, (5), 20-26.

(Cimitile, A., De Lucia, A., Di Luca, G.A., & Fasolino, A.R. (1999, January). Identifying objects in legacy systems using design metrics. *Journal of Systems and Software*, 44 (3), 199-211

Flint, E.S. (1997). The COBOL jigsaw puzzle: fitting object-oriented and legacy applications together. *IBM Systems Journal*, 36 (1), 49-65.

Melro, E., Gagne, P., Girard, J., Kontogiannis, K., Hendren, L., Panangaden, P. & De Mori, R. (1995, January). Reengineering User Interfaces. *IEEE Software*, 12 64-73.

Noffsinger, W.B., Niedbalski, R., & Blanks, M. (1998, December). Legacy object modeling speeds software integration. *Communications of the ACM*, 41 (12), 80-89.

Robertson, P. (1997, May). Integrating legacy systems with modern corporate applications. *Communications of the ACM*, 40 (5), 39-46.

Chapter IX

Understanding Distributed Object Oriented Systems

Alex Podaras
Hewlett Packard, USA

Distributed objects, as applied to the term *distributed object oriented systems*, can be defined as those objects that have many locations on a system (network), but stemming from the way they interact with one another, appear to be coming from just one location (Taylor, 1996, p. 263). Obviously, this presents distributed-object oriented systems with *design complexities* because the hardware and software are *not located* in one place but, to the user, must look as though they are. These complexities can be well appreciated by looking at the literature. Montlick (1999) uses the very term *complex* in a chapter heading related to distributed object oriented systems. He attributes this building complexity to the fact that object oriented technology is in its infancy. Given that distributed object oriented systems are complex and in their infancy, it is hard to decipher a clear definition of *distributed object oriented systems* and the client/server (frontline computer/back-line computer) model or environment. Some such as Berson (1996) say that client/server computing is a form of distributed computing, while others such as Taylor (1996) say that client/server computing is different from distributed computing. Understanding the client/server environment adds to the complexity of understanding distributed object oriented systems.

The purpose of this chapter, then, is to provide an understanding of what distributed object oriented systems are, no matter how complex they may appear to be. To provide a foundation for this understanding, the "building block" evolutionary process leading to the development of distributed object oriented systems will be given first. To foster an understanding of the systems themselves, it will be shown that no matter how complex, for a system to be distributed object oriented, basically several key ingredients must be in place. Accordingly, it will be shown that, fundamentally, distributed object oriented systems must have two object oriented properties or characteristics: encapsulation (the ability to hide code from the user) and messages (the way objects communicate). Additionally, it will be shown that software components (objects) of the distributed object oriented systems must have certain inherent features. Aside from the two object oriented properties and the certain inherent features, any critical system must have the ability to keep its data in a consistent state. This is particularly important when concurrent (at the same time) transactions (a unit of work) are executed.

It was determined that because distributed object oriented systems are complex and in their infancy, in order to produce a basic definition and understanding of what they are, it would be necessary to analyze a cross-section of the current literature: i.e., information found in books, articles, journals, and Internet sources as well as information obtained from interviews with an IT expert.

What We Already Know

Evolution: Host-Based Environment to Object oriented Model

As was mentioned in the above text, there are at least two ways of defining a client/server model (structural design) or environment (surroundings). One way is to say that distributed computing and client/server are the same (Berson); the other is that they are two separate entities (Taylor). For the purpose of obtaining a clear definition and understanding of distributed object oriented systems, Berson's (1996) client/server rationale is used in this section.

Host-Based Model

In the host-based environment there is one processing computer (host) with several "dumb" terminals attached to it. "Dumb" terminals do not have the ability to process application components, which are application fragments; they are only used to communicate with the host and display output to the user. Application components in

Figure 1. Host-Based

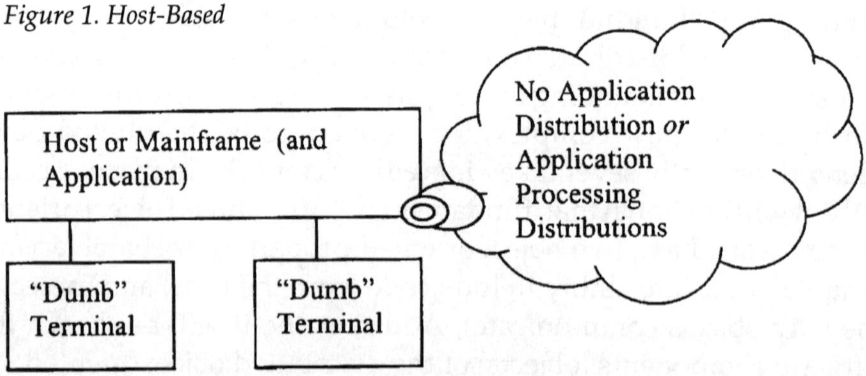

turn make up an application.

In a host-based environment, the main computer or the host computer does all the application processing for the system. The application resides only on the host. The output is then displayed on "dumb" terminals or compiled in a pre-formatted report and routed to a host-based printer. In the host-based model the host computer is a mainframe. Typically, these host computers were large IBM mainframes (see Figure 1).

When the host-based model first came out it was referred to as a client/server environment. The "dumb" terminals were the clients and the server was the mainframe. Some IT professionals will claim that host-based computing is a client/server environment but most will argue that a client/server environment does not mean host-based. Originally, the clients did not do any of the processing; they were just "dumb" terminals. Today, clients must do part of the application processing (along with other measures which will be mentioned in a later subsection) to be considered a client/server environment, although the application processing is not necessarily evenly dispersed. The current meaning of a client/server model will also be discussed in a later subsection.

Master-Slave Model

The next model to evolve from the host-based model was master-slave. In a master-slave model, there is one computer (master) with additional computers (slaves) attached to it. These slave computers can do some limited local processing as directed by the master computer. In other words, the master computer dictates to the slave computers what application processing to perform but the application processing is unidirectional (master to slave). The application processing is distributed, unlike in the host-based environment. *Webster's Dictionary* defines distributed as divide among many. The application processing is divided across the system; the slave does limited local application processing as directed by the master. An important part of distribution is cooperation among the computers. The computers can not be performing independent tasks to be considered distributed.

In a master-slave model, the application resides only on the master computer, just like the host-based environment. Even though the slave is doing some limited local application processing, the actual application processing is distributed, not the application. Typically, these master computers were large IBM mainframes. A slave computer was typically a smaller mainframe or minicomputer such as an IBM System 36 or Digital Equipment Corporation VAX. A process that could have been performed in this environment would have been data entry from "dumb" terminals accessing the slave computer, which performs data editing, formatting and batch uploading to the master computer. The master computer would then perform other operations such as additional editing, database updating and execution of specific programs as requested. Intelligent terminals can act like "dumb" terminals to access the application on the master computer or be disconnected from the system and flipped into stand-alone PCs to do such things as word processing or spreadsheets. As technology developed, replacing " dumb" terminals with intelligent terminals became more and more of a viable option than was using dumb terminals (see Figure 2).

Shared-Device Model

The next model to evolve from the master-slave model was shared-device. In a shared-device model, the PCs - not yet true clients - share resources such as files or a printer via a local are network (LAN). These resources are located on a server's (device) disk drive, which is attached to the PCs. File servers can be thought of as back-line computers that receive requests. The PCs do all of the application processing and the server only does shared-file or print processing. The application resides only on the PCs.

Shared-device environments were a significant step for a fully

Figure 2. Master-Slave

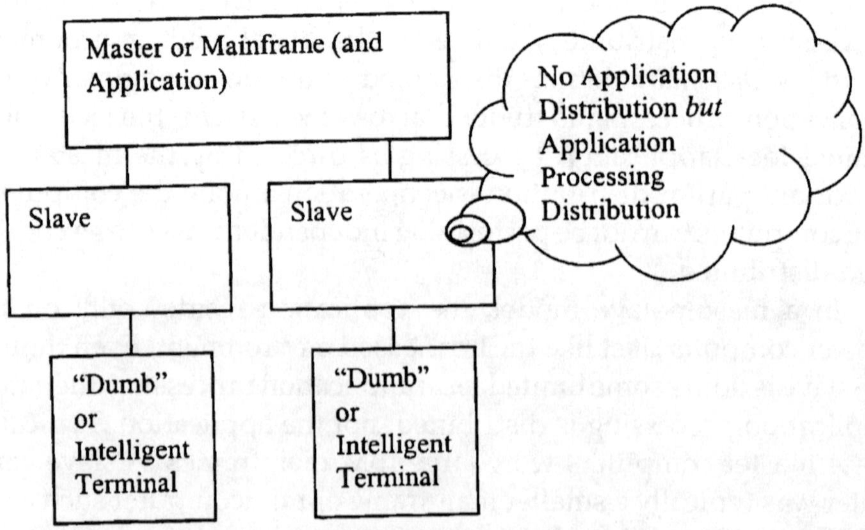

transparent distributed environment. In a shared-device environment, the user does not know where the file is located on the system; the file could be local and reside on the PC, or remote. If the file is remote and located on the file server, then the file is shared by the PCs (see Figure 3).

As these shared-device environments grew into WANs (wide area network), so did the number of PCs and servers on a system. And just as a natural progression, their power grew as well. These systems were becoming client/sever environments in which the PCs or rather workstations, as they became to be called because of their increased power, were becoming clients of the servers. Clients can be thought of as frontline computers that make requests to the server. Servers started to handle more than just file and print requests from clients. The application and its processing were being divided among or distributed between the client and server. Part of the application components reside on the client and server, although not necessarily evenly. The client and server are cooperating together to process the application but not unidirectional, like the master-slave model (see Figure 4). However, problems evolved with the management of the clients. The difficulty of managing clients was inherent in the design of client/server applications and led to the evolution of "thin-client" applications, which were much easier to deploy and manage. For

Figure 3. Shared-Device

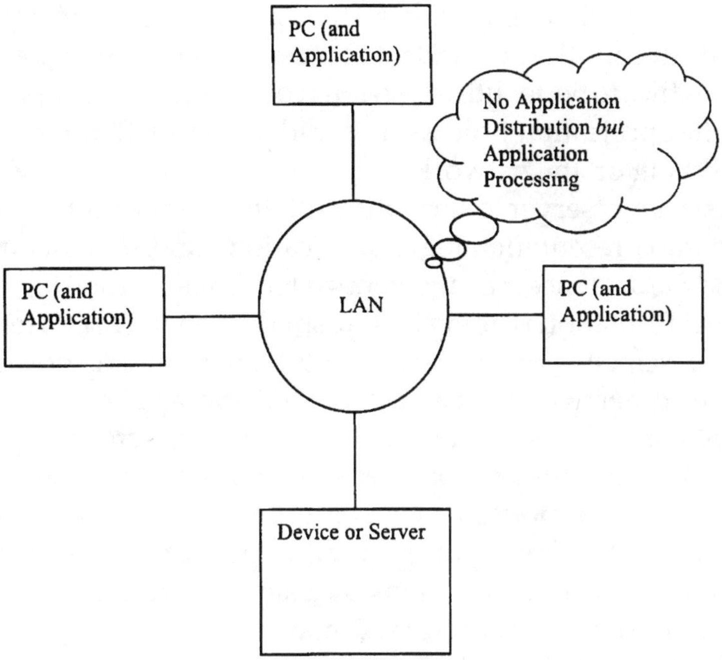

Figure 4. Client/Server

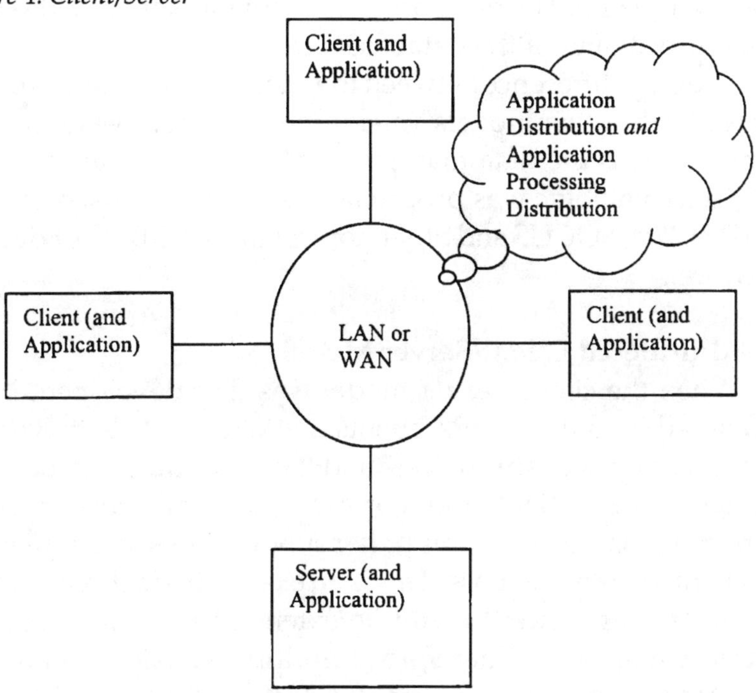

example, every time the application was upgraded, it had to be upgraded for all of the clients. It also became more efficient to distribute the application and its processing, along with the data that composes files to better utilize various computing resources. Distribution of the application processing could lessen such things as system bottlenecking on the network.

This client/server distribution of the application is typically divided into presentation logic, application logic, data manipulation logic and the database management system. Presentation logic handles how the information is going to be displayed on the user's terminal or computer screen—for example, text, graphs, dialog boxes and so fourth. In other words, it is the part of the application code that interacts with the user's terminal or computer screen. Application logic implements business policies from inputted data (from pointing devices such as a mouse or keyboard and/or a database). In other words, application logic is the part of the application code that decides what to do in various situations by using *if, then and else deduction*. Application logic is also referred to as business logic. They are the same. Data manipulation logic is the part of the application code that manipulates the data within the application by using SQL (structured query language). The database management system (DBMS) does the actual processing of the database data.

The only difference between the client/server application components and the other models' (mentioned in the above text) application components is the data manipulation logic. Specific data manipulation/retrieval logic was proprietary, such as that used by ADABAS, MODEL 204, FOCUS and other non-relational DBMS or data retrieval software.

Multitiered Client/Server Model

When the client/server model was first developed, it was only two tiered. In other words, clients made requests to servers and that was it. Today, a client/server model can be multitiered. This means that servers are clients too. For example, a mid level manager in a corporation is a server to his or her subordinates and at the same time is a client to his or her boss. This is an example of a three tiered system. However, this concept could be extended to include several other layers of managers. Therefore, a multitiered client/server model is more than two tiers (see Figure 5). Additionally, the mulitiered client/

Figure 5. Multitiered

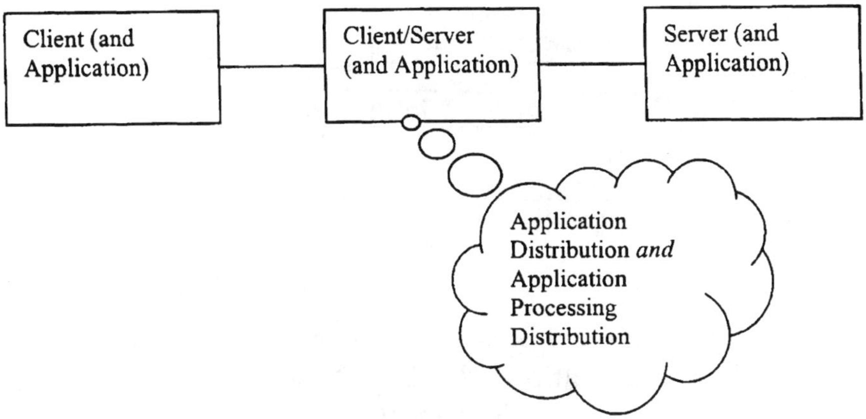

server model can support different LAN or WAN topologies or configurations.

Client/Server Measures.

In order to have a tiered or multitiered client/server model, several measures must be in place. First, there must be *cooperative processing* between the client and server. Second, the processing must be *distributed* between the client and server. Third, it must be an open system: the client/server model must allow for growth (scalability); must provide the ability for the client/server systems to talk to one another (interoperability); and must allow the application to run on any hardware platform (portability). Additionally, standards must be in place. Today, the client/server model is still evolving. The client/server model is now starting to incorporate distributed objects.

Object oriented Properties

Encapsulation

Encapsulation is the process of hiding the internal code or data of an object's implementation (Taylor, 1996, p. 52). Access to the code is through a defined interface, such as a command box. For example, a command box in Visual Basic (an object oriented programming language) that says, "Calculate 2 Multiplied by 2" and displays the results in a text box is an example of encapsulation. The code is hidden

Figure 6. Encapsulation

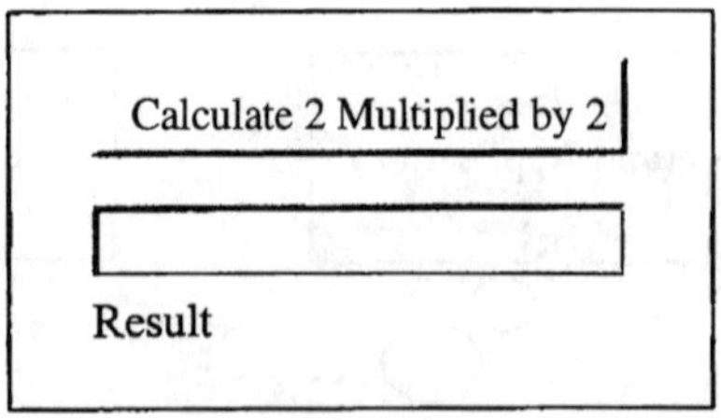

underneath the command box. The user only sees the box with the caption "Calculate 2 Multiplied by 2," not the code (see Figure 6).

Perhaps a simpler example of encapsulation would be to consider an actual calculator. If a user wants to multiple 2 times 2, first he/she presses the 2 button followed by the times button. Then he/she presses the 2 button again, followed by the equal sign. At this juncture, all the user sees is the answer 4, in a small glass display area. The user can not see into the calculator to see how the operation was actually executed. Plastic is covering the circuitry that performs this operation. The actual execution of the operation is encapsulated in the calculator, just as the programming code is encapsulated in an entity or object like the command box in Figure 6 above.

As Lowe (1997) states, an advantage of encapsulation is that it provided the first opportunity for software programmers to reuse code. Encapsulation made it possible for software programmers to stop *reinventing the wheel.* Code that has already been coded and tested once in a program can be used again in another program.

However, as Garber (1998) notes, some people believe that reusable code, which is encapsulated or hidden in software components, has not lived up to its potential. Encapsulated reusable code (it can also be original code) is or can be in any software component or object, just like the command box in Figure 6 above. Some software developers believe that reusing code is neither practical nor cost effective. Others are concerned that code can be used that was actually developed by someone else. And still other developers simply believe that code should be built from scratch.

According to Garber (1998), three main infrastructure elements for software components can ease the concern over reusing code. First, there must be a uniform design notation for the software components.

This would allow for reusable software components to have the same functions and properties as other code that is encapsulated into it. Secondly, there must be a standardized interface. If a standardized interface is not used, it is like trying to run a Microsoft program on a Macintosh machine. Thirdly, there must be a library of reusable software components that describe their features or what they can be used for. Other aspects of software components, not including encapsulation, will be discussed in a later section.

Messages

Before messages can be discussed, methods must be examined. A method returns a value from a set of instructions. As Rob and Coronel (1997) explain, a method can also be thought of as a procedure or subroutine. The procedure is an object. A method has a body and name. Each method is defined by a name. For example, the body of a method calculates the average salary earned per day, for two months of work, with an equal amount of days (31) in each month and a total of 62 days for two months. The method is named XAM (Average Amount of Money). In this method XMA = total_salary_for_two_months/62 and returns the worker's average salary earned per day. Total_salary_for_two_months is an attribute. An attribute is a data value of an object. For example, a data value for total_salary_for_two_months could be sixty-two dollars.

In this example and all other cases, to invoke the method a message is sent to the object. Messages are the way objects communicate to each other to carry out an activity (Taylor, 1996, p. 49). As Page-Jones (1995) notes, in order to send a message, three things must be known. First, in order to send a message an object must know which object to send the message to. It is like sending an envelope; an address is needed for the mailman to send the letter. Second, the method to be executed must have a name. In this case, Object 2. Third, any parameters or arguments must be specified. Parameters are the actual returned values of the object. In the average salary earned per day example, the parameter would be one dollar if the total salary for two months was sixty-two dollars (62 dollars/62 days = 1 dollar earned per day) (see Figure 7).

Perhaps another example will further illustrate this point. Suppose two people (A and B) are each holding an end of a string to which they have tied a can. The two cans and the string represent the system.

Figure 7. Messages

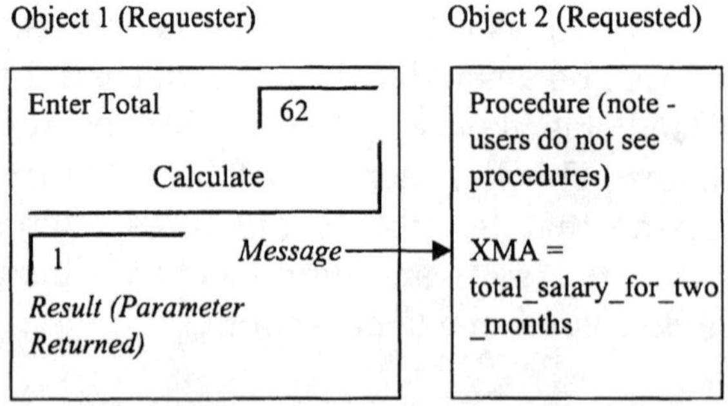

Person A, talking to person B, is located in a different place than B. They (A and B) represent distributed entities or objects. Person A is talking through one of the cans and person B is listening to person A through the other can. Person A tells person B to add 2 plus 2 and send the message back. As person A is speaking, he is invoking the message to person B. Since the two cans are connected to each other, person A knows whom to *send* the message to and the person or object's *name* - B. Next, person B performs a set of instructions to obtain the answer (4). These instructions or methods are to take 2 plus 2 and add them together. After person B obtains the answer, person B sends the answer (4) back to person B. The answer (4) represents the *parameter*.

Before leaving this section it should be noted that object oriented or rational database management systems (RDBMS), such as Oracle, have objects but differ from distributed object oriented systems in a few ways. For one, they do not have messages. Therefore, objects cannot communicate with one another to carry out an activity, such as person A and B did in the above example. Secondly, they do not have encapsulation. Looking at the code in a RDBMS is like looking at code on a piece of paper. The code is not hidden like in distributed object oriented systems.

An object in a RDBMS can be a trigger. A trigger is a set of instructions that initiates an event. For example a system shuts down when the office is closed for a holiday.

Software Components (Objects)

A few points will be reiterated before talking about software components. As mentioned above, objects are procedures and so are software components. Software components in turn can or cannot be procedures in which the code is encapsulated. A note though, these are not the only possible objects a program can have. For example, a form in Visual Basic is an object as well. As long as the object is an abstract description of a real-world entity with a unique identity (embedded properties) and can interact with itself and other objects, it is an object (Rob and Coronel, 1997, p. 548). Since Lowe (1997) contends that software components must have four features, a discussion of each of these follows.

Software Components Work Well Together

Objects are independent of other objects but can work together, such as the calculate button or procedure in Figure 6. When one object of the application is being used, another object can be "sleeping" or inactive. There also must be platform independence to truly be an open system. In other words, distributed objects do not care what computer architecture (structural design) or operating system is being used. The end result will be the same.

Software Components Transparently Downloaded Themselves

When a user requests a distributed object from the network, it is automatically located on a server. Also, the object is transparently downloaded to the user's computer (the client), except for the time delay that occurs as the object is being downloaded to the user's computer.

Software Components Will Not Damage Anything

Users must feel secure that distributed objects will not steal their credit cards or damage their hard disks. Security becomes important but it is not a deterrent from having distributed object oriented systems. To minimize this from happening, special software certificates are used to authenticate the object.

Software Components Are Dwarf

Distributed objects must not take too long to download. Users do not mind waiting 30 to 40 seconds but they will not tolerate 5 to 10 minutes.

Transactions

As Montlick (1998) notes, any critical system must have the ability to keep its data in a consistent state. This is particularly important when concurrent (at the same time) transactions (a unit of work) are executed. Transactions solve two problems. The first problem that they solve is concurrency. For example, say that two users (Stan and Laura) are using an object oriented system to add a row of data to a field or column in a database. Lets assume that the presentation logic is on the client and the rest of the application components on the server. Also, assume that both users want to decrease total inventory. Stan wants to decrease the current inventory (200 units) by 100 units and Laura by 50 units. Both access the row at the *same exact time*. Initially, both see the same data on their computer screens. However, Stan finishes the update first. His update will be lost and Laura's update will be committed to database. This is because his update superseded the first user's update, or as it is in this example, Laura's update. This is known as ***race condition***. The current inventory would read incorrectly 150 units. If Laura finished first, her update would be lost. In this case, the current inventory would read incorrectly 100 units. Either way the update is wrong. The inventory should reflect a change of 150 units and read 50 units as the current inventory count. If the inventory was 50 units, then the data would be in a consistent state.

Transactions solve this race condition problem by using locks. To keep the data in a consistent state, during current transactions, locks are used. Locks prevent more than one person from accessing a row at the same time. After the transaction is completed, the lock is released (Lowe, 1997, p. 266).

As Montlick (1999) explains, the second problem that transactions solve is a ***fail condition***. Say for example, that Stan and Laura want to add a row to a database, but this time there are two copies of the database on the object oriented system. These database copies are located in two different buildings. Let us also assume that the presentation logic is on both of the clients, and the rest of the components are on the two servers. There are then two copies of the database on each of the servers. One is in New York and one is in Maryland. Stan, who is located in New York, updates his inventory on the database through a client. This time, the database in Maryland is updated as well. Later on Laura, who is located in Maryland, updates her inventory on the Maryland database through a client. This time though, the database in New York is not updated. Consequently, the databases' data and the system are not consistent, for they both should read the same inventory (i.e., 50 units each).

Transactions solve this race condition problem by making sure that the *whole* update is fully completed. This keeps the data in a consistent state. In the above example, when Laura updated the Maryland database and the New York database was not updated, the whole transaction would have failed.

Findings

What Distributed Systems Are Missing

Today, there are standards available for distributed object oriented systems, such as COBRA, ActiveX and OpenDoc. Each has its advantages and disadvantages. These standards keep track of the objects and route or direct requests to the correct object on the system (Lowe, 1997, p. 260). However, there are no strategies available for implementing distributed object oriented systems. For example, two people meet in the streets of Spain. Half of the people there, including residents and visitors to the country, speak Spanish, while the other half speaks English. Upon meeting each other, if theses two people shake hands, it is understood that they want to speak English. They are agreeing on a standard way of speaking to one another. Computers work the same way, a standard is needed for them to communicate with each other. The standard could be CORBA, ActiveX or OpenDoc. CORBA has a different standard for distributed object oriented systems than ActiveX or OpenDoc. However, the problem is not with setting up a standard or way of communicating with one another but rather with implementing a strategy to distribute the objects. For example, the two people meet and one is a resident of Spain, while the other is a visitor. The visitor had asked the concierge for directions to a particular restaurant but decided to ask someone else too, just after he left the hotel. When the visitor discovered that he and the person he just met both spoke English, he asked the man for directions and the man gave them to him. The visitor then realized that both sets of directions were different but that they both got him to the correct place. The same is true for distributed object oriented systems; there is no agreed strategy for implementing distributing object oriented systems, just like there was no agreed upon way of getting to the restaurant, as seen in the different (but accurate) directions given by the concierge and the Spanish resident.

Where Are Distributed Object oriented Systems Going

If you look at where things are going, there will be a trend away from "proprietary clients" such as a PowerBuilder client accessing an Oracle database, replaced by browser-based clients that can be accessed in the office/at home/on the road easily and uniformly via the Internet. Companies are designing custom portals (think of a Yahoo or Web like main menu for corporate information available to its employees) for employees to access a wide variety of corporate data stored in data warehouses. A data warehouse is similar to a very large database that stores data for 5 - 10 years. Management of this architecture is centralized, but access is simple and ubiquitous. All you need is access to an ISP (Internet Service Provider) and a browser installed on your PC. Obviously, security would have to be a major concern (IP authentication processes), but this is not a showstopper. E-mail is evolving using this model and applications are following suit (B. Messina, personal communication, March 15, 1999).

This new model has 5 layers instead of 7. What is happening is that the Internet is allowing for this relatively new 5-layer OSI (Open Systems Connection) model, which was adapted from the 7-layer OSI model, to take advantage of the Internet. By using the Internet to connect PCs together, two of the layers are no longer needed. You should notice two things about this model. One, it is a client/server model. Two, it also meets the client/server measures as noted in that section.

Conclusion

There will never be an agreed upon definition or understanding of distributed object oriented systems. You can go through numerous books and find several definitions of the same thing, such as the many different definitions of client/server. Finding an agreed upon definition or understanding of distributed object oriented systems will not get any easier as the technology develops but keeping abreast of different definitions will help. The trick is to break things down into their smaller parts and go from there. Having done that with regard to distributed object oriented systems, this chapter should help someone get a better definition and understanding of distributed object oriented systems.

References

Berson, A. (1996). *Client/server architecture.* New York: McGraw-Hill.

Berson, A., & Smith, S .J. (1997). Data warehousing, data mining, & OLAP. New York: McGraw-Hill.

Kiely, D. (1998, February). Are components the future of software? *IEEE*, pp. 10-11.

Lowe, D. (1997). *Client/server computing for dummies.* Foster City: IDG Books Worldwide, Inc.

Montlick, T. (1999). *The distributed smalltalk survival guide.* Cambridge: Cambridge University Press.

Page-Jones, M. (1995). *What every programmer should know about object oriented design.* New York: Dorset House.

Purao, S., Jain, H., & Nazareth, D. (1998). A comprehensive approach to effective distribution of object oriented systems in loosely coupled networks [On-line]. Available: http://www.cis.gsu.edu/~spurano/research/oodistcs.html

Purao, S., Jain, H., & Nazareth, D. (1998). Effective distribution of object oriented applications. *Communications of the ACM*, 41,100-108.

Rob, P., & Coronel, C. (1997). *Database systems design, implementation and management.* Cambridge: Course Technology.

Singer, G. (1996). *Object technology strategies and tactics.* New York: SIGS Books & Multimedia.

Chapter X

Distributed Object Business Engineering: Digital Legos for the Enterprise

David H. Patton
USWeb/CKS Corporation, USA

Tomorrow's business environment will make it increasingly difficult for businesses to operate efficiently. To gain the needed edge, in the global economy, many businesses are looking towards information technology. By utilizing technology as a conduit, companies are able to leverage their greatest asset: their internal knowledge base. This chapter presents a framework for architecting enterprise-wide object based information systems. These next-generation systems maximize information value throughout the enterprise, while reducing development time and effort throughout the system lifetime. By presenting a complex concept in a pragmatic fashion this chapter should provide benefit for both information architects and business managers.

Distributed Object Business Engineering: Designing Enterprise Information Portals for Tomorrow's Business

Information is power. Yet this mantra of the next-century paradoxically poses a statement and a question. In the coming age data, information and the knowledge derived from it equate to real-world power just as traditional forms of capital equated to power in the industrial age.

This study seeks to introduce and define a theoretical model describing a new approach to information age enterprise computing in the global marketplace. The implications of this study are that they provide business a new approach to process engineering offering the enterprise a strategic edge in decision making at all levels.

Decision-making theory, specifically the *rational actor model*, assumes decisions are made based on the availability of all current, timely, and relevant information available. The goal of information systems is to provide an infrastructure that acts as a repository for data and to provide a mechanism for the extraction and transformation of this data to information. However, the rapid increase in the pace of business has placed increased pressure upon the enterprise to make decisions more quickly in order to remain competitive.

This study is based on a survey of current literature and the authors observation within academia and industry incorporating current theories and models from object oriented technology, client/server computing, and business process engineering. The study seeks to provide some background on the characteristics of the emerging business environment, as well as past and contemporary information system theory as a starting point for defining the new business environment and a new model of Distributed Object Business Engineering.

Discussion

Business in the next century will be remarkably different from the manner in which it is currently conducted. In recent years, there have been two separate but parallel revolutions within business and technology that are impacting the business landscape of today (Fingar & Strikeleather 1996).

Business:

- New organizational structures - New structures are reshaping businesses from the traditional hierarchical models to flatter, more networked organizational models. The results of this are smaller organizations with fewer layers between the top and the bottom, thereby decreasing the reaction time of the organization as a whole. The networked structures disregard traditional "chain of command" structures by establishing interoperating teams that work together on specific projects. Each team is self-sufficient with regards to mission goals, with the overall organization providing administrative support.

- Globalization of business - The last twenty years have seen a boom in the number of companies conducting global operations. This trend was accelerated by the widespread adoption of the Internet and is sure to continue. Traditional business hours are a thing of the past in the new global marketplace. Business must adapt to conducting business 24 hours a day, seven days a week. In addition, business must adapt its products and services to fit language, economic, regulatory, and cultural differences.
- Market capitalization - Within the last five years, small-time individual investors have become a dominant player in the stock market. As the number of individuals continues to grow, market capitalization of many high profile, some say overexposed, companies will continue to swell. Case in point, the market capitalization of Microsoft stands at $380 billion, while the market capitalization of the remainder of a well-known Internet stock index (ISDEX) stands at 95% of Microsoft's valuation (Harmon, 1999).
- Restructuring of distribution channels - Traditionally goods and services were put to market through well-defined distribution channels. These channels were comprised of one or more middlemen who would each increase the total cost in return for some kind of "value-added" service. A recent trend within the business world is to reduce the overall length of distribution channels or to eliminate them altogether and sell directly to consumers. This is called disintermediation.

Technology:

- The desktop computer - The introduction of the desktop or personal computer revolutionized business and the world, allowing people to work faster, smarter and more efficiently. But the PC also facilitated other more subtle changes that are currently taking place.
- Graphical user interfaces - Back in the dark ages of computing users were relegated to performing work on a computer through a command line interface such as DOS. In the 1980s, Apple introduced the Macintosh computer. The Macintosh was the first consumer level computer that offered the graphical user interface

or GUI. A GUI allowed users to interact with their machines through the use of easy to understand icons and drop-down menus for performing tasks. No longer did you have to remember specific syntax to perform actions such as copying or moving a file.

- Advanced network infrastructures (LAN's, WAN's, Internet) - Networked computing has been a major force in the widespread adoption of computers in business. Networking allows users to share data and common system resources such as disks and printers. In the past installation of a network was a time-consuming, expensive endeavor with a steep learning curve. Added to this problem was the number of proprietary protocols and products available. The introduction of the Internet with its standardized protocol (TCP/IP) has overcome many of these barriers, allowing every business and many individuals to build and operate their own local area networks. These LAN's are interconnected either through proprietary networks called wide area networks (WAN's) or to the Internet, the granddaddy of all WAN's.
- Client/Server computing - The advent of the network required system designers to develop an underlying architecture that defined the relationship between a server and its client machines. Initially designs were based on a simple terminal-to-host model, where multiple dumb terminals connected to a massive server (usually a mainframe) on a time-sharing basis. This type of architecture is called a two-tier model. To offset the high maintenance required of these systems the three-tiered model was introduced. This model inserts an additional layer between the client and the server to handle business logic, rules, and data access. This middle tier is a logical layer, and does not require the addition of hardware for implementation (Clarke, Bowman & Strikeleather, 1996). Examples of a three-tiered system are most LAN's found in business today.
- Object oriented technology (OOT) - OOT is a computing paradigm that allows applications and systems to be modeled on real-world concepts (Fingar & Strikeleather, 1996). OOT has benefited developers by allowing rapid application development and re-use of existing code. The primary benefit for business is that OOT

has allowed the design of systems and application that were previously impossible to design and build.

- Widespread adoption of open standards - The rise of the Internet has focused attention away from proprietary protocols to the adoption of open standards such as TCP/IP. The result of this has been that systems designers are better able to tie together disparate and separate systems. Additionally, open standards have opened the way for a wider base of end users. As an example, you are now able to perform most banking functions at home through your PC without the purchase of additional software. Before the adoption of open standards this would not have been possible.

The effect of these two concurrent revolutions, within business and technology, is the creation of new business environment that is fundamentally different from the current business environment. What is this new environment then, and what are its characteristics? The new environment creates a global market that continuously operates twenty-four hours a day, seven days a week, and is defined by the following characteristics:

- Increased global competition.
- Global distribution of organizational resources.
- Increased pressure to continuously improve core business processes.
- The acceleration of the decision-making cycle.
- Increased demand for information throughout the enterprise.

Businesses that are to survive must obtain a mastery of the complex and dynamic environment. To gain an advantage in the coming age, many businesses are looking to redesign core processes (engaging in Business Process Redesign) by transitioning to a "knowledge-based organization." These two terms have appeared in much of the current literature, but what exactly are they and what is their relationship to IT?

Business Process Redesign (BPR) is "the analysis and design of workflows and processes within and between organizations" (Davenport and Short, 1990). It seeks to find fundamentally better ways to serve customers, partners, and the organization itself. Furthermore, Davenport and Short (1990) define a business process as "a set of logically related tasks performed to achieve a defined business outcome." With this definition we can define three main factors that comprise a business process:

- Entities
- Objectives
- Activities

Information technology is a key enabler of BPR that should be used to recognize and break away from outdated business rules and underlying assumptions (Hammer 1990). Malhorta (1998) states that IT and BPR have a recursive relationship, where IT supports business process that in turn should be expressed in terms IT can provide. It should be noted that although BPR had its roots in IT, it is primarily a business initiative.

The knowledge-based organization provides employees at all levels with access to information to make necessary tactical and strategic decisions. It seeks to leverage an organization's knowledge base as a tangible asset of the organization. The knowledge-based organization can be viewed in some ways as a logical outcome of BPR. The ultimate goal of these two is to align IT, business strategy, business process and structure into a cohesive whole.

The confluence of these two has created an explosive demand for information. Business must draw together diverse and separate islands of information into a seamless and integrated information system that is accessible at all levels of the enterprise. From a technical standpoint, this means universal access that is both transparent and adaptive (Fingar and Strikeleather, 1996). This creates system requirements of enormous complexity and sophistication, that current tasked based and procedural methodologies and architectures are incapable of handling. A new paradigm to information system design must be developed that is capable of handling these requirements: a next generation information systems model.

As an additional challenge, this new computing model must be placed within a global environment characterized by a distribution of end users and resources, and the immateriality of time; that time in our new system is relative. While client-server-computing models have existed for a number of years they have proven to be inefficient. Not until the full-scale use of the Internet did client-server models develop to the necessary level of sophistication with three-tier and n-tier models. These models have given system architects a robust framework to develop distributed applications by separating business logic from application logic from the user interface. However, we are still left with the fact that system architects predominately utilize the old procedural and tasked-based methodology. This is the current state of enterprise computing today. With the requirements of the new business environment defined, we can begin the construction of this next generation information systems model. Appendix A shows a logical flow of the dynamics that necessitate this new model.

Definition and Characteristics

Distributed Object Business Engineering (DOBE) is the new model; it draws together distributed object computing within the context of the knowledge-based organization.

DOBE is a framework for developing object based distributed enterprise-wide information systems. This framework defines a process and an open architecture for system design that fulfills the requirements of operation in the emerging business environment. Although this is a broad definition, it may help to define some characteristics of DOBE:

- Process oriented - The traditional model of tasked-based systems that seek to break task down into smaller and smaller sub-task is inadequate in a distributed environment. Rather, the process of work should be the focus for systems. Visualizing how workflows within the enterprise occur will offer a basis for system modeling.
- Uses a cognitive based interface - New and improved interface methodologies must be adopted that place greater emphasis on human cognition. Systems must present information in a manner that reflects our own perception of reality and not the computers.
- User centered - Today business processes are a human phenomenon, and systems must be designed in accordance with this principle in mind. Most end users within the enterprise have attained a level of computer mastery far below systems architects. Yet these same architects ignore this and design systems that are unsuited for end users needs.
- Based on real world concepts not technology - The conduct of business is done in the real world and systems that are used in business must reflect this facet. It is more natural to think in terms of the real world concept than to think about data structures and procedures (Fingar and Strikeleather, 1996).
- Technology is a conduit - Technology is not the basis for a solution but merely a tool that draws together the information architects

Figure 1. Relationship between the component parts of Distributed Object Business Engineering.

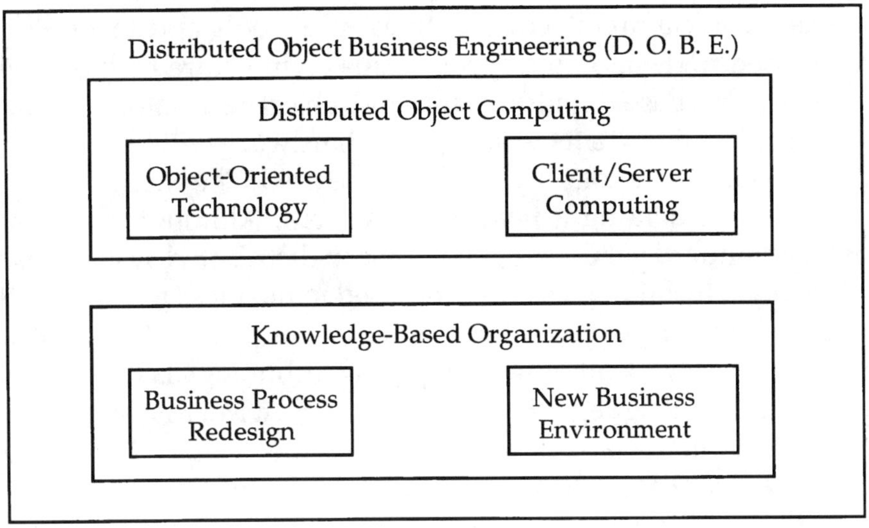

and the end users into a holistic approach (Young, 1997).

- Component based - A component-based system has four main advantages over existing procedural models as defined by Fingar and Strikeleather (1996). Components reflect the real world, are considerably more stable, reduce system complexity, and are reusable. The result of this is systems with a reduced codebase, reduced development time, consistent behavior, and improved quality of information.

The defining characteristics discussed above provide a skeletal framework from which to begin design and construction of our new system. As with any engineering project, there must be an architecture and a process to provide the underlying groundwork. Architecture provides a technology independent framework for systems design. Tangential to architecture is process, which describes a methodology to follow for system implementation and enterprise integration.

Architecture

Just as a building is based on an architectural design, so must any information system be based on a solid architecture. If the foundation of our model is not solid, it will not work in the real world. When designing an information system there are two fundamental architectures that must be considered equally. These two separate, yet congruent, architectures are the technical architecture and the information architecture (Clarke, Strikeleather & Fingar, 1996).

The technical architecture defines what tools and technologies will be used to develop the system. This architecture includes what hardware, databases, middleware, and object technologies will be used. To a certain extent defining what hardware will be used sets a path for what technology and tools will be used. The exception to this is when implementing a Java based system. Although there is no industry standard yet developed for use in distributed systems, there are two main technologies currently used in business today: CORBA developed by the Object Management Group, and Com/DCOM developed by Microsoft. A new emerging technology is RMI which is part of the Java language set developed by Sun Microsystems.

The information architecture describes the heart of the system. It includes a definition of system objects, their content, behavior, and interaction. This enables developers to assemble and integrate self-contained objects into an integrated solution. It is within the information architecture that the strengths and limitation of client-server computing become apparent. The information architecture can be seen as a seven-layered model to assist in proper semantically based architectural design.

What exactly does this model describe? Each object is divided to its own intrinsic layer depending on the object's purpose. These individual layers are then grouped into one of three object categories that also represent the different tiers of a typical three-tier distributed application.

The bottom two layers represent application and data objects. These two layers provide for the underpinning technology infrastructure, object life-cycle persistence, and system intrinsics and metrics e.g., defining time, money, and date formatting standards.

The next four layers represent the business logic of the system, which governs exactly how data is manipulated. The entities layers represent objects that define business objects such as customer, employee, inventory item, or truck. The processes layer is where the entities are put together to define a specific business process such as selling, buying, or auditing. The events layer is an insulation layer to provide a mechanism for response to external stimuli such as a competitor price change. The workflows layer can been seen as the assembly line where the previous three layers come together. This

Figure 2. Seven layered architectural model of Distributed Object Business Engineering.

	Layer Name	Example	Description
Interface Objects	View	• End-User Interface	Provides System Interface
Business Objects	Workflows	• Logical combination of processes	Sequencing of Events
	Events	• Competitor Price Change	Representation of actions that insulate or influence scenarios
	Processes	• Buying, Selling, Auditing	Assemblage of entities representing a business function or process
	Entities	• Objects, Associations, Roles	Definition and interaction of application objects
Application Objects	Intrinsics and Metrics	• Metrics Definitions of underlying objects	Semantic definition
	Infrastructure	• CORBA, COM/DCOM, RMI	Provides life-cycle persistence

layer assembles entities, processes, and events into logical workflows.

Lastly there is the presentation objects or the view layer. This layer represents objects that are responsible for data and information presentation, as well as end user to system interaction.

DOBE is the synthesis of object oriented technology and client-server architecture. However, what emerges is greater than the sum of its parts. The technical advantages to adopting this architecture is:

- Legacy assets can be easily integrated and leveraged through the use of legacy object wrappers.
- Ease of object integration through the assemblage of objects.
- Allows for business models to be developed that are simulation of the real world business environment.
- Business objects can be reused.

Process

Process should serve as a guide while traversing the complexity of designing a next-generation computing system, offering guidelines for implementation and enterprise integration. Process can be seen as the methodology to be followed in designing system architecture and implementation. At the macro level, process is divided into the phases of assessment, planning and execution.

Assessment - what are the goals and objectives of the organization? This assessment also determines what organizational resources are available and what is their current state.

Planning - How are the goals and objectives stated above realized? This is the most critical aspect of the process. A successful outcome will only come through diligent and thoughtful planning. Here is where the system architect must determine how legacy assets are to be integrated, what technology base and hardware, and what development tools are to be used, etc. "Systems created under a well-defined architecture will exhibit the qualities of conceptual integrity. In the short-term, this quality helps organize and manage the development process. In the long-term, it facilitates business and technical evolution" (Read, 1996, p. 18). This planning phase should be dynamic in nature allowing for the inevitable changes that will come during the project life cycle.

Execution - This should take a staged approach by rolling the system out in various stages throughout the enterprise, or as modules that are gradually implemented.

As with any new technology adoption, change must be carefully managed at all levels of the enterprise. Industry experience has shown there are several characteristics to a successful technology adoption (Read, 1996):

- Preserving and leveraging legacy assets - Most businesses have invested too much time, money and effort in their legacy systems to just have them discarded as newer systems are implemented. Legacy systems will add value to the new systems through their semantic contents which will distribute knowledge throughout the enterprise. In addition, they can also provide a translation service that maps internal data to object structures of the new system. The combination of this is to provide a pathway for the gradual transition of legacy systems.
- Investing in advanced infrastructure - New infrastructures will be based on object oriented and client/server technologies. Together these two technologies greatly increase the efficiency of the enterprise. This type of "infrastructure can empower businesses to construct new era applications that were once technologically impossible" (Read, 1996, p. 13).
- Transitioning staff to new skills - Existing development staffs represent a considerable knowledge base that may not exist in written form. As such, developing new systems based on these

advanced technologies, may require developers to change from the procedural methods they have relied upon and adapt to entirely new problem-solving approaches, tools, processes, and organizations. Within industry development groups are transitions to a team-based approach, where teams work together from across the entire enterprise.

- Emphasizing architecture to facilitate system evolution - As was noted earlier the speed of business is increasing. This places enormous pressure upon architects to build flexible and scalable systems. Change may come from a shift in business priorities, or methods, or it may come from new technology; the only sure thing is that it will come. Planning for this inevitable change is perhaps the greatest challenge facing architects. This fact has directly contributed to the creation of formal procedures and notations to describe systems and the inter-operation of their component parts. "Formalizing procedures and notations helps us evaluate system architecture within the context of system goals" (Read, 1996, p. 16).

This combination of architecture and process provides the underlying groundwork for systems design. The bulk of the time should be spent within the planning phase of the project. Within this phase, it is vital that careful consideration be given to component design. Specifically, what constitutes the objects at each of the seven layers within the architectural model. Good planning here will pay off in the future. Well-designed objects based on real-world concepts will be stable, yet remain flexible to business or application rule changes. This sort of "Digital Lego" design paradigm will offer information architects a way to rapidly design systems in response to an ever-changing business environment.

Future Trends and Conclusion

We are only scratching the surface of what is really the start of an entirely new paradigm in enterprise computing. The concept of "Digital Legos" is only now starting to make headway into the business realm. In the future, meaning the next five to ten years, enterprise information systems will undergo a radical transformation. Within this time we will see the last of the monolithic mainframes

Appendix A.

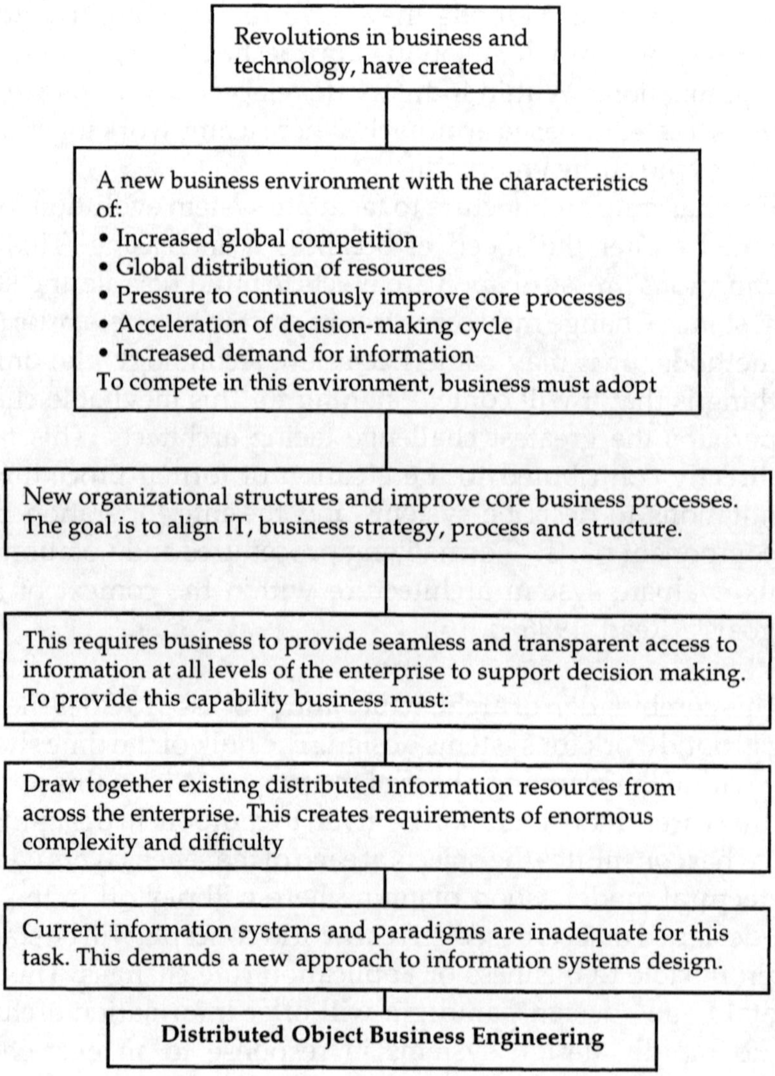

and procedural application phased out, in favor of lightweight distributed systems run off of UNIX, Windows 2000 and/or Mac OS X Servers. The groundwork has already been laid for the backend of these systems (server architecture and object design). The real work ahead lies within the realm of adopting a true standard for distributed systems, designing robust transaction models for objects, and system usability.

Usability, which once stood in relative obscurity, will gain in importance. As data sets grow in complexity, the need to visualize them in a manner consistent with user cognition will also grow. The traditional spreadsheet method of presenting information is insufficient to present multidimensional data sets, or data not based on alphanumeric symbology such as multimedia data. Other methodologies must be developed to present these types of data, including 3D hyperbolic views, and data fly-through.

Systems based on the DOBE framework provide for the requirements of next-generation enterprise information systems. DOBE systems are scalable, flexible, reusable, dynamic, and stable. Without object oriented technology, systems of this nature would not be possible. The possibilities presented through advanced technology design either through DOBE or another framework must be tempered with the ultimate goal in mind: to ensure the alignment of information technologies with business goals.

References

Clarke, J., Bowman, T., Strikeleather, J. (1996). Client/Server Architectures (The Next Generation Computing Series). The Technical Resource Connection, Inc. Available at: http://www.trinc.com.

Clarke, J., Strikeleather, J., Fingar, P. (1996). Distributed Object Computing for Business (The Next Generation Computing Series). The Technical Resource Connection, Inc. Available at: http://www.trinc.com.

Davenport, T.H. & Short, J.E. (1990 Summer). "The New Industrial Engineering: Information Technology and Business Process Redesign," *Sloan Management Review*, 11-27.

Fingar, P. & Strikeleather, J. (1996). Getting Started with Object Technology (The Next Generation Computing Series). The Technical Resource Connection, Inc. Available at: http://www.trinc.com.

Hammer, M. (1990, July-August). "Reengineering Work: Don't Automate, Obliterate," *Harvard Business Review*, 104-112.

Harmon, Steve (1999). Many-To-One: Total ISDEX Market Cap Equals Microsoft. Internetnews.com. Available at: http://www.internetnews.com/stocks/column/article/0,1087,archive_41_72661,00.html.

Malhorta, Y. (1998). Business Process Redesign: An Overview. @Brint

Research Institute. Available at: http://www.brint.com/papers/bpr.htm.

Read, D. (1996). Enterprise Computing: The Process (The Next Generation Computing Series). The Technical Resource Connection, Inc. Available at: http://www.trinc.com

Young, E. (1997). "An Integrated Knowledge Environment," *DM Review Magazine*. Available at: http://www.dmreview.com/issues/1997/nov/articles/nov97_20.htm .

Chapter XI

What Are the Actual Industry Expectations and Needs with Regard to Object Oriented Technology?

Luis F. Proano
Pan American Health Organization

This chapter is a review of journals and printed articles published during the last two years. It will give you an idea of the current needs in the industry due to object oriented technologies. It also analyzes factors like the lack of mainstream products and object standards influencing the development of skilled professionals in working with object databases. It will show industry trends and needs and make recommendations for training approaches in order to develop skilled professionals who will satisfy these needs. It will tell you what you need to know to make yourself more marketable in an ever-changing industry.

It seems that the industry agrees that object oriented databases can outperform relational databases at handling complex relationships among data. It has been mentioned that an object database could model the supply chain based on a mix of product, storage and transportation attributes. However, object databases have not caught on in supply-chain management. This is mostly due to the need for specialized skills and the exotic nature of object oriented databases.

The question that this chapter will answer is: What are the actual industry expectations and needs in regard to object oriented technology?

This chapter will focus on current industry trends. The implications of following those trends will be explored as well as the availability of resources. It will address the lack of mainstream products and object standards that make it more difficult to develop skilled professionals. It will make recommendations for training approaches in order to develop skilled professionals who will satisfy these needs. It will tell you what you need to know to make yourself more marketable in an ever-changing industry.

This chapter is a review of journals and printed articles published during the last two years. This study has been able to identify the current and future industry requirements.

Industry experts predict that in the near future the object paradigm will be adopted as the dominant approach to systems analysis, design, and implementation. Jones, Hilton, and Lutz (1999) mention that the promise of the object-oriented approach to systems analysis hinges on correctly partitioning the problem domain into essential classes and objects. Most developers agree that this is no easy task.

Object Databases

Object databases have the potential to solve problems in any industry in which processes are so complex that relational databases can't keep up. For example, in Baer's (1999) article he explains how manufacturers, distributors, shippers and retailers must constantly juggle when to manufacture product, where to deploy finished goods inventory and how to choose the most economical routes or carriers to get it there. A food manufacturer with a mix of packaged and perishable products might have to weigh the optimizations differently by product. An object database could model the supply chain based on a mix of product, storage and transportation attributes.

Baer's agrees that even vendors face the '"weird product" syndrome as they try to accustom customers to objects. Analyst Merv Adrian at Giga Information Group in Norwell, Mass. said that "it's hard to ask someone to sell something they haven't heard of. Until now, object databases have been more for rocket scientists." Adrian expects the object-database market to double this year, spurred by the growth of object-oriented languages such as Java. It still seems that information technology managers have to weigh the benefits of object-oriented databases versus the pain of developing and maintaining them.

Finally, Baer warning: "It's harder to find developers and database administrators who can handle objects than it is to find specialists in more common relational products" seems to apply to other issues of object oriented technologies as well.

John Kerin, from the Chicago Stock Exchange, spent nine months finding the specialists he needed to maintain his application. "Just knowing C++ and syntax wouldn't cut it," he says. "You need to know how object databases and ORBs (object request brokers, which allow objects to communicate) really work.

Limited research has been done to date regarding class and object identification and refinement. Jones et al. (1999) paper presents the findings of an empirical study that assesses the frequency of use of various strategies for identifying and refining classes and objects during systems analysis and tests the hypothesized relationships between strategy usage and several respondent characteristics. Results suggest analysts should learn a base strategic repertoire complemented by selected strategies targeted to the application type and the analyst's previous background.

Organizations have moved beyond the pilot project stage and are now using object technology to build large-scale, mission-critical business applications. Unfortunately they are finding that the processes which proved so successful on small, proof-of-concept projects do not scale very well for real-world development. Today's organization needs a collection of proven techniques for managing the complexities of large-scale, object oriented software development projects, a collection of process patterns.

Business Wire magazine (1999) reports that Ardent Software, Inc. (NASDAQ:ARDT), a global data management company and a leading provider of advanced object database technology, announced today the signing of its 200th academic customer and the subsequent formation of the Ardent Object Technology Academic Partner Program. This new program, designed for colleges and universities worldwide, provides students and faculty with access to Ardent's advanced object oriented software technology.

"With the increasingly widespread use of the Web and other multimedia applications in the business world, Ardent sees a growing demand for developers who are educated in distributed, object oriented systems like O2," according to Francois Bancilhon, vice president and general manager with Ardent's Object Technology business unit. "The signing of our 200th Academic Partner and the demand for the expansion of our Academic Partner Program are clear signs that the academic community also recognizes this opportunity."

Colleges and universities in 34 countries use the O2 ODBMS to support instruction and research in object oriented programming and database management, providing crucial hands-on experience to more than 6,000 students each year, better preparing them to meet the market's demand for experienced object-oriented developers. Participating institutions include: Johns Hopkins University; Stanford University; University of Alberta, Edmonton Canada; University of Pennsylvania; Brigham Young University; Hartford Graduate Institute; Centre de Recherche en Informatique de Montreal (CRIM): University of Rio de Janeiro; CNAM Paris; University of Paris XI; University of Dortmund; University of Mexico; Buckingham University; University of London; University of Tokyo; and University of Osaka.

Software and Applications Development

In most implementations of OOT, both encapsulation and polymorphism are available in one way or another. Purists would argue that only implementation inheritance fully satisfies the requirements of an object oriented programming concept. Languages such as C++, Java, and Smalltalk support both implementation inheritance and interface inheritance.

An important concept supporting only interface inheritance is Microsoft's Component Object Model (COM). Instead of reusing the actual software code, only the specifications of an object are reused. This is a significant simplification, making it possible to work around the lack of standards on how to bind binary objects together; also, objects implemented in different languages can be combined into one application. The objects become software components.

The development of object technology has altruistic roots. The concepts of pure object orientation stem from an academic pursuit for capturing real-world entities and providing a more intuitive method of interacting with computers than through standard procedural programming constructs.

However, commercial constraints have put pressure on the ideological foundations of object oriented technology as vendors vie for larger shares of this rapidly expanding market. Specifically, the complex but idealistic goal of distributed object computing to allow companies to build and rebuild business applications by assembling and purchasing interoperable objects that conform to a single object model has been hijacked by the debate surrounding competing approaches to object middleware.

Recently, pragmatic choices about rival middleware architectures—should companies invest in Microsoft's Distributed Component Object Model (DCOM) or a union of Sun Microsystems' Java technology with the Object Management Group's Common Object Request Broker Architecture (CORBA) — have replaced the commendable concepts of pure object technology. This situation is exacerbated as simplified objects such as JavaBeans or ActiveX components increasingly find use as the software building blocks of choice within Internet protocol-based (IP-based) networks.

However, in spite of the rapid growth of simple reusable components and graphical user interface objects that find use in World Wide Web environments, large-scale distributed object projects are not yet common within corporate information environments. The major stumbling block to widespread robust object architectures is the immaturity of DCOM and, to a lesser extent, CORBA as mission-critical middleware. Although vendors are beginning to offer some key services such as transaction processing, application and system management functions, and data integrity guarantees within object middleware products, many IT architects remain confused about the next step in object technology adoption.

The driving principle behind OOT is that it creates a model (i.e., a software program) that emulates the real world. If at all possible, software objects should be based on the objects we surround ourselves with. The main benefit is a design that is comprehensible and has a greater chance of remaining as intended during the entire life of a software product. Real-life objects stand the challenge of time and changing conditions. A software object based on the same principles should do the same.

Reuse has often been termed OOT's greatest benefit. While this may be true in the long run, it is the author's opinion that reuse is a beneficial result of a well-thought-out design with durable objects.

Without a proper design, there will be no more reuse with OOT than without it. This is one reason why so many reuse initiatives have failed. OOT is an important enabling technology for reuse because it provides us with advanced abstraction mechanisms. But reuse will only happen when the underlying design is sound.

A simplified inheritance model has created an emerging software component market. This may well be the largest impact of OOT; it is possible to buy components that perform well-defined operations. And, contrary to previous days, it is easy to integrate these components into a program. A quick search on the World Wide Web opens up a new world of reusable components; the object bazaar is becoming a reality.

Although object oriented code may be inherently more reusable than functionally oriented code, most object oriented legacy systems were not designed with reuse in mind. OO code, due to the very aspects that make it desirable, tends to suffer from a wide scattering of the code that performs even a fairly simple task. It is considered to be good object oriented programming style to write small member functions, which results in an OO system consisting of a large number of small modules. Through inheritance, a class may inherit one or more classes, each with its own associated methods, but few defined locally.

These aspects of object oriented code underline the need for good, semantically based tools to aid in the understanding, and thus the reuse, of object oriented code.

Peter Ruber (1997) mentions that object-oriented technology (OOT) development is difficult and expensive, and it has not worked out for everyone. However, a new class of development tools and object request brokers (ORB) has made the difference for some companies. Although the promise and future benefits of OOT are becoming more enticing to IS managers, many are apprehensive about the up-front costs associated with object migration. Building an object-based enterprise requires IS managers to rethink the entire development process. With CORBA 2.0 now firmly entrenched as an industry standard, third-party developers are coming up with some intriguing packaged solutions. Some are delivering ORBs that will provide as much as 80% of the application logic for certain industries. Despite gains made during the past year, the object landscape is still going to be littered with difficult development hurdles and competing technologies.

Chin, White, and George (1997) also mentioned that dramatic shifts in the landscape of industrial control are already visible on the horizon as new software, lower-cost hardware and advances in networking technologies combine to create next-generation control systems. Helping to shape the future are object oriented technologies. They will make control systems more open, more flexible, more intuitive to use and offer increased productivity, regardless of the control system, whether programmable logic control, distributed control system, or PC-based controls. The greatest benefit of object technology is a new capacity for designing control systems that bridge diverse requirements. Distributed objects communicate over a network system. Currently, the largest and the best known computer network is the Internet.

Nesi and Querci (1998) state that due to the growing diffusion of the object oriented paradigm and the need of maintaining under control the process of software development, industries are looking for metrics capable of producing satisfactory effort estimations and predictions. These metrics have to produce results with a known confidence since the early phases of software life cycle in order to establish a process of prediction and correction of costs. To this end, specific metrics are needed in order to maintain under control object oriented system development. New complexity and size metrics for effort evaluation and prediction are presented and compared with respect to the most important metrics proposed for the same purpose in the literature. The validation of the most important of these metrics is also reported.

Languages

It is not the intention of this chapter to start an argument about which object oriented language is the best. The question is, in many cases, irrelevant; it all depends on what level of support the software development environment provides.

Until 1995, the two leading object oriented languages were C++ and Smalltalk. C++ still has the largest installed base. Smalltalk is, in many cases, a more elegant and simpler programming environment, but it has lost a lot of its market momentum to Java.

Java is the most exciting and important development in the field of OOT today. It started out as a platform-independent programming development and execution environment. Its syntax resembles C++ with some of the more complex mechanisms and limitations removed (e.g., pointers and garbage collection). The programming model, however, strongly resembles Smalltalk. While still in its infancy, the momentum behind Java is such that the language will without doubt play a significant role during the next 5 to 15 years.

Rick Whiting discusses Java's current status. He states that Java is clearly a winner as a development language. IT managers report productivity gains by factors of 2, 4, even 10 times compared to other languages. Corporations are increasingly using Java to build business-critical, server-based software, particularly self-service programs that provide employees and customers with access to corporate applications and databases. Adopters are coming to understand the benefits of utilizing Java as a universal integration technology. Java's ultimate success hinges on the availability of more robust development tools and application servers and support from online transaction processing software and other mission-critical systems. Corporate IS is turning to Java for reasons other than making their programmers more productive. Some see Java as the first real embodiment of the dream of object-oriented development and reusable code. For others, Java's cross-platform capabilities and thin-client approach to deployment are the attractions. Java's biggest drawback is its reputation for being deficient in the performance department. Java is also being hindered by a lack of capabilities and robust third-party products.

Leilani Allen (1998) agrees that once viewed as a geeks-only language, Java is now being embraced by the pinstriped crowd. IBM has invested $200 million in Java and has 2,500 developers worldwide working on applications. The biggest factor driving Java is its promise of platform portability. Part of the appeal of Java is that it is cheap. It is also very easy to learn for those who have mastered object-oriented programming. Java still has its problems, notably a lack of robust tools that support team-based development. Java's biggest challenge will be retaining its nonproprietary status.

Don Kiely (1998) concluded in his article that a decade ago, object oriented development was hailed as a key solution to the software productivity problem, but objects have fallen short of their promise for several reasons. Objects created in one language are generally usable only in that language because of a lack of protocols for crossing boundaries, and organizing objects in repositories has proven to be a nightmare.

Kiely also found that component-based development represents the next stage in the evolution of software development, promising to shorten development cycles, reduce skills requirements, and cut costs associated with custom development. Component development solves many of the shortcomings of object oriented programming and focuses on capturing business logic rather than solving esoteric technical issues. For components that are adaptable to various uses on any platform, component-based development depends not only on binary code reuse but on design reuse to assemble many kinds of smaller components into frameworks. Component-based development's promise is great, but the vendors and users of the process are in for some work to make it a reality. One of the most promising ways to realize the benefits of component-based development would be for members of vertical industries to jointly develop standard components.

Standardization Efforts

In the last few years some experts tried to standardize object-orientation. There are different efforts to define a unique object oriented data model.

First let us discuss why there is a need for standards. We can identify the following reasons:

1. Standards allow computer systems to communicate and provide common services.
2. Standards ensure interoperability among systems.
3. Standards facilitate communication of people (they talk about the same thing).
4. Standards ease the portability of applications.
5. Standards make it easier to learn new systems.

But there are also some problems with standardization of object-oriented topics. See the list below:

1. Different areas have different needs (OOPL, OODB, ...).
2. It's difficult to categorize OIM technologies. There are different views of Object Orientation (conceptual view, user oriented view, view of interoperation levels).
3. There is only little communication between groups (vendors, researchers, users).

Some groups have tried to establish a single terminology for object oriented languages, systems, databases, an abstract framework for object oriented systems, and a set of architectural and technical goals.

Four areas of standardization have been identified:

1. Object Request Broker: A communication element for handling distribution of messages between application objects.
2. Object Model: A single design-portability abstract model.
3. Object Services: Provide the main functions for realizing basic object functionality.
4. Common Facilities: Comprise facilities which are useful in many application domains.

The primary purposes of standardization are:

1. To establish a working definition of the term "object-database",
2. To establish relationships between object-database technology and object oriented technology in related fields, and
3. To establish a framework for future standards activities in the OIM area.

What to Teach

Object technology offers tremendous possibilities for making the teaching of software much more effective and more exciting for the students than ever before.

As the software community recognizes the value of the object oriented approach, the question increasingly arises of when, where and how to include object oriented concepts, languages and tools in a software curriculum — university, college or even high school.

There are some articles proposing a coordinated approach to structuring such a curriculum, based on systematic reliance on the best aspects of the object-oriented method. It suggests a radical departure from the traditional methods of teaching programming, design and analysis: the progressive opening of black boxes, also known as the "inverted curriculum" and based on the systematic use of object-oriented libraries of reusable components. It also offers ideas for university departments that are in search of ambitious, multi-year federating projects.

Although the discussion will mostly address the question of academic education, some of it is also applicable to courses taught to professionals, either in public seminars or as part of an in-company training plan.

Start early, the earlier the better. The object-oriented method provides an excellent intellectual discipline; if you agree with its goals and techniques, there is no reason to delay bringing it to your students; you should teach it as the first approach to software development.

Beginning students react favorably to object-oriented teaching, not just because it is trendy, but because the method is clear and effective.

This strategy is preferable to a more conservative one whereby, you would teach an older method first, then unteach it in order to introduce object oriented thinking. If you think object oriented development is the right way to go, there is no reason to delay.

Teachers sometimes have an unconscious tendency to apply an idea that used to be popular in biology: that ontogeny (the story of the individual) repeats phylogeny (the story of the species) — a human embryo, at various stages of its development, vaguely looks like a frog, a pig etc. Transposed to education, this means that a teacher who first learned Algol then went on to structured design and finally discovered object orientation may want to take his students through the same path. There is little justification for such an approach which, transposed to elementary education, would mean that students first learn to count in Roman numerals, only later to be introduced to more advanced "methodologies" such as Arabic numerals.

One of the reasons for recommending (without fear of fanaticism or narrow-mindedness) the use of object orientation as the first method that students will learn is that, because the method is so general, it prepares students for the later introduction of other paradigms such as logic and functional programming — which should be part of any software engineer's culture. If your curriculum calls for the teaching of traditional programming languages such as Fortran, Cobol or Pascal, it is also preferable to introduce these later, as knowledge of the object oriented method will make it possible to use them in a safer and more reasoned way.

The object oriented method is also good preparation for a topic which will become an ever more prevalent part of software education programs: formal approaches to software specification, construction and verification. The use of assertions and more generally of the Design by Contract approach (Meyer 1993) seems to be an effective way to raise the students' awareness of the need for a sound, systematic, implementation-independent and at least partially formal characterization of software elements. Premature exposure to the full machinery of a formal specification method such as Z or VDM may overwhelm students and cause rejection; even if this does not occur, students are unlikely to appreciate the merits of formality until they have had significant software development experience. Object-oriented software construction with Design by Contract enables students to start producing real software and at the same time to gain a gentle, progressive exposure to formality. Some recent developments in the area of object-oriented formal specification such as Object-Z may ease that transition by providing a natural bridge between the two areas.

How to Teach?

Not only does object orientation affect what can be taught to students of software topics, the method also suggests new pedagogical techniques. Here are a few suggestions based on discussions with university professors as well as Bertrand Meyer's (1993) own experience.

Progressively Opening the Black Boxes

It was mentioned above that an object oriented course on data structures and algorithms could be organized around a library. This idea deserves further consideration, as it may actually be applied to courses on introductory programming and many other subjects.

A frustrating aspect of many courses is that teachers can only give introductory examples and exercises so that students do not get to work on really interesting applications. One can only get so much excitement out of computing the first 25 Fibonacci numbers or replacing all occurrences of a word by another in a text — two typical exercises in an elementary programming course.

With the object oriented method, a good object oriented environment and, most importantly, good libraries, a less traditional strategy is possible if you give students access to the libraries early in the process. In this capacity students are just reuse consumers and use the library components as black boxes in the sense defined above; this assumes that proper techniques are available for describing component usage without showing the components' internals.

With this technique students can start building meaningful applications early: their task is merely to combine existing components and assemble them into systems. In many respects this is a better introduction to the challenges and rewards of software development than the toy examples that have been the traditional mainstay of introductory courses.

Almost on day one of the course, the students will be able to produce impressive applications by reusing existing software. Their first assignment may involve writing just a few lines enough to call a pre-built application and produce striking results. Then they are invited to take the components making up the application and recombine them in different ways so as to produce variants of the application, or apply them to new uses.

This black-box use of preexisting components is only the first step. As students progress, a process of progressive opening of the black boxes will take place. The students are encouraged to start looking into the components themselves. The teacher may wish to specify the order in which the components are to be thus examined.

Initially the purpose of this progressive opening is simply to let students understand the components, which provide models of good object oriented designs. Then little by little the students are induced to adapt the components to new purposes — either by copying them and modifying the copies, or by using the inheritance mechanism, whose very purpose is indeed to support a combination of reuse and adaptation. In the process the need for new software elements will most likely arise, so the students will start writing their own classes; they only do so after having had extensive exposure to the best possible examples of quality object-oriented software — library classes.

For this process to work, good abstraction facilities must be present, making it possible to understand the essentials of a component without understanding all of it: a short form (which can be produced by tools of the environment) is an abstracted version of the class, revealing only the specification of the class, that is to say the properties which can be used explicitly by client classes. The short form lists the exported features with their assertions, but hides implementation properties. After students have seen and understood the short form, they may selectively explore the internals of the class — again under the guidance of the instructor.

Apprenticeship

The technique of progressive opening of black boxes is the application to software teaching of the time-honored technique of apprenticeship: learning from the previous generation of master practitioners of your chosen craft, and once you have understood their techniques trying to do better if you can. For lack of available masters, one-on-one apprenticeship is necessarily of limited applicability; but here we do not need the masters themselves, just the results of their work, made available as reusable components.

This approach is the continuation of a trend that has influenced the teaching of some topics in software education before object orientation became widely popular. The evolution of the standard Compiler Construction course of computer science departments is a good example. In the seventies and early eighties, the typical term project for such a course was the writing of a complete compiler or interpreter from scratch. In practice, because the front-end tasks of compiler construction, lexical analysis and parsing, require significant development effort, the project could only be a compiler or interpreter for a very small toy language. Then tools for lexical analysis and parsing (such as Lex and Yacc on Unix) became widely available and started to be used more and more frequently for course projects; this made it possible to spend less time on these front-end tasks and to include work on the more challenging aspects of compiler construction, such as code generation. The approach outlined above may be viewed as the generalization of this trend.

The Inverted Curriculum

The pedagogical technique of progressive opening of the black boxes has an interesting analogy in a neighboring discipline—electrical engineering. There has been much talk in recent years, in electrical engineering circles, of an educational policy known as the inverted curriculum (Cohen 1991). The proponents of this approach criticize the classical electronics curriculum (field theory, then circuit theory, power, device physics, control theory, digital systems, VLSI design) as "reductionist" and suggest instead to use a more "systems-oriented" approach. In order:

1. Digital systems, using VLSI and CAD.
2. Feedback, concurrency, verification.
3. Linear systems and control.
4. Power supply and transmission, impedance matching requirements.
5. Device physics and technologies, using simulation and CAD techniques.

The ideas seem similar: rather than repeating phylogeny, start by giving students a user's view of the highest-level concepts and techniques that are actually applied in the most advanced industrial environments then, little by little, unveil the underlying principles.

A Long-Term Policy

The "progressive opening" approach has an interesting variant applicable by professors who are in a position to define a multi-year educational strategy. This variant is relevant for courses on application-oriented topics such as operating systems, graphics, compiler construction or artificial intelligence.

To teach such an application area, it is interesting to have the students build a system by successive enhancement and generalization, with each year's class taking over the collective product of the previous year and trying to build on it. This method has some obvious drawbacks for the first class (which collectively serves as advance man for future generations, and will not enjoy the same reuse benefits), and experts confess they have not yet seen it applied in a systematic way. But on paper at least it is an attractive idea.

There hardly seems to be a better way of letting the students weigh the advantages and difficulties of reuse, the need for building extendible software and the challenge of improving on someone else's work.

The experience will prepare them for the reality of software development in their future company, where chances are they will be asked to perform maintenance work on an existing system long before they are asked to develop a brand new system of their own.

A practical note is in order here. Even if the context does not permit such a multi-year strategy, instructors in charge of software education should try to avoid a standard pitfall. Many undergraduate curricula include a "software engineering" course, which often devotes a key role to a software project to be carried out by the students, often in groups. Such project work is necessary, but often disappointing because of the time limitations stemming from its inclusion in a one-trimester or one-semester course. If the academic administration can at all be convinced, it is much preferable to run such a project over an entire school year (even the total amount of allocated work is the same). Trimester projects, in particular, border on the absurd; they either stop at the analysis or design stage, or result in a rush over the last few weeks to code at any cost and using any technique that will produce a running program — often defeating the very purpose of software engineering education. It is desirable to have a little more time on your hands, so as to let the students appreciate the depth of the issues involved in building serious software. A year-long project, whether or not it is part of a longer-term policy as suggested above, favors this process. It is a little more difficult to fit into the typical curriculum than the standard trimester or semester course, but well worth the fight.

An Object Oriented Plan

The idea of a long-term teaching strategy based on reuse, as well as the earlier suggestion of organizing an entire curriculum around object oriented concepts, may lead to a more ambitious concept which goes beyond the scope of software education to encompass research and development. Although this concept will be appealing to certain institutions only, it is worth some thought.

This discussion applies to a university department (computing science, information systems or equivalent) which is in search of a long-term unifying project — the kind of project that produces better teaching, development of new courses, faculty research, sources of publication, Ph.D. theses, Master's theses, undergraduate projects, collaborations with industry and government grants. Many a now well-respected department originally "put itself on the map" through such a collective multi-year effort.

The object oriented method provides a natural basis for such an endeavor. The focus of the work will not be compilers, interpreters and development tools (which may already be available from companies) but libraries. What object oriented technology needs most to progress today is application libraries (also called domain libraries). With a good object oriented environment, as already noted, will come general-purpose libraries covering such universal needs as the fundamental data structures and algorithms of computing science, graphics, user interface design, parsing. This leaves open entire application domains – from financial software to signal analysis, computer-aided design and many others — in which the need for quality software components is crying.

The choice of such a library development project as a unifying effort for a university department presents several advantages:

Even though such an effort is a long-term pursuit, partial results can start to appear early.

Compilers and other tools tend to be of the all-or-nothing category: until they are reasonably complete, distributing them may damage your reputation more than it helps it. With libraries, this is not the case: just a dozen or two quality reusable classes can render tremendous services to their users and attract favorable attention.

Because an ambitious library is a large project, there is room for many people to contribute, from advanced undergraduates to Ph.D. candidates, researchers and professors. This assumes, of course, that the application domain and the breadth of the library's coverage have been chosen judiciously so as to match the size of the available resources in people, equipment and funds.

Talking about resources, such a project may start with relatively limited means but is a prime candidate to attract the attention of funding agencies. It also offers prospects of funding by industry if the application domain is one which is of direct interest to companies.

Building good libraries is a technically exciting task which raises new scientific challenges, so that the output of a successful project may include theses and publications, not just software.

The intellectual challenges are of two kinds. First the construction of reusable components is one of the most interesting and difficult problems of software engineering, for which the method brings some help but certainly does not answer all questions. Second, any successful application library must rest on a taxonomy of the application domain, requiring a long-term effort at classifying the known concepts in that area. As is well known in the natural sciences classification is the first step towards understanding. Developed for a new application area, such an effort (known as domain analysis) raises new and interesting problems.

The last comment suggests the possibility of interdisciplinary cooperation with researchers whose specialty is in the application domain rather than in software engineering. Cooperation should begin with people working in neighboring fields. Many universities have two groups pursuing teaching and research in software issues, one (often "computing science") having more of an engineering and scientific background, the other (often "information systems") more oriented towards business issues. Whether these groups are administratively separate or part of the same structure – both cases are common — the project may appeal to both, and provides an opportunity for collaboration.

Finally, a successful library providing components for an important application area will be widely used and bring much visibility to its originating institution.

The Future

As usual, anticipation of the technology's impact has far exceeded our ability to use it. We are beginning to see the impact now, but it still takes much longer than expected to design and implement a practical application of OOT within industry.

Recent developments, including open systems, convergence to fewer software and hardware platforms, emerging de facto software industry standards, the World Wide Web, and an industry providing components that can be integrated into complete applications, have accelerated the use of OOT. It is possible today to make entirely object oriented MES applications.

OOT's effectiveness does not depend on how academically correct the object-oriented principles are in an MES application. Rather, it depends on how the technology adheres to standards and principles used by the emerging software components industry.

Driven by user demands for open architecture, object oriented technology is finding an increasingly important role in systems development

In conclusion, it's clear that OOT is here to stay, and it is maturing. We have gone through a phase of adapting OOT to the problems we are trying to solve. From a purely technical point of view, the general application of OOT today does not use all of the capabilities of the concept. However, by simplifying it, the benefits of OOT have become more accessible and easier to apply.

When looking for an MES solution, emphasis should be put on how configurable the solution is to the problem it is intended to solve. A future scenario puts the MES vendor together with the end user of the solution, building a model of the application based on existing components and generating the system from the model.

This scenario puts requirements on the MES vendor as well as the customer. MES vendors must have an object oriented implementation of their solutions based on software components and general de facto and real industry standards.

The customer must focus on problems to be solved and distance himself/herself from the details of how the solution is implemented. Instead, the focus should be on openness and using industry standards, powerful configuration tools accessible to the end user, the extent to which the solution fits into the domains of control systems, from instrumentation to enterprise resource planning (ERP) and from plant design to maintenance.

References

Allen, L. (1998). A sip of Java? *Mortgage Banking, 58*(12), 107-108.

Ambler, S. (1998). An introduction to patterns. *Software Development, 6*(7), 70-72

Baer, T. (1999). Object databases. *Computerworld, 33*(1), 66-67.

Bock, C., & Odell, J. (1998). A more complete model of relations and their implementation: aggregation. *Journal of Object-Oriented Programming, 11*(5), 78-70.

Business/Technology Editors, (1998). Ardent Software Launches New Academic Partner Program to Meet Industry Demand for Object-Oriented Programming Skills. *Business Wire*, 1.

Calvanese, D., & Lenzerini M. (1994).Object-oriented schemas more expressive

Chih-Ting Du, T., & Wolfe, P.M. (1997). An implementation perspective of applying object-oriented database technologies. *IIEE Transactions, 29*(9), 733-742.

Chin, K., White, P., & George, G. (1997). Controlling the Future. *Chemical Engineering, 104*(12), 74.

Chu, B., Long, J., & Matthews, M. (1998). FAIME: an object-oriented methodology for applications plug and play. *Journal of Object Oriented Programming, 11*(5), 20-26.

Etzkorn, L., & Davis, C (1997). Automatically Identifying Reusable OO Legacy Code. Computer,30(10), 66-71.

Hardgrave, B.C., & Douglas, D.E. (1991). Object-oriented education: Trends in information systems and computer science curricula. *The Journal of Computer Information Systems, 39*(1), 1-6.

Hoske, M.T. (1998). Objects make software behave like hardware. *Control Engineering, 45*(13), 70-72.

Jones, C. G., Hilton, T.S.E., & Lutz, Charles M. (1998). Discovering objects: Which identification and refinement strategies do analysts really use?. *Journal of Database Management, 9*(3), 3-14.

Kaindl, H., & Carroll, J.M. (1999). Symbolic modeling in practice. *Communications of the ACM, 42*(1), 28-30.

Kiely D. (1998). The component edge. *Informationweek, 677*, 1A-6A.

Kiely, D. (1998). Objects fall short of promise. *Informationweek, 677*, 4A.

McGregor, J.D. (1998). Now where did I put those bugs? *Journal of*

Object-Oriented Programming, 11(6), 9-14.

Meyer, B. (1993). Towards an O-O Curriculum. *Journal of Object-Oriented Programming,* 585-594.

Moriarty, T. (1998). Borrowing from OO. *Database Programming and Design, 11(5),* 13-15.

Nesi, P., & Querci, T. (1998). Effort estimation and prediction of object-oriented systems. *The Journal of Systems and Software, 42*(1), 89-102.

Noffsinger, W.B., Niedbalski, R., Blanks, M., & Emmart, N. (1998). Legacy object modeling speeds software integration. *Communications of the ACM, 41*(12), 80-89.

Olsen, D.H., & Sudha, R. (1999). An empirical analysis of the object-oriented database concurrency control mechanism O2C2. *Journal of Database, 10*(2), 14-26.

Patrizio, A. (1997). Object theory is fine, practice is better. *Informationweek, 624,* 12A-14A.

Potok, T. E., &Vouk, M. A. (1997). The effects of the business model on object-oriented software development productivity. *IBM Systems Journal, 36*(1), 140-61.

Ruber, P. (1997). Object relief. *InfoWorld, 19*(4), 85-86.

Whiting, R. (1998). Is the Java cup half full or half empty? *Software Magazine,* 18(13), 43-46.

Chapter XII

Business Process Reengineering with Object Oriented Technology: Is the Gamble Worth the Risk?

Robert M. Gittins
American University, USA

The rise of Object Oriented (OO) technologies has been nothing if not spectacular in the past few years. The IT world has witnessed the next generation of cutting-edge technology with the advent of OO programming languages, OO analysis and design, OO CASE tools, OO database management systems (OODBMS), and OO modeling. While the potential for this new technology has IT and business professionals extremely excited, the burgeoning field is undeniably immature and currently lacks the stability necessary to be considered mainstream or a reliable option for companies that are about to reengineer their business processes. Despite the growing popularity of OO technology, there are numerous issues that have contributed to its inability to firmly entrench itself and take over from the older, proven technologies. Object Oriented technology's image problem has created a highly difficult decision- making process for corporations about to embark on business process reengineering (BPR) projects. At this time, reengineering with OO technology is a significant risk for companies to make, and those who have moved forward with OO technology have not, for the most part, seen the results that they were hoping for and their organizations are now suffering as a result of this decision.

The rise of Object Oriented (OO) technologies has been nothing if not spectacular in the past few years. The IT world has witnessed the next generation of cutting-edge technology with the advent of OO programming languages, OO analysis and design, OO CASE tools, OO database management systems (OODBMS), and OO modeling. While the potential for this new technology has IT and business professionals extremely excited, the burgeoning field is undeniably immature and currently lacks the stability necessary to be considered mainstream or a reliable option for companies that are about to reengineer their business processes.

Despite the growing popularity of OO technology, there are numerous issues that have contributed to its inability to firmly entrench itself and take over from the older, proven technologies. Object Oriented technology's image problem has created a highly difficult decision-making process for corporations about to embark on business process reengineering (BPR) projects. The benefits and challenges of this new technology, as they relate to the BPR process, are discussed below.

What OO Technology Can Bring To Companies Seeking To Reengineer

The mainstream press has picked up on the enthusiasm of OO technology vendors in portraying this new technology as an IT messiah of sorts. This being the case, IT managers are beginning to feel pressure to start implementing OO technology in order to reap the rewards that the pundits are discussing in the appropriate journals, magazines, and newscasts. This pressure stems from the numerous benefits that OO technology has over the technologies that are currently being used.

If OO technology lives up to its hype, companies may expect to see substantive benefits from its implementation, including:

Reuse of Code. One of the inherent advantages of OO technology is that once an object has been created, it may be recycled any number of times to meet similar needs. Minor modifications may be necessary, but that will likely be a trivial task. Code reuse will save companies time and money during the development process, once they have developed objects that may be reused, or once they have access to an object library.

Simplified Maintenance. Another inherent benefit of OO technology is the ease in which objects may be modified and maintained. Once the change to the object has been made, the modification is reflected in all of the applications that make use of this object. It will no longer be necessary to make numerous changes to existing code or spend time testing the code to ensure that the changes did not adversely affect another part of the system.

Improved Productivity. Albeit a long term benefit, companies that implement OO technology should witness an increase in productivity. This increase will be a function of the ease of creating, modifying, and maintaining OO systems, and the ability to generate high quality applications in a shorter amount of time than is now possible. Code reuse and qualified OO programmers, systems analysts, and network managers must all be present in order for this advantage to be realized.

Complete Support of GUI's. OO technology allows end-user applications to be created in a "user friendly" way. Graphical User Interfaces make applications easier for end users to learn and to use them more efficiently once they become familiar with the new system.

The Ability to Support System Complexity. Building a system with OO technology is similar to a child playing with Legos. Once a solid foundation has been built and the user becomes familiar with how the technology works, the size and complexity of a system may continue to grow and expand. This will be a key factor as companies begin to recognize the need to reengineer and create complex systems to meet their business needs and retain their competitive advantage.

The potential of OO technology is great and a good number of companies are beginning to look toward OO technology as a catalyst and as a means of change. For example, High Tech Systems, Inc. has developed extensive training materials in order to provide the skills necessary to succeed in the OO field. The Object Discovery courses materials conclude:

> ...the urgent need to integrate these powerful business technologies into one methodology has not been explored or applied until quite recently. Exciting developments are now

being produced by combining BPR with the well-established procedures of class and object modeling. The application of object modeling techniques to business process reengineering provides an effective and timesaving method for rethinking and redesigning business processes, thereby improving critical measures of performance such as cost, quality, service and turnaround. More importantly, applying these integrated techniques to the reengineering process quickly leads to the discovery of solutions that can be easily understood and quickly implemented at all levels of a corporation (High Tech Systems, Inc., 1997).

Those companies that have already reengineered their business processes under an OO paradigm have witnessed mixed results. For some, OO technology has lived up to the promises of the vendors, and the press, and has propelled the company towards higher profits and an expanded customer base. However, other corporations have not been so lucky and have had a difficult time during this process, and the obstacles they have encountered are discussed below.

OO Technology Challenges For BPR

Lack of OO Tools, Standards, & Practices. While there are numerous OO programming languages available for OO systems development, there are decidedly few proven systems analysis and systems design tools available for OO programmers to utilize. Until these tools are developed and implemented, it will be difficult for OO technology to establish a substantive foothold from which it may expand. Additionally, developers have spent a great deal of time and money with the legacy tools that they currently use, and they will not work within an OO framework. There will have to be a convincing argument for developers to give up their existing tools. Without new OO tools, companies run the risk of implementing a technology that may well hinge on the individual efforts of a small number of their IT staff. This is not a good way of encouraging people to accept a new technology.

Java was supposed to be the saving grace of the OO programming world, "In the beginning of Java's life, the vendor and user community reacted with overblown optimism to the promise of an object-oriented, platform-independent saviour (Burger, 1999)." However, Java has not lived up to its hype, or expectations, and Sun Microsystems Inc. is now struggling to define Java in such a way that it will prove to be a useful OO language. In fact, no one can really determine if Java is a programming language or a platform in and of itself. As the situation currently stands, companies that are thinking about reengineering with OO technology are forced to decide the ultimate outcome of the Java debate and they have little guidance in making this decision. If they decide to move toward Java, they are faced with the possibility that Java will be defunct within five years which would leave the company in a very precarious position.

If companies are required to invent their own OO tools, they must also wrestle with the issues of standards and practices; "Although object-oriented technology seems promising,...the lack of consensus on the object-oriented model is the most important problem to be resolved in object-oriented technologies, a fact confirmed by the different interpretations appearing in different object-oriented prototypes (Du & Wolfe, 1997)." This translates into an uncomfortable situation for anyone contemplating reengineering with OO technology, especially when it becomes obvious that while OO technology application development tools will allow a corporation to customize its products at a highly detailed level, it does possess a high learning curve and requires a long development process (Freeman, 1997).

Furthermore, a lack of standards will also disrupt the role of database management systems (DBMS) within the corporate structure; "Many people believe that object-oriented architecture has the potential to form the basis for the next generation of database management systems. However, a lack of consensus and standardization are hindering the widespread adoption of object-oriented concepts (Du & Wolfe, 1997)." The DBMS has become an integral and invaluable tool in a company's IT arsenal. It is an imperative system that many companies cannot operate without. If a corporation must decide to reengineer with OO technology and have to worry about the functionality of their DBMS, they are unlikely to reengineer with that technology. To do so would be to put their company at grave risk without a safety net.

Without an overarching way of enforcing common programming, design, and analysis policies and procedures, it will prove to be an enormous task to find a way to pay for the implementation of this new technology. Companies that jump onto the OO bandwagon may also place themselves in jeopardy of having to reevaluate and reengineer their standards and practices to conform to industry standards and practices as they are created and accepted. At the present time, there are not very many companies ready to gamble with implementing OO technology before it really solidifies itself as the latest IT standard due to the overriding belief that, "if we are ever to reap the rewards promised by distributed objects, we need a single standard to emerge for communicating between objects. It is bad enough we have to deal with two major standards, CORBA and Distributed Component Object Model-there are multiple versions of each (Petreley, 1998)."

Expense. At this stage in its development, OO technology can become a rather costly investment for companies that attempt to implement it. The technology itself requires a significant investment and may include OO tools, development of a new design environment, modeling tools, hardware, training, end-user support, and many other expenses associated with the implementation of any new technology. In fact, Chuck Lewis, CEO of Financial Technologies International in New York maintains that, "...if time and costs are crucial factors for your company and your developers are unfamiliar with object technology, components, rather than true object-oriented application development, may be your best bet (Freeman, 1997)."

According to Norman Kerth, a Portland Software Development Consultant, the reusability "benefit" of OO technology may be an expensive endeavor:

> Building reusable objects requires extensive analysis and design. You really need to understand what the generalities are...Then you will need to invest extra time in testing and quality assurance, optimization, and documentation. All this takes time and labor, which increase the cost of the code. IT departments must also add to the payback equation the cost of tools to support reuse, such as version control and repositories. Finally, the cost of administering an ongoing reuse program must be considered. With all these elements, it becomes apparent that reuse doesn't come cheap (Radding, 1998).

This is but one of the areas in which OO technologies will impact a company's reengineering budget.

A corporation that decides to move toward OO technology would be wise to continue to support its existing systems which would incur the cost of maintaining that system. There would be additional costs associated with the reengineering process itself. Most companies witness a drop in productivity and efficiency during a period of reengineering which can be an expensive process. As the reengineering process begins to take place, there will be significant expenses for staff training. Most people find, IT personnel included, that OO technologies have a fairly high learning curve and it can take upwards of 8 months to a year before the staff becomes competent to function on their own with the new OO system.

There are also costs associated with distributed objects being accessed over the corporations network:

> Estimates vary, but once distributed objects are added to the corporate net, overall performance could dip from 5 percent to 35 percent. This decrease can be traced to two causes: network overhead and processor overhead. A negligible source of network overhead will be the messages exchanged by the objects themselves. A more significant source will occur at the machines that invoke the objects. Objects require more processor time. This will result in delays as objects traverse a net. End-users on interactive applications will likely see degraded response times. The situation is only going to get worse as more and more applications are distributed and traffic volumes will climb, particularly as desktop applications are rewritten and deployed across the corporate network...But what about processor overhead? This is the performance decrease that can be linked to all the ORB components that must be processed. (Since ORBs are middleware, they by definition force processors to do more work.) Not all ORB software is well-optimized. Processor overhead will have a definite impact on latency. Once again, end users will see slower response times (Golick, 1998).

As the new system comes on-line, many companies will find that they will have to replace a high number of end-user workstations in order to support the new applications. Depending on the size of the organization and the complexity of the system developed, this can be an extremely large expense.

Finally, as with any reengineering effort, there will be numerous unforeseen costs that tend to bombard the organization throughout the reengineering process. While it is difficult to find exact numbers and budget information that covers this topic, it is a generally accepted belief in the industry that these costs are extensive and often found to be prohibitively expensive. Budget forecasts for reengineering projects often fail to take into consideration the monetary impact on end-user departments which invariably present themselves during the reengineering process. Object Oriented technology is clearly a large investment with a great deal of risk in the current marketplace.

The bottom line on this issue is simple:

> Although there have certainly been object success stories, most people tend to remember the expensive failures. Object development is difficult and expensive, and it hasn't worked out for everyone...Although the promise and future benefits of OOT are becoming enticing to IS managers, many are apprehensive about the up-front costs associated with object migration. Companies deep into their object-development cycle say that you can't measure the investment of money and labor...As enticing as object technology has become, its drawback is the high cost and associated high risk of getting started (Ruber, 1997).

Companies that decide to reengineer with OO technology must be prepared for the extensive budget and resource impact that comes with their decision.

Relational Technology vs. OO Technology. A great majority of the world's data is contained within relational technology despite the fact many of these legacy systems are being developed using OO technology. The sheer volume of this data frightens many people as they begin to consider a paradigm shift away from relational technology:

> Object-oriented technology, like almost all new technologies, must overcome different legacies on its way to acceptance. There is the legacy of old systems that have been built in a

> more traditional, structured way and don't mix easily with objects. As a matter of fact, structured software-development techniques have only now, after about a decade of promotion, firmly established themselves (Kozaczynski & Kuntzmann-Combelles, 1993).

It is difficult for many people to fathom moving enormous data stores from a firmly entrenched technology into a technology that is just beginning to show promise.

Many people struggling with this issue have come to the conclusion that, "At present, the most frequently used approach to developing systems involving complex data types employs some form of a hybrid relational database or an object-oriented database. Much work remains to be done before it becomes clear which of these approaches will become dominant (Du & Wolfe, 1997)." If this is in fact a commonly held belief, under what circumstances would OO technologies be implemented over the proven relational technologies? It seems fairly obvious that few people would benefit from moving directly into the world of OO DBMS at this point unless there was an overwhelming advantage for doing so. Even so, this "advantage" would be placing the organization at risk in order to obtain their reengineering goal, especially when the current status of OO DBMS is taken into consideration; "Object-based databases have not been popular, even though most new developments use object-oriented programming. These environments go through horrible contortions to map from an object-based view of data into relational columnar views-a time consuming and error-prone process (Morgenthal, 1998)."

With the current dependence on legacy relational systems, it has become a daunting task to obtain the necessary skills to make a transition to OO technology; "the main concern of any object enthusiast should not be whether object technology will be around in the future, but whether the OO concepts can avoid the kind of dilution that have plagued structured techniques. If everything is advertised as object-oriented, the burden is on the buyer to ascertain what is OO and what is not (Meyer, 1998)." OO technology requires a fundamental shift in programming, development, design, analysis, implementation, and testing. With this being the case, many companies are concerned about such a shift, largely due to a lack of qualified personnel required to make this type of transition. There simply does not appear to be an overwhelming reason for companies to move away from the proven relational technologies that have become entrenched in corporate structure and in the mind set of people making the IT decisions for these companies.

Training. OO technology has a decidedly high learning curve for everyone involved in the process, "[T]he investment in people whose experience and expertise are in other ways of doing things. To become accepted, the object-oriented way of thinking must become the natural way of doing things. Now it presents a steep learning curve (Kozaczynski & Kuntzmann-Combelles, 1993)." Management is faced with making a decision that will profoundly alter the way their systems are created and the way their staff performs their responsibilities:

> Despite the hype, the technology created by Sun Microsystems, Inc. is still maturing, and companies are still learning how and when to use it, particularly in Internet, intranet and extranet environments. Object oriented programmers with the necessary Java and business experience are hard to find. Many corporate information technology staffs are fully occupied wrestling with more pressing year 2000 and enterprise resource planning projects (Sliwa, 1998).

System programmers, systems analysts, database developers and administrators, and system administrators will all have to become familiar with a completely different way of doing their jobs. This transition will be both costly and time consuming if the transition is made by current staff. If new staff members are brought in, this process will be similarly costly and many companies will have problems finding qualified people from a relatively small pool of qualified candidates.

Once these hurdles have been cleared, there will have to be a clear and focused approach for dealing with end-users. They will have to be introduced to the new OO paradigm and encouraged to look for the benefits of the new system. Additionally, numerous training exercises and mentoring programs must be developed and implemented to acclimate the end-users to the new system. Companies that ignore the cultural change aspects of this transition will find themselves consumed by an unhappy staff, a loss of productivity, and a staff unwilling to work with the new system.

Again, CEO Lewis provides valuable insight into this process as he concludes that, "Object-oriented techniques have enabled our organization to establish itself as a leading provider of next generation applications for the securities industry...[b]ut it's taken us three years to reach the top of the learning curve, and counting everything, we've invested more than a hundred million dollars in developing a complete architecture and application set for the financial industry (Freeman, 1997)." As Financial Technologies International has learned first hand, reengineering with OO technology has a high cost, both in terms of budget impact and personnel, as well as with the training of qualified individuals that are a mandatory component to the OO reengineering process.

Testing & Metrics. OO technology offers new challenges for developing and interpreting test results for the newly designed systems. There is little guidance on the market for dealing with testing and how one should gauge the results. This is truly an instance of having to think outside of the box, however, in this case the box has never been completely opened before. Companies may well find this issue to be prohibitively expensive both in terms of budget impact and also in terms of time and development costs.

The issue of metrics will also present obstacles for many people. There have been countless ways of measuring productivity for current technology, however, it does not appear that these metrics will be viable with OO technology. Again, companies will be largely on their own to develop these metrics until industry standards are developed and implemented. It is unlikely that a large number of corporate executives will want to position their business for the future in this manner.

Risks vs. Benefits. When a company that is seriously considering moving towards OO technology takes a look at all of the issues discussed above, they will be forced to analyze the benefits that they are expecting to see against the many growing pains that this new technology is going through. This process is likely to be confusing, and companies will be forced to run the risk of making a premature decision that will limit their ability to remain competitive and productive. The decision to implement OO technology must be made carefully with realistic expectations. Furthermore, organizations must determine if the benefits that the proponents and vendors off OO technology are continually testifying to are actually as beneficial as they are claimed to be. Case in point, reuse of code is often listed as a significant advantage of OO technology; yet, code reuse has been a relatively common practice, cutting and pasting for example, with many of the older technologies that are widely utilized throughout the business and IT industries. Organizations that have gone through the OO reengineering process have consistently maintained that, "[w]hen IS managers first began hearing about object-oriented technology years ago, they heard a compelling story: Develop a software object once and reuse it as many times as you like in different applications, thereby, saving on application development costs...But such thrifty recycling is easier said than done...OO is known for reusability, but reusability is overrated (Freeman, 1997)." Another fairly common perception of this "benefit" of OO code reusability maintains, "Many say code reusability is the point of OOP. Bzzt. Wrong. Code does not have to be object-oriented in order for it to be reusable. Programmers have long had at their disposal a number of fascinating non-object-oriented technologies for the reuse of code. There's cut-and-paste and link libraries, to name but two examples (Petreley, 1998)." There are many such "benefits" involved with OO technology that companies need to carefully examine to make an accurate assessment of this new technology.

Top level management at Premiere 100 companies have begun to turn away from OO technologies for their reengineering projects because, "they'd rather wait until the edge is off new technology-and keep any wild, risky experiments as far away as possible from core business systems, since exposing key corporate data to those risks makes no sense at all. There's a good reason such old reliables as mainframes, Cobol and IMS still reign over most core IT operations (Hayes, 1998)." As Charles Popper, VP of Corporate Computer Services at Merck & Co., put it, "[it] doesn't mean these and other Premier 100 companies don't make bets on advanced technology. But they'd rather be 'fast followers,' waiting until the odds of success are a bit more in their favor-and the edge is a little less bleeding (Hayes, 1998)." This appears to be wise advice in the current IT environment, advice that many of the Premiere 100 companies are heeding.

Conclusion

OO technology has established itself as the wave of the future; the problem is that the future is not quite upon us yet. An MIT study found that, "object-oriented technology will be considered experimental for a long time to come. This implies that developers will try to avoid using it on large, visible, or critical projects in the near future (Kozaczynski & Kuntzmann-Combelles, 1993)." While it may be possible to obtain significant advantages from implementing the technology before it is entrenched as an industry-accepted technology, it is more likely that companies will make the move too early. Due to this premature entry into the world of OO technology in the business process reengineering environment, companies will likely encounter costly obstacles from the time-consuming process that may well decrease productivity and wreak havoc on the business as a whole.

At the present time, reengineering with OO technology is a gamble. The Premiere 100 companies have recognized this gamble; "On average, object oriented technologies are only moderately important to Premier 100 companies. Only 30% of respondents say that they are very important. But the secret to handling hot technologies-especially when they seem to be major gambles-is to manage these projects like the high-risk investment they are (Hayes, 1998)." Corporations that decide to reengineer their business processes with OO technology, will be wagering that all of the benefits that they hear about from their vendors are true, not will be true, but are true right now. If code reusability is not an option and there are not object libraries available, if OO systems are not easily developed and modified, if OO technology does not facilitate the development of complex systems, and if OO technology fails to increase productivity then companies that attempt to reengineer with this technology will find themselves holding a losing hand with a large pot on the table and no way to fold. The simple promise that OO technology is coming of age should not be a deciding factor for corporations that are contemplating using OO technology to reengineer their business processes.

The health care industry has found itself wrestling with these exact issues and their response has been less than supportive of OO technology:

> If Wall Street offers clues about technology headed for the mainstream, then it's a good bet that the makers of health care software will continue to focus on the conventional. Of 31 companies going public between 1992 and 1997, most didn't base their stock offerings on new-generation technologies, according to an analysis conducted by Health Care Investment Visions, Alameda, Calif...That means the Internet, artificial intelligence, object-oriented systems, and speech recognition-the very technologies needed for electronic medical records-may be years away from wide-scale use in health care (Tech Tomorrow, 1998).

If the health care industry has drawn this conclusion, it seems likely that other companies seeking to embark on a reengineering project are making similar decisions in regards to the maturity, reliability, and benefits of OO technologies.

There will always be new technologies, however, in order to maximize the benefits of these new technologies, it is often wiser to be patient and allow the technology to mature rather than risking the productivity and livelihood of the organization by being on the cutting, or bleeding, edge of technology.

References

Brown, David (1997). *Object-Oriented Analysis: Objects In Plain English* . New York: John Wiley & Sons, Inc.

Burger, Dale (1999, January 1). Java 2 receives a lukewarm welcome. *Computing Canada, 25,* 4.

Du, Timon Chih-Ting & Wolfe, Philip M. (1997, September). An implementation perspective of applying object-oriented database technologies. *IIE Transactions, 29,* 733-742.

Freeman, Eva (1997, March). Is OO app dev worth the cost? *Datamation, 43,* 82-86.

Golick, Jerry (1998, November 21). Dealing with distributed objects. *Data Communications, 27,* 62-69.

Hayes, Frank (1998, November 16). Pragmatic risks. *Computerworld, Premier 100 Supplement,* 38-39.

High Tech Systems, Inc. (1997). Business process reengineering? A practical introduction to business process reengineering and object modeling (On-line). Http://www.objectdiscovery.com/bpr/index.htm.

Kozaczynski, Wojtek & Kuntzmann-Combelles, Annie (1993, January). What it Takes to Make OO Work. *IEEE Software, 10,* 21-23.

McKeen, James, D. & Smith, Heather A. (1997). *Management Challenges in IS: Successful Strategies and Appropriate Action.* New York: John Wiley & Sons, Inc.

Meyer, Bertrand (1998, January). The future of object technology. *Computer, 31,* 140-141.

Morgenthal, J.P. (1998, June 1). OODBMS can save you lots of work. *Internetweek, 717,* 11.

Petreley, Nicholas (1998, September, 14). Mr. Spock and Dr. McCoy give an object-oriented programming tutorial. *InfoWorld, 20,* 112.

Radding, Alan (1998, November 9). Hidden costs of reuse. *Informationweek, 708,* 1A-8A.

Ruber, Peter (1997, January 27). Object relief. *InfoWorld, 19,* 85-86.

Semich, J. William (1995, September 15). C/S manufacturing: Build, buy, or reengineer? *Datamation, 41,* 84-93.

Sliwa, Carol (1998, August 24). Java use limited in critical apps. *Computerworld, 32,* 1,76.

Taylor, David A., PhD. (1990). *Object-Oriented Technology: A Manager's Guide.* Reading, Massachusetts: Addison-Wesley Publishing Company, Inc.

Tech tomorrow: More of the same? (1998, February 20). *Hospitals & Health Networks, 72,* 38.

About the Authors

Book Editor

Rick Gibson is an Associate Professor at the American University in the Department of Computer Science and Information Systems. His research has been focused on global software development and software process improvement.

Dr. Gibson has over 20 years of software engineering and management experience. He has managed major projects in support of commercial, government and educational organizations for development of computer applications. He has trained project teams around the globe in project management, defect prevention, quality metrics, ISO 9000, and Y2K remediation.

Dr. Gibson's background includes system development using structured and object oriented software development methodologies. As a Software Engineering Institute authorized lead evaluator, he has conducted software evaluations of over forty different software development organizations. He has extensive experience in the development of process improvement and corrective action plans for evaluated organizations.

Chapter Authors

Gerold E Cameron is manager of the Document Imaging Center for American University-Enrollment Services. He holds a bachelor's degree in accounting and a master's degree in computer information systems both from American University.

Hernán Cobo is a systems engineer graduate from the Universidad Nacional del Centro de la Provincia de Buenos Aires, Argentina. Now he is a Professor in the Computer and Systems Department of the Exacts Sciences Faculty. He is in charge of organizing the Systems and Communications aspects of the University. His research interest is software engineering.

Jane Fedorowicz holds the Rae D. Anderson Chair in Accountancy and

Information Systems at Bentley College where she is teaching accounting and information systems courses. She received her M.S. and Ph.D. degrees in Systems Sciences from Carnegie-Mellon University. She has previously taught at Carnegie-Mellon University, Northwestern University, Boston University and the University of Massachusetts at Boston. Professor Fedorowicz currently serves on the editorial boards of *Information Systems Research,* the e-journal *Communications of the Association for Information Systems* and the *Review of Accounting Information Systems.* Her primary research interests involve the impact of information technologies on individuals and organizations, especially enterprise information systems and object oriented technologies. She has published in *Decision Sciences, Journal of Management Information Systems, Information and Management, ACM Transactions on Database Systems, Communications of the ACM, International Journal of Technology Management, Decision Support Systems,* and many other venues. She is a frequent speaker for research and practitioner groups.

Mehdi Ghods is an Associate Technical Fellow with The Boeing Company. He earned graduate degrees in physics, computer science and measurement. Prior to joining The Boeing Company, he was a faculty member in the radiology department at Michigan State University. His current research interests and work include operations research, management information systems, technology transfer, and in particular, measurement and research in information technology.

Robert M. Gittins is in his final semester in the Management Information Systems (MIS) Master's Program in the Computer Science and Information Systems (CSIS) Department at American University (AU) in Washington, DC. In May 1996, he graduated with a bachelor's degree from AU while majoring in political science and criminal justice. Mr. Gittins plans to attend law school starting in the 1999 fall semester to pursue a career as an intellectual property attorney and consultant with a focus on information technology (IT) and Internet policy. During the course of his education, Mr. Gittins has worked as a member of AU's Office of Information Technology's IT staff, and he currently holds the position of Information Systems Manager in the Department of Continuing Education & Special Programs at AU. Mr. Gittins has also taught undergraduate courses in the CSIS department at American University and will continue to do so in the foreseeable future.

Gretchen Irwin is a Senior Lecturer in the Management Science and Information Systems Department at the University of Auckland. Her research focuses on the teaching, learning, and the effective use of information technology by systems developers and end users. Her work has been published in the *Communications of the ACM, Journal of MIS,* and *Human-Computer Interaction.* Gretchen completed her Master's Degree and Ph.D. in Information Systems at the University of Colorado, Boulder.

Denis M. S. Lee is a Professor of Computer Information Systems in the

Sawyer School of Management at Suffolk University. He holds mechanical engineering degrees from Columbia University and MIT, as well as a Ph.D. from the Sloan School of Management at MIT.

Dr. Lee's research interests are related to the management of computer-based technologies and the management of technical professionals. He is currently the Principal Investigator of a research project funded by the National Science Foundation on the knowledge acquisition behavior of young information systems workers. His research articles have appeared in the *Academy of Management Journal, Management Science, MIS Quarterly,* the *IEEE Transactions on Engineering Management, Journal of Engineering and Technology Management* and the *Journal of Educational Computing Research.* Dr. Lee is also active in a number of professional societies and serves on the editorial boards of the *IEEE Transactions on Engineering Management* and the *Journal of Engineering and Technology Management.*

Holly Lee is the CIO/CFO of a small office supply company in Illinois. She holds an M.B.A. with a major in Information Technology from The University of Kansas. Ms. Lee previously worked in the banking and export industries, and has extensive experience in Japanese business. Her interests include enterprise system integration, IS personnel expertise, and object oriented technologies.

Virginia Mauco received her systems engineering degree at the Universidad Nacional del Centro de la Provincia de Buenos Aires, Argentina. She is an Assistant in the Computer and Systems Department, Exacts Sciences Faculty, of the same University. Her principal areas of research interest are systems reengineering and OO systems.

Jim Nelson is a lecturer of Information Systems at the University of Kansas. He received his B.S. in Computer Science from California Polytechnic State University, San Luis Obispo, and his M.S. and Ph.D. in Information Systems from the University of Colorado, Boulder. His research interests include developing theoretically grounded models and metrics for business processes and investigating the problems people have shifting to emerging technologies.

Kay Nelson has both national and international experience in the fields of information systems and engineering management. She is currently an Assistant Professor at the University of Kansas. Dr. Nelson earned her Ph.D. from the University of Texas at Austin in Management Information Systems. Her current research interests include the measurement of software maintenance quality and maintenance effectiveness, the role of tools and methods in software maintenance, and the use of information systems for strategic communication and coordination. Dr. Nelson has previously published in *MIS Quarterly.*

David Patton holds a B.A. in International Affairs and a M.S. in CyberMedia Science, both from The American University in Washington, D.C. David currently works for USWeb/CKS in Bethesda, MD. where he spends his time building Internet-based applications for electronic commerce, knowledge management, and enterprise collaboration. In the past David has conducted research on information operations and interface design.

Alex Podaras has a B.S.B.A with a double major in business administration and computer information systems from American University. He also has a M.S. degree in computer information systems from American University. Alex Podaras has experience in working in business and information technology areas. He has worked for such large companies as Hewlett Packard (HP) and has first hand experience with their computer information systems.

Edward Sim received his Master of Science Degree in Management Information Systems from George Washington University and his Ph.D. in Information Systems from the University of Maryland, Baltimore. He has taught in the areas of system analysis and design, database and decision support systems, and information systems. He is currently a member of Association of Information Systems, Decision Science Institute, INFORMS and the Society for Computer Simulation International. He is also a member of Phi Kappa Phi. His current research interests include information system development methodologies, Object Oriented technologies and methodologies, and requirements engineering.. Dr. Sim is an assistant professor of Management Information Systems at Loyola College in Maryland

Chamini Wasalathantry is a consultant with Ernst & Young in New Zealand. Chamini completed her Master's Degree in Information Systems at the University of Auckland in 1998.

Index